Postcinematic vision

posthumanities

CARY WOLFE, SERIES EDITOR

(continued on page 239)

Postcinematic Vision

The Coevolution of Moving-Image Media and the Spectator

Roger F. Cook

posthumanities 54

University of Minnesota Press
Minneapolis
London

Published by the University of Minnesota Press
111 Third Avenue South, Suite 290
Minneapolis, MN 55401-2520
http://www.upress.umn.edu

Printed in the United States of America on acid-free paper

The University of Minnesota is an equal-opportunity educator and employer.

Library of Congress Cataloging-in-Publication Data
Names: Cook, Roger F., author.
Title: Postcinematic vision : the coevolution of moving-image media and the
    spectator / Roger F. Cook.
Description: Minneapolis : University of Minnesota Press, 2020. |
    Series: Posthumanities | Includes bibliographical references and index.
Identifiers: LCCN 2019019310 (print) | ISBN 978-1-5179-0766-2 (hc) |
    ISBN 978-1-5179-0767-9 (pb)
Subjects: LCSH: Mass media—Philosophy. | Mass media—Audiences. |
    Visual perception. | Digital media. | Cinematography.
Classification: LCC P90 .C6815 2020 (print) | DDC 302.23—dc23
LC record available at https://lccn.loc.gov/2019019310

UMP BMB

Contents

Introduction

As digital technology has radically altered the media landscape and liberated the screen from the confines of an auditorium equipped with a projector and fixed seats, some media theorists have declared that the "cinematic century" has ended and that we have entered a "postcinematic" and even "post-televisual" age (Friedberg 2006, 242).[1] In the last few years a number of film scholars have mounted a concerted effort to delineate the salient characteristics of this transition to a radically new constellation of visual media. This endeavor gained focus and steam when in his 2010 book *Post-Cinematic Affect* Steven Shaviro explored how the emergent forms of digital media were generating a substantially different "structure of feeling" (1). More recently, an extensive online collection of both new and previously published work, *Post-Cinema: Theorizing 21st-Century Film*, has provided a comprehensive overview of what is at stake in this theoretical pursuit and pointed toward new avenues of investigation (Denson and Leyda 2016).

In her groundbreaking work toward a phenomenology of cinema, Vivian Sobchack had already laid out in 1992 the basic contours of what distinguishes cinematic spectatorship in the electronic age:

> Postcinematic, incorporating cinema into its own technologic, our electronic culture has disenfranchised the human body and constructed a new sense of existential "presence." Television, video tape recorders/players, videogames, and personal computers all form an encompassing electronic system whose various forms "interface" to constitute an alternative and virtual world that uniquely incorporates the spectator/user in a spatially decentered, weakly temporalized, and quasi-disembodied state. (300)

This passage from the conclusion of *Address of the Eye* was written just as digital imaging was beginning to alter cinema profoundly. Anticipating some of the key changes in the media environment over the next two decades, Sobchack cites those aspects of film viewing that would be affected most strongly: the involvement of all the senses in conjunction with the primary role of vision and hearing; spatial and temporal orientation; and the new sense of presence that the postcinematic image would generate. While I agree with her characterization of the new spectating position as "spatially decentered, weakly temporalized," her suggestion that it is "quasi-disembodied" or that "our electronic culture has disenfranchised the human body" broaches questions about the way moving-image media have affected human perception since cinema became a global cultural dominant. In this study, I address the convergence of cinema and digital media with respect to the role film has played in the coevolution of the human and technology over the last hundred years. Challenging the notion that our engagement with visual media is ever actually disembodied, my account of this process contributes to our understanding of how our increasingly mediated relation to today's digitized cultural environment is altering lived experience.

For some, the term postcinema seems to suggest that the film image will not survive the development and success of diverse forms of new media. Once restricted to the movie or television screen, moving images are now viewed on all manner of mobile devices and in almost every possible location. As these changes continue to take effect and new forms of media are invented at a rapid pace, there is little consensus about how this will affect cinema or whether it will succumb to the onslaught of new visual media. This popular cultural medium has, however, overcome comparable challenges in the past. Media technologies that enable new forms of entertainment either in the home (as had occurred with TV) or in public venues (such as IMAX theaters or video and VR installations) have always posed a threat to the movie industry (Young, xii). But cinema has proven resilient, both when TV became the dominant visual medium in the second half of the twentieth century and now as mobile moving-image devices have become commonplace. A quick assessment of the current state of cinema finds a robust medium that exhibits at least on the surface more continuity than mutation. Moviegoers still flock to theaters to be entertained by films of roughly the same length and narrative composition as the conventional feature film that took shape in the first two decades of the previous century. Faced with the strong disruptive potential of digital technology, the Hollywood film industry has responded in the same manner it has to all developments in film technology since the 1910s, assimilating digital imaging to its standard practices much as it had previously adopted innovations like sound, color, and the mobile camera. Economic, cultural, and social forces have ensured that advances in moving-image technology are deployed to bolster feature-film exhibition and reinforce the existing mode of spectatorship.

While those who fear that cinema's days are numbered seek reassurance from its continuing popularity, theorists of postcinema contend that the ubiquity of digital devices has already ushered in a new media regime with fundamentally different conditions for spectatorship. Still, the prefix "post" does not indicate a clean break from the inherited cultural forms of moving-image viewing to one shaped entirely by either new embodied sensibilities or epistemologies of perception (Denson and Leyda, 6–7). Rather, it designates a period of transition in which both traditional film aesthetics and inherited ontologies of the image continue to play a role. As David Bordwell has argued with his assertion of an "intensified continuity" (2006, 24, 50), digital imaging has the power to create even more compelling simulations that reinforce narrative continuity and representational realism. However, the ability to harness the power of digital technology in this way can also undermine the belief in an indexical connection between the chemical reaction that takes place on a strip of celluloid film and a profilmic reality. The digitally altered cinematic image threatens the traditional realist ontology of film. For some, this loss of indexicality has unleashed a fundamental "crisis in perception" (Brown, 70–71) or "crisis of realism" (Lowenstein, 2) and stoked the fear that digital technologies "are inherently deceptive and, therefore, dangerous" (Tyron, 47).

For the theorists of postcinema, this development has not spurred nostalgia for a grounding of film in material reality, but rather reveals the mediated nature of the indexical trace:

The relationship between an image and its profilmic referent is thus never fully given in the image itself. It is always
mediated by other elements, such as the screened or printed
representation, the sound accompanying it, the context in
which it is appearing, and the spectator's prior knowledge
and expectations about the process by which the image has
come to be what it is. Most or all of these variables remain
in place in digital cinema, even if the expectations themselves are changing (Ivakhiv 2016, 727).

This idea did not originate with postcinema. It is however made
manifest in the age of new media not only by the remediation of
the digital image into cinema, but also by our mediated engagement with a culture saturated by digital technologies. Moreover,
as Michel Chion explains, this idea was also already inherent in
the audiovisual image of classical cinema. The audio is never a
direct reproduction of naturalistic sound, but rather always rendered to enhance the affective dimension of the visual perception.
This distortion of auditory reality invalidates the indexical relation between film sound and the events on screen (109–14; Shaviro
2016b, 378).

The incorporation of digital imaging into cinema has shaken the
epistemological underpinning of realist film theory in another way
as well. The penetrating impact of film was due to a novel capture
and rendering of movement that simulates the temporal and spatial
constructs of consciousness. This aspect of film enables the viewer
to engage the image in such a way that, as Gilles Deleuze articulated
it, "the brain *is* the screen" (1986a). Notwithstanding this, the practices of classical cinema left the viewer bound to the camera, fixed
in a spectatorial relation to the screen, such that the participatory
potential of film remained largely unrealized. The crisis unleashed
by digital technology involves its ability to generate a more participatory viewing experience and to disrupt the mode of spectatorship
that has dominated since narrative integration became the operative paradigm for mainstream cinema. In this respect, the current
situation is analogous to that created by the invention of synchronized sound. In both cases, the new technology could be employed
to produce embodied forms of spectatorship that rely on all the

senses and threaten the hegemony of vision. The film industry re-sponded by developing production practices that reinforce classical narrative by making audio subservient to the image. Today, Holly-wood has dealt with digital technology in a similar fashion, finding ways to use CGI to enhance cinematic storytelling.

Critics who want to reassure us of cinema's sustainability have emphasized the resilience of the film industry to assert that digital techniques function "as additions or enhancements to the basic psychological and cultural experience of cinema" (Rodowick, 182). Even conceding this point, postcinema theory pushes back against the claim of an intensified continuity. Shaviro counters that the use of special effects in action blockbusters since the 1990s has spawned a postcontinuity style of filmmaking: "a preoccupation with imme-diate effects trumps any concern for broader continuity—whether on the immediate shot-by-shot level, or on that of the overall nar-rative" (2010, 123). He does not claim that these films no longer adhere to the basic continuity rules, but rather that it is no longer important, at least in the way it was prior to digital imaging. Clas-sical continuity, he explains, is not primarily about storytelling, but rather its main function has always been to orient the viewer securely within the spatiotemporal matrix of the film. Thus, con-tinuity no longer matters not because story no longer plays a role, but rather because our spatiotemporal orientation to the digitally mediated environment of the twenty-first century has changed and, consequently, so too has our orientation to the film image (Shaviro 2016a, 51).

The insistence on intensified continuity also downplays im-portant shifts that have occurred beneath the conscious level of psychological and cultural experience. Digitally produced dis-tortions of classical space, time, movement, rhythm, and sound operate outside the conventional narrative register that depends primarily on story patterning, character development, or ideologi-cal considerations. As our senses are assailed by dynamic imagery, accelerated movement, and penetrating sound, complex character development and psychologically motivated cause-and-effect logic give way to action generated for its own sake. As a result, there has been an aesthetic shift away from classical narrative and toward spectacle. The artistry of special effects often generates a strong

affective charge in the viewer that supplants desire or identification associated with characters or events in the narrative. These
pulses of undifferentiated affect inform the viewing experience
in crucial ways. Rather than a traditional form of identification
or alignment of subjectivities, they produce a kinesthetic melding
with the movement of characters and bodily engagement with the
film world. This new dimension of effects evokes for the most part
subphenomenal responses that demand bodily attention, but not
mental awareness. They are part of a paradigm shift away from
the scopic regime of modernity that is dominated by disembodied
vision to a mode of spectatorship where the invisible plays a pro-
gressively important part.

The explosion of digital technologies at the end of the last century has sparked a surge of theoretical work on the role media in
general and visual media in particular play in the coevolution of
the human with technology. As media theory focuses its attention
more on the transformational power of digital technology, it has
for the most part overlooked cinema's role in this process. Scholars working in this area often dismiss the cinematic image as one
that addresses the viewer almost strictly at the level of phenomenal
consciousness. This is perhaps not surprising, given the resilience
of mainstream narrative filmmaking. Moreover, the rapid proliferation and ubiquity of digital media, particularly in the form of
mobile, handheld devices, may well be reconfiguring our brain circuits in a more dramatic, or at least more rapid and thus more observable, manner than cinema has over the course of its existence.
Consequently, much has been written about how digital imaging is
changing and possibly even heralding the end of cinema, and there
has been correspondingly less interest in investigating cinema's
place in the coevolution of visual technology, cultural media, and
the human faculties that interface with them.

In this study I seek to rectify this situation. I engage contemporary media theory together with some of its important predecessors to argue that film, as the first moving-image technology to
have widespread and intensive influence across various cultures
globally, has substantially altered how the body processes external
images. My study tackles the question of the evolution of spectatorship with a two-pronged approach. First, it focuses on the in-

dividual spectator and examines how the audiovisual medium of cinema engages the body during film viewing in a way that reorganizes the neural networks that process sensory data and guide the body's movements. This analysis draws on two related views about the human that stem from recent studies in cognitive neuroscience and media theory. One contends that cognition is not a mental process restricted to higher consciousness, nor does it take place only within the human body. Rather, nonconscious cognitive processes contribute significantly to all higher mental operations, as do technical systems that humankind has developed to serve as prosthetic extensions to its biological capabilities. The other maintains that because cognition is embodied and extended in this manner, *human* evolution is not purely or even primarily a biological process but rather a coevolution of the human with the technology it is compelled to continuously advance so that it can successfully manage the existing technical systems. My first chapter argues these points and then analyzes how the moving-image medium of cinema engages the embodied spectator and influences the coevolution of the biological and the technological. In the last two chapters the focus shifts to the historical progression of media and the process of remediation. Examining film and cinema at two key points of convergence with other media, this second part of the book reinforces the arguments made in chapter 1. Just as cognition involves technical systems outside the body, the dynamic of remediation and reverse remediation between existing and new media extends into nonconscious cognitive processes in the body as well. Remediation between film and the dominant media around 1900 and then between cinema and digital media at the end of the twentieth century manifests the imbrication of the biological and the technological that pervades all aspects of the human coevolution with the cultural environment it has created.

Moving-Image Media and Embodied Spectatorship

Postcinematic vision refers to a new way of seeing both inside and outside the movie theater. It characterizes a contemporary stage in the complex development of visual media that is constantly transforming not only spectatorship, but human perception itself.

In the abundance of theoretical work that addresses the significance of digital imaging for cinema, scholars have for the most part
assumed that the human biological processes involved in audiovisual experience have remained constant. In his influential 2007
work *The Virtual Life of Film* David Rodowick offered an extensive
exploration of how digital technology has altered both the material and conceptual basis for constructing film images. Focusing
largely on how cinema shook up traditional aesthetic theory, he
argues that the continual movement of the celluloid film strip
through the projector disrupted the ontological stability of the
traditional aesthetic object. As a consequence, cinema studies has
always been more "a constantly shifting terrain for thinking about
time-based spatial media" than a conventional discipline with an
established object of study (12). Still, for Rodowick the essential
aspect of cinema as a new medium in the history of the arts was
the analog capture of moments of duration on film, a process that
extends but does not fundamentally alter the indexical character
of the photograph (12–14).

In what Shaviro has aptly described as a "beautifully elegiac
book" (2016b, 377), Rodowick affirms the radical disruption caused
by the technological innovation of new media, while insisting
that the essential aesthetic character of cinema and the basic set
of concepts in cinema studies still dominates the current cultural
practice. More specifically, he contends that "the social and technological architecture of theatrical film viewing and the basic
structure of classical Hollywood narrative have remained remark-
ably constant since 1917." And he claims that this is still the case,
even now that the synthetic, digital production of perceptually
realistic images has abolished cinema's indexical link to the dura-
tional existence of an actual past (182–83). I agree in general with
this assessment of the theatrical cinema experience. As I assert
in my analysis of films from the end of the 1990s in chapter 3, the
Hollywood film industry often employs digital imaging to enhance
the impression of a synthetic film reality, in much the same way as
they have utilized various other technological innovations over the
last century.

While I agree with Rodowick on these matters, there are key
differences in our evaluations of the effects of digital technology on

the cinematic experience and on spectatorship more broadly. My study focuses its attention largely on changes that occur beneath the level of phenomenological consciousness and entail cognitive faculties distributed across human, biological, and technological systems. Rodowick also discusses in some detail how the technological and material components of digital imaging alter the cinematic experience. For him, a crucial factor is that the human cannot read the coding of machine languages as a phenomenological image without technological intervention, and thus the digital image must always be converted into an analog format to become humanly perceptible (111–12). But of course, as he points out, analog systems of moving-image media also require technological interfaces, such as the film projector. Ultimately, what renders the use of digital imaging in cinema problematic for him is that, in contrast to the celluloid film image, it is not authentically cinematographic. As opposed to the analog transcription involved in film capture, the computational operation required to create the digital image merely mimics how "cinematography automatically creates . . . movement in and through space" (102). Motivated by a faulty notion of perceptual realism, filmmakers ignore, he argues, the intrinsic characteristics of digital imaging and employ it to simulate how the film world was constructed spatially through the medium of film. In Rodowick's view, the computational mode of image construction breaks the connection between the technical medium and human perception, but cinema continues to operate as if it were intact: "perceptual realism retreats from the physical world, placing its bets on imaginative worlds—in other words, a projection of mind into image that conflates mental images with perceptually real events" (105).

Rodowick's critique targets both the aesthetic practice of cinema in the digital age and film theory's failure to identify the misconceptions about media that plague contemporary cinema studies. Rather than address the particular arguments he makes about the digital image, I want to examine how his basic assumptions about the relationship between the human and media differ from those at work in this study. First, in distinguishing between the analog versus the digital cinematic image, he asserts that in the case of the former the cinematographic properties of the medium shape cinematic realism "automatically." By contrast, the latter depends almost exclusively on an intentional act informed by conscious choices and decisions. In both cases, he segregates the operations of higher consciousness from nonconscious processing that involves both the human biological system and the technical systems of cinema. We see this most clearly when he declares that the digital cinematic image has lost its reference to physical reality (its indexicality) and derives only from mental events, or "the free reign of the imaginary in the creation of images *ex nihilo* that can simulate effects of the physical world" (104).

In contrast to the gap Rodowick posits between conscious and nonconscious responses to images, I adhere to a more expansive view of cognition that has emerged out of convergent research areas in neuroscience, philosophy of mind, and related disciplines since the 1990s. Recent findings in these various fields reinforce ideas generated by cognitive scientists who have produced the so-called 4EA model of how the mind functions (Protevi, 25–26). As opposed to the classical cognitivist idea that the brain controls all nonconscious bodily processing in a top-down mode much like the central operating system of a computer, they argue that cognition is distributed across different modes of conscious and nonconscious processes (*embodied, embedded, enacted, extended, affective cognition*). This new conception of the mind-body attributes a greater role in our mental life to automatic, subcortical circuitry in the brain. An increasing number of studies across a wide range of the biological and cognitive sciences have contributed to the idea that in all situations nonconscious neural processing contributes to higher consciousness in an integral manner. This model of how humans process lived experience rejects the traditional idea that human cognition is a process that only operates inside the body in conjunction with incorporeal thought processes. According to the extended cognition piece of the 4EA model, higher-order mental processing is not confined to the biological processes within the body. Rather, it includes operations occurring in cognitive systems distributed widely across both natural and technical environments. This applies to human interaction with all technical systems, including the computational operations in computer code that produce digital images. This concept of distributed cognition contradicts Rodowick's assumption that the mathematical process that simulates classical cinematic realism occurs in a technical realm that is cut off from the human system of perception. Even in the case of such a complex interface between visual perception and an external image, our sensory processing works in conjunction with the technical system that produces the image.

The second area of theory that supports my account of post-cinematic vision and marks a clear distinction with Rodowick postulates that *human* evolution is not exclusively biological, but rather is first and foremost a coevolution of humankind with the technology it has created. The idea that our biological systems of perception work integrally with computer codes at the subphenomenal level in the production and reception of digital images only makes sense if we assume that our bodies are changing and adapting to digital technology in a fundamental way. That is, the prevalence of digital imaging in cinema and other (audio)visual media is altering our relation to the image in a way that is part of a larger collective process of cultural and biological evolution linked to the development of technical systems. Drawing on evidence and arguments from interrelated fields (paleoanthropology, neuroscience, cybernetics, and media theory, among others), I seek to establish the idea that the prosthetic extension of our neural systems into external media has been the primary motor of *human* evolution since early tool use. My analysis embraces the concept of technogenesis to address a notion that has demonstrated remarkable staying power not only in mainstream film theory but also in areas of recent media theory that emphasize embodied responses to external images. This is the idea that cinema presents the viewer with a discrete image that works almost exclusively at the level of phenomenal consciousness. Throughout this study I call on recent discoveries in neuroscience to argue that even in the case of conventional narrative cinema, spectatorship cannot be limited to the passive receipt of information in the form of what some theorists have called the *phatic image*.

This focus on cinema's place in the coevolution of the human and technology marks another point of distinction between my assessment of digital cinematic imaging and Rodowick's. In his description of how the cinematic imaginary relates to the nonconscious processing that produces spatial orientation he charges that "the concept of realism in use by computer graphics professionals . . . does not correspond to an ordinary spatial sense of the world and actual events taking place within it, but rather to our perceptual and cognitive norms for apprehending a *represented* space" (103). Rodowick is certainly correct in differentiating between how the viewer orients herself spatially to the film world versus outside the movie theater in a real (nonmediated) spatial environment. However, throughout his discussion of the spatial orientation produced by a cinematic representation based on what he terms perceptual realism, he assumes an "ordinary" spatial sense of the world that has remained constant since the emergence of film at the end of the nineteenth century. The theory of the coevolution of the biological and technological that informs my work suggests that pervasive moving-image media such as cinema and more recently digital media change how our bodies process not only technically produced external images but also our interaction with real environments as well. Recent studies in cognitive science and media theory have shown how the omnipresence of digital technology has altered both how we negotiate our movements through space in complex cultural environments and our perceptual and cognitive apprehension of space. At the end of this study I analyze how the digital cinematic image embodies changes that have occurred to the human biological systems for maintaining spatial orientation even as it also contributes to these changes produced by lived experience in a cultural environment increasingly mediated by digital technology. According to a central thesis of this book, the cinematic image has had a similar effect on the human systems of sensorimotor processing over the hundred-plus years since the invention of the film camera and projector.

In her recent exploration of how higher consciousness always works in conjunction with nonconscious cognitive processes, Katherine Hayles advocates persuasively for increased attention in the humanities to the role nonconscious cognition plays in every area of human decision-making. This includes both decisions that are largely reached and executed automatically with the help of highly complex technical systems, such as autonomous trading algorithms, and ethical decisions that determine the social and cultural environment we inhabit. Expanding the concept of extended cognition to explain what she calls a *planetary cognitive ecology* (2017, 3), she provides a broad theoretical framework that supports my central thesis of a coevolution of humans and moving-image media that has produced new networks (or "assemblages" as she prefers to call them) of complex interactions between conscious and nonconscious human operations, biological and technical systems, and human and nonhuman cognizers.

My study takes a similar approach to consider postcinematic vision both in terms of perception and at the subphenomenal level of sensory processing. It draws on recent work in neuroscience to show how in film viewing, the two sets of neural networks that support these operations do not function independently of each other in distinct brain areas. Rather, changes in the material composition and temporal properties of external images alter not only the body's motoricity, but reverberate throughout the entire chain of both pre-personal affects and mental imaging activated by contact with a medium. Even without stirring conscious awareness, media images can disrupt fixed perceptual images and transform how we perceive and think about the world. Describing how the film effect depends on this reciprocity between sensations and meaning, Sobchack asserts that the "meaning-making capacity of [the] senses . . . are always acculturated and never lived as either discrete or raw" (2004b, 61). As new media exert their effect on the various sensorimotor images produced by automatic bodily activity (not only visual images, but also aural, tactile, and kinesthetic ones, among others), they also give rise to new modes of image generation in higher-order mental operations.

At the beginning of her book *Unthought: The Power of the Cognitive Unconscious*, Hayles draws a distinction that serves my work as well. She differentiates between nonconscious cognitive processes at work within individual subjects and systemic nonconscious cognitive assemblages "which include human, biological, technical and material components" (2). Although I have not adopted Hayles's terminology, my account of how the human has coevolved with moving-image media since the invention of film also alternates between these two scopes of investigation. At times, I concentrate on nonconscious cognitive processes occurring within the individual spectator, and at other times, the focus expands to networks of biological, material, and technical systems that extend across a larger cultural environment. "Spectatorship" refers to such a collective systemic network that has continually evolved and adapted to developments in moving-media technology and its corresponding cultural practices.

In analyzing the evolution of spectatorship, my study also assumes a generalized spectator unmoored for the most part from particular national, historical, or social circumstances. There is of course no such actual being, and theoretical studies that speak in terms of "the spectator" inevitably evoke from some the objection that individual, historical, and cultural factors have a constant and profound effect on how we engage with film. I am certainly not denying that point. It would be absurd to do so. By the same token, the existence of these factors does not invalidate theoretical work that brackets them out in order to analyze basic aspects of the film experience shared by all. Indeed, film theories that focus on spectatorship, whether they follow a semiotic, psychoanalytical, cognitivist, or Deleuzian model, must consign social and historical variances to a secondary position. The media-theoretical approach I have chosen does this, but in doing so it avoids shortcomings of the main two spectator-centered theories that it challenges, apparatus theory and cognitivist film theory. The former presupposes an unchanging, monolithic sociocultural frame that has determined viewer response throughout the history of cinema. The latter posits the viewer as an organism with a basic set of bodily properties and mental processes that have been fixed for several millennia. By situating cinema in the coevolution of the human with technology, my study emphasizes the ever-changing construct of both the cultural environment and the human organism as an essential aspect of "the spectator."

Media Convergence and Remediation

To assess the effect cinema has had on spectatorship and the human system for processing external phenomena more generally it is necessary to analyze it as part of an ongoing process of mutual interchange among the various media that are driving culture at any one time. In the last two chapters of the book the primary focus shifts from the individual, embodied spectator to the evolution of media and the convergence of film and cinema with other major media. The history of media is a cumulative process whereby new dominant forms may eclipse old media in prominence, or even supplant them, but never totally leave them behind. As recent theorists have asserted, the historical development of media always involves both the remediation of material and formal elements from past technologies into new ones, as well as the reverse transaction whereby existing media are altered by new ones. Or, as W. J. T. Mitchell stated in axiomatic fashion, *"all media are mixed media"* (399). Marshall McLuhan declared that the study of this dynamic was key to understanding how media drive human evolution in the modern age. He writes with respect to photography: "To understand the medium of the photograph is quite impossible, then, without grasping its relations to other media, both old and new. For media, as extensions of our physical and nervous systems, constitute a world of biochemical interactions that must ever seek new equilibrium as new extensions occur" (1994, 202). The constellation of overlapping media is such that a significant alteration in any one area is like a stone thrown into a pond. It sets off a series of waves across the whole spectrum that triggers changes in other media as well as the whole cultural environment and leads to a reconfiguration of the human sensorium.

A brief discussion of the 1999 work that reintroduced the concept of remediation into contemporary media theory will help clarify what is at stake in my analysis of how the material medium of film and the cultural practice of cinema converged with other media. In *Remediation: Understanding New Media*, Jay Bolter and Richard Grusin distinguish between traditional forms of transparent media and the hypermedia of the digital age to explain what is distinctively new in the present. Their account of this historical development toward nontransparent media hinges on whether older forms that have been remediated into the new are acknowledged or concealed. The concept of hypermedia refers specifically to the way digital media remediate older forms aggressively and comprehensively, while still marking their presence openly. And they contrast this mode of remediation to film. Echoing the prevailing view

in contemporary film and media theory, they contend that mainstream cinema excels in rendering its own apparatus transparent and concealing elements of other media that have become its
content. In this way, film, like other predigital technologies, fuels
the desire for *transparent immediacy* and promotes the principle
of indexicality that underlies it: "The common feature of all these
forms [of transparent immediacy] is the belief in some necessary
contact point between the medium and what it represents" (30). At
the same time, Bolter and Grusin maintain that both transparent
media and hypermedia are manifestations of the same desire to
"achieve the real" (53). Furthermore, they declare: "The work of art
today seems to offer 'an aspect of reality which cannot be freed
from mediation or remediation,' at the same time that new media
seek to present us precisely with 'an aspect of reality which is free
from all mediation'" (75).

In characterizing the evolution of media in this manner, Bolter
and Grusin appear to be reducing remediation to a mechanism
whereby "'new' media borrow conventions of the 'old' in the process of constructing their new brands of realist representation"
(Young, xx). This is evident, for example, when they argue that in
computer animation and virtual reality the movement of the image
enables new strategies for achieving immediacy and "involving the
viewer more intimately in the image" (28). In my analysis of how
cinema has shaped how we see the world, the movement in and of
the image plays a crucial role. However, rather than focusing on
absorption in the image ("involving the viewer more intimately"),
I explore how it engages the viewer at the level of automatic bodily
experience and, in doing so, has altered our technologically mediated relation to the moving image. By linking the process of remediation to the coevolution of the human and technology, my
approach opens new perspectives on how film has served as an
active agent in the evolution of media that shaped culture at both
the beginning and the end of the twentieth century.

To illustrate how this difference in the understanding of remediation highlights my book's main contribution to the current
theoretical discourse revolving around film and digital media, I
turn to Bolter and Grusin's critique of McLuhan. They cite his now
axiomatic declaration that "the 'content' of any medium is always

another medium" (1994, 8), and acknowledge that their concept has its roots in his work. However, reiterating a view made popular by Raymond Williams, they see McLuhan's work tainted by a strain of technological determinism that the information industry now employs for commercial gain. Holding his writings responsible for how they are now used to justify "the excesses of technologically driven capitalism in the late twentieth century," Bolter and Grusin assert that they "can reject McLuhan's determinism and still appreciate his analysis of the remediating power of various media" (76–77).

I take issue with precisely this point. There is an element of technological determinism in McLuhan's theory, albeit not of the kind attributed to him by Williams, Bolter and Grusin, and others. Near the end of his seminal 1964 work *Understanding Media: The Extensions of Man*, he asserts that we cannot free ourselves from our relation with technology: "It is the theme of this book that not even the most lucid understanding of the peculiar force of a medium can head off the ordinary 'closure' of the senses that causes us to conform to the pattern of experience presented" (1994, 329). In McLuhan's formulation, "closure" refers to the body's reaction whenever our sensorium has been reorganized through the body's interaction with new media. Dramatic shifts in the existing media complex produce a shock in the biological organism and result in the closure of the remaining sensorimotor circuits around the gap that was produced by the prosthetic extension of the others into external media. This process, which McLuhan calls "autoamputation," establishes a new equilibrium among the senses that alters how the body perceives and interacts with the external world. Given this intrinsic connection between the biological and technological, media appear and operate as part of an overarching coevolution of the human and technology that does advance with an irresistible force. As humankind develops new technology, it is perpetually driven to embrace and modify it, evolving along with it to more complex forms of existence.

This does not mean however that any specific medium is endowed with the irresistible force of technological progress, such that its effects are predetermined, already manifest in the technology itself. The charge of determinism leveled at McLuhan contends, wrongly in my view, that according to his theory media in and of themselves determine our economic and social order. In fact, his analysis of media always includes the broader process of mediation, whereby various social forces, cultural practices, and media constellations influence how humans interact with a technology over time. In the case of film, production companies and the institutional structures that govern filmmaking, movie theaters and other exhibition sites, the aesthetic paradigms for products such as a feature film, and the subsequent innovations in moving-image technology are all factors that comprise cinema as a medium. Film and media theory has long argued that these elements have served to render the apparatus transparent, leading to a dominant film style that caters to the desire for the real and situates the viewer as a disengaged observer of an extant reality. Underwritten primarily by semiotics and psychoanalysis, apparatus theory dominated in the 1970s and into the 1980s. Even after cognitivist film theory challenged it directly in the 1980s and cultural studies approaches replaced it as the dominant paradigm in the 1990s, it has continued to exert its influence in media theory's assessment of cinema.

This is evident in Bolter and Grusin's account of media convergence in the digital age. Even as they assert that in the digital age hypermedia have discarded the principle of transparency, they hold to the notion that the desire for the real and the logic of immediacy dominate our relation to the image. In doing so, they elevate the cultural practices that have shaped dominant cinema into a universal principle (a historically inflected "logic of immediacy" [31]) that remains constant across all phases of the human interface with visual media. In my analysis of cinema's convergence with other media I seek to unpack this collapse of medium and mediation that clouds Bolter and Grusin's work as well as the film theories that influenced them. By framing their theory of remediation in terms of transparent immediacy, they do not merely obscure the role cinema has played in the coevolution of the human and media. They efface the essential relation between the biological and the technological that distinguishes human evolution. In doing so, they also belie the essential idea at the heart of McLuhan's understanding of media. He proclaimed that all technology is a prosthetic extension of the body into the external environment, and that the essence of what it means to be human is that we coevolve with the cultural changes it produces. In his analysis of a wide array of modern media, he casts them not merely as a means for conveying knowledge or information, but rather as an expansion of our cognitive system that works its effects back onto the body and changes our whole nervous system: "Physiologically, man in the normal use of technology (or his variously extended body) is perpetually modified by it and in turn finds ever new ways of modifying his technology" (1994, 46). As new forms of media emerge, certain patterns of sensory processing are extended through them into the external environment. This disrupts the existing distribution of the senses in the body and alters how we interact with the world in a significant manner (1994, 45–46). According to McLuhan, this is the essential dynamic that drives our evolution as humans.

Maintaining that this is key to understanding how media function, my study considers the historical evolution of cinema as a continual transaction between moving-image media and changes in the human sensorium produced by the rapid growth of technological culture throughout the twentieth century. Arguing against the grain of most contemporary media theory, I claim that the moving image of cinema has always served to disrupt the spectatorial relation of the viewer to the image and challenge the ocularcentric nature of modern culture. My central thesis asserts that the invention, development, and dissemination of film and other moving-image technology have continuously altered the underlying relation between media and human perception in ways that counter the scopic regime of modernity and visual realism. Through the engagement of neural networks that produce subperceptual signals, the moving image in all its formats has continuously altered the existing relation between the various senses and reorganized the human sensorium. However, rather than attempting what would be a thinly stretched study of cinema's interaction with other media over its long history, I have chosen to focus on two critical points of media convergence—one at the beginning and the other at the end of the twentieth century. At these two junctures film underwent a dramatic process of remediation with the major media of the time. An analysis of the larger cultural environment in which this occurred and of the reaction of writers, scholars, and filmmakers to the transformative force of new media will provide insight into how advances in technology were not only changing spectatorship in a fundamental way but also modifying both the conscious and nonconscious human systems for interacting with the external world.

The invention of the film camera and projector and the rapid growth of public film exhibitions at the end of the nineteenth century sent shock waves through the network of dominant media at the time and triggered a wave of remediation and reverse remediation between film and its predecessors. The most significant reaction did not come from the effect film had on other visual media, but rather from its encounter with the dominant medium that had propelled human culture forward for more than three millennia: alphabetic writing. The spectacular new moving-image medium challenged the hegemony of writing and sparked responses from the literary world in a way that previous visual technologies had not. As devices that were born of the mechanized urban life around the turn of the century, the film camera and projector were attuned to a human sensorium that was adjusting to the faster-paced culture and the deluge of new impressions afforded its neural networks. The new moving-image medium was a prosthetic extension of these sensory networks that supported adaptation to the fast-evolving technologies of the twentieth century. According to McLuhan's concept of autoamputation, when these new networks of sensory processing are formed they challenge the current dominant sense and produce a new equilibrium in the human sensorium. When film burst onto the scene around 1900, it encountered an ocularcentric culture. As a result of writing's position as the preeminent medium driving cultural evolution for millennia, vision had become firmly entrenched as the dominant sense. With respect to film's effect on the sensory systems of the spectator, this leads to the counterintuitive conclusion that the rise and spread of film challenged the status of vision. My discussion of the remediation between film and writing around 1900 and cinema and digital media around 2000 will support this idea. My account of cinema's role in the coevolution of humans and technology throughout the twentieth century contends that it and other moving-image media have promoted primordial tactility, a state of bodily processing in which the senses operate in a more unified manner. The second pivotal period of convergence comes after cinema had had far-reaching effects on modern culture for a hundred years. This time it is the established medium that is challenged by a new field of technology and a whole set of new media that it had spawned. The explosion of digital technology at the end of the twentieth century constituted a major threshold event in the evolution of media. Cinema offers one of the most obvious instances where the remediation of accepted conventions into emerging media and the reverse remediation of new technology back into the existing medium play a crucial role in shaping the human interface with a fast-changing cultural environment. Media theorists have assessed cinema's influence on new media differently. In *The Language of New Media* (2001) Lev Manovich famously declared that the cinematic window onto the world had become the determinant aesthetic principle that was framing our interface with computer technology (86). Others have latched onto this idea to support their belief or hope that cinema would remain a vibrant cultural medium despite the rampant spread of the digital image. Rodowick, for example, claims that in the age of digital cinema "the varieties of now-overlapping moving-image experience could be called 'cinematographic'" (187). While I do not disagree, my analysis of how these media have converged with the fusion of analog and digital imaging suggests that cinematography has evolved in a more complex fashion than Rodowick assumes when he argues that the basic concepts of traditional film theory remain the best framework for understanding audiovisual culture in the digital age (188–89). To be sure, digital forms of moving-image media have adopted the basic toolset of conventional cinema to provide structure and coherence to their sequences and narratives. As these techniques are remediated back into cinema, cinematographic elements/principles employed in digital media have undergone transformations and are now altering the cinematographic image in substantial ways.

This ever-progressing interchange among a diverse set of moving-image media is not confined to audiovisual instruments and aesthetic techniques. With the advent of digital devices, the physical and cultural contexts for spectatorship have changed and expanded dramatically. Moving-image media have become tailored more to a user than a spectator in the traditional sense of a movie-goer or even a television viewer. Even more important, digital technology has radically transformed how the individual interacts with the complex environment of a contemporary culture saturated with technical interfaces. Our engagement with the external world has become heavily, and almost incessantly, mediated through digital tools. The cinematographic techniques that are remediated from digital moving-image media back into cinema bring with them this fundamentally new relation of the user/spectator to the image. As a composite of biological and technological systems that have evolved in relation to both audiovisual media and technical culture at large, postcinematic vision manifests how remediation is an essential dynamic not only in the progression of media but in every facet of *human* evolution.

The following provides an overview of the book's structure and approach. My study begins by laying the groundwork for its claim that cinema has played and continues to play a major role in the coevolution of the human and technology. The first part of chapter 1 sketches a broad historical account of how the capacity to make and refine tools propelled humans out of the slow progression of biological evolution into an ever-accelerating co-advance with the technological culture it was producing. The next section counters the idea that cinema only offers what Paul Virilio has termed a "phatic image" (62–65), one that has lost the power to engage sensorimotor systems directly and alter neural circuitry in the brain. I argue that, as an essential element of the viewing experience, movement in and of the image activates the sensorimotor systems of the viewer, such that tactile, somatosensory, kinesthetic, proprioceptive, and other embodied responses are always engaged at the level of both affect and cognition. After countering the view that film spectatorship is disembodied, my analysis shifts around to deal with the inverse problem, namely that the recent focus on the role of subperceptual processes has led to the devaluation of the conscious, deliberative dimension of the film experience. Rejecting the dismissive conclusion that "consciousness is an epiphenomenon," I suggest how understanding cinematic spectatorship requires insight into the conjoined neural networking of automatic microprocesses and conscious macroprocesses. This is particularly relevant with respect to moving-image media. Like all media, film, I argue, incorporates the dual temporality of automatic, subphenomenal processes and deliberative, conscious processes that is operative in the human biological organism. The final section of chapter 1 offers a brief discussion of two films—*Strange Days* (Kathryn Bigelow, 1995) and *Abre los ojo* ([*Open Your Eyes*] Alejandro Amenábar, 1997)—whose narratives and application of digital technology reflect cinema's belated awareness of this ability to mirror in its own medial properties the basic structures of human mental processing. My reading of these films maintains that as they recognize cinema's technogenetic disposition, they also help restore its ability to effect change.

Chapter 2 examines how cinematic spectatorship was shaped by the convergence of film with the dominant media around 1900. It begins by assessing how the distanced, disembodied viewing position that had prevailed in the visual arts since Renaissance painting influenced film practices. Tracing a gradual shift that occurred as a series of new moving-image devices appeared in the course of the nineteenth century, my analysis contends that the more refined cameras and projectors developed around the turn of the century presented the viewer with a compelling prosthetic extension of visual consciousness. The next section examines how film was the product of a mechanized urban society at the beginning of the twentieth century. Adhering to the concept of technogenesis, it explores how film came into being when changes in the human sensorium produced by a faster, more complex mechanical culture were extended into external media images. As evidence of this effect, my account cites early film theorists who observe how film afforded itself to the "apperceptive apparatus" (Benjamin 1969b, 250) of the modern urban dweller in a way that supported adaptation to the mechanized culture of the day.

The second half of chapter 2 focuses on the clash between this vibrant new visual technology and the long-standing dominant cultural medium of writing. This discussion first recounts how contemporary literary authors and film critics evaluated the progressive impetus of film versus the more conservative interests of the established literary sphere. The attention then turns to later theorists who articulate the fundamental opposition between writing and film in terms of how they configure the constellation of the human sensorium. In the last two sections of the chapter, I investigate the reciprocal process of remediation that occurred between these two media as the reach and popularity of film grew rapidly. Assuming first a bird's-eye view of the dynamic at work as a standard feature-film format took shape, my analysis targets the particular issue of embodied spectatorship. This discussion addresses the remediation of literary elements into film as part of a much broader framework of mediation, one that considers how the entire set of conditions that structure readership (cultural forces, commercial interests, bodily disposition, and aesthetic forms, among others) work their way into film viewing. The last section of the chapter takes a different approach to explore the reverse remediation of film practices back into literature and writing more generally. It offers a case study of how early cinema influenced the life and writing of Franz Kafka and sparked an ambivalent resistance to its effects. The first part of the section chronicles Kafka's fascination with cinema and his eventual rejection of it because of its detrimental effect on his work as a writer. The second part argues that the personal and professional crisis provoked by film contributed substantially to a sustained analysis in his later works of the pervasive, deterritorialized control that writing exerts throughout modern society.

Chapter 3 returns to the end of the twentieth century to map the fault lines in moving-image spectatorship created by the convergence of cinema and digital media. The first part of the chapter charts the changes that the incorporation of digital technology into filmmaking has produced in the cinematic mode of representation and film viewing. It pays particular attention to the ways in which the aesthetic techniques of digital media that cinema employs are in fact cinematographic practices that were remediated into the new media and altered by them before being remediated back into cinema. This section then discusses films at the end of the 1990s that offer metareflective commentary on the shift in cinematic spectatorship that is occurring even as they employ digital imaging in ways that generate a new spectating position. The next section expands the discussion to include other films that also address the convergence of film and digital media. Here the analysis demonstrates how digital imaging enables new modes of dynamic movement, penetrating sound, and spatiotemporal orientation that alter cinematic spectatorship in a significant manner. Reflecting on the conventional continuities of classical cinema even as they fracture them, these films activate new sensorimotor systems and engender more fully embodied modes of spectatorship. Furthermore, I argue, as they engage the neural networks required to establish spatial and temporal orientation to the digitally altered film world, these films also promote adaptation to our mediated interface with the digitized cultural environment outside the theater.

The final section of chapter 3 investigates how the science-fiction scenarios of these films probe the relationship between the postcinematic image and our digitally mediated interface with a highly computerized cultural environment. As they envision a future where the posthuman subject can exist without the physical medium of a body, they reveal how this idea stems from the representational realism of classical cinema. My analysis claims that they address this question implicitly, rejecting in the end the fear that digital technologies could lead to a disembodied singular consciousness. However I contend, in contrast to other film scholars, that even as they implicate the classical mode of cinematic spectatorship as a source of this misconception, they fail to suggest that it should or even could be completely eliminated. Rather, they see the digitized postcinematic image as a hybrid construct that requires a corresponding shift in the spectating position and the embrace of our posthuman embodied being in a world mediated through digital technology.

In the conclusion I offer some parting thoughts about how this study has sought to contribute to our understanding of the interlacing of the biological and technological that constitutes human existence. Reiterating the structural correspondence between the evolution of neural networks in the brain and the advance of technology, I emphasize here how the hybrid forms generated by the confluence of cinema and new media mirror the way lived experience is mediated through increasingly sophisticated technologies.

I also contend that this convergence modifies our physical existence and produces a new conception of the human. This closing
discussion reframes my account of how a digitally altered cinema
contributes to the expansion and deterritorialization of the human
sensorium, giving particular attention to the way it promotes adaptation to a technologically saturated cultural environment. It also
re-articulates the crucial point that cinema did not just assume
this cloak when it became postcinema, but rather that it has served
this function since its emergence.

{ 1 }

Film and the Embodied Mind

Technogenesis: The Coevolution of the Biological and Technological

To comprehend the changes cinema has produced in the way humans "see the world," both in terms of presubjective modes of perception and higher-order forms of visual consciousness, we need to situate them in the long history of the coevolution of the human with the cultural environment humans create. According to the concept of technogenesis, the integral coupling of the biological human with the technologically altered external environment defines the originary condition of the human and drives the coevolutionary process that now determines the progress of the species. As a major innovation in visual media, the moving image of film has played a significant role in this process of cultural evolution over the last century. Placing new demands on the affective, perceptual, and cognitive networks for processing visual input, it has altered both automatic bodily interactions with external images as well as the higher-order cognitive processing of them. By virtue of its wide circulation via cinema, film has established a prosthetic relation with the human that extends beyond each individual to a collective process of technico-cultural evolution. Before making the case for film's place in this process as part of the progression of modern media since 1900, the first part of this chapter establishes the theoretical foundation for positing the integral fusion of the biological and the technological.

The key element that separates the human from all other species is the ability to change the environment through technics and to evolve along with those technological changes (technogenesis). Humans share many essential cognitive processes, including among others perception, memory, attention, and categorization, with other primates (Tomasello, 10–12). The capacity to archive and retrieve traces of key evolutionary events in the external world propelled the human species out of the slow, plodding advance of biological evolution and into an ever-accelerating cycle of bodily changes that occur in response to the alterations it makes in the world. Insisting that changes to the human body are mediated through culture and technology, Klaus Theweleit offers this provocative description of the human condition: "*This* is evolution: the use of technics. There is no such thing as 'biological' evolution" (260).

Paleoanthropologists have long promoted the basic idea expressed by Theweleit in his dramatic, and purposely overstated, formulation. In his classic work *Gesture and Speech*, André Leroi-Gourhan describes how the human had already reached the ceiling of its anatomical evolution as much as a million years ago when its main characteristics were already in place: upright posture, the emancipated hand, tools, and rudimentary language. At this point the cortical fan had already opened out as wide as it would extend. The development of *Homo sapiens* remained then a matter of shifting proportions between different parts of the brain and changes in its neural organization. According to Leroi-Gourhan, the gradual development of tools and technology was the crucial factor that enabled the reengineering of the brain. They formed the medium, or culture, in which memory could be offloaded and stored outside the body. This exteriorized mode of memory served as a prosthetic extension of the internal forms of memory stored genetically in the DNA and neurally in the nervous system.[1]

More recently, Bernard Stiegler has elaborated the consequences of this early threshold shift in human evolution for understanding our existence as humans. In his account of the inception of human technology he asserts that the memory of the stereotype for the first tools, choppers, and rudimentary bi-faced blades resided first in the material trace, that is, in the tool itself. The steps needed to produce the tool required anticipation and foresight. The tool was the reservoir or medium where the memory of those steps was stored. The earliest technical memory of how to produce the simple flaked pebble resided outside the body as a prosthetic memory that enabled *Homo habilis* to act with foresight and to reproduce the tool. Stiegler explains that the production of tools started the long process of specifically human evolution whereby "the differentiation of the cortex is determined by the tool just as much as that of the tool by the cortex" (158). The tool as an external medium for memory is then not merely the first instance of the coevolution of the human and technology. It is technogenesis at its origin, the "coup" where technical innovation began to shape the cortex and the human emerged. These first instruments are also not just primitive prosthetic devices that support and extend already existing systems of biomechanics in the prehuman biological makeup. The shaping of the brain (functionally and anatomically) through the tools we produce is the central dynamic in the emergence of the human and remains so throughout human evolution: "The prosthesis is not a mere extension of the human body; it is the constitution of his body *qua* 'human'" (Stiegler, 152–53). While most biological organisms evolve directly within natural environments, adaptation to the cultural and technological innovations introduced by humans involves a process of technical mediation. Pushing this position to its techno-logical conclusion, Stiegler claims that it is impossible then to separate human evolution from advances in culture. The former is the interior and biological and the latter the exterior and material instantiation of a unified process that he calls "technico-social-cultural *differentiation*" (155). In charting the transition from materiality to interface in contemporary media arts, Louise Poissant reveals how our most advanced cultural achievements depend on the same basic creative process that produced the first tools: "The technique restores for us the state of advancement of our knowledge, crystallized in the tools that we have shaped but also our way of asking questions, of looking at solutions and of our way of representing a situation. There would be a whole technogenesis linking human development to technical innovations and to the materials produced" (230–31).

As central as technical mediation is to Stiegler's account of this evolutionary process, he resorts to conscious mental content to describe it. He argues that the exteriorization of mental representations, that is, of the steps required to make a tool, is an essential part of the restructuring of the brain that drives human evolution. Other proponents of technogenesis maintain that the technologically mediated relation with the world via sensorimotor-based images accounts for the emergence of the human and has continued to directly alter mental processes throughout human evolution.[2] I return to this point later in a different context, drawing on cognitive neuroscience to explore similarities in the temporal properties of neural networks in the body to those of external, technological systems. While this issue remains open to debate, recent findings in neuroscience have bolstered the view that nonconscious technical mediation was the crucial driving mechanism in human cognitive evolution. In *Origins of the Modern Mind*, Merlin Donald sketches three major transitions that occurred in the course of the long evolution that produced the present stage of human intelligence. The first two entail biological adaptations and culminate with the emergence of *Homo sapiens* and the human speech system. The third adaptation began with the human capacity for "visual symbolism and external memory" (6). Donald argues that the development of external systems for symbolic representation led to a cognitive advance of the same magnitude as that produced by Darwinian evolution. New media for the external storage of mental images entail "a *hardware* change in human cognitive structure," Donald asserts, "but the 'hardware' supporting this adaptation is technological rather than biological" (15–16). He draws on neuroscience to explain how extended cognition leads to a coevolutionary intertwining of technology and the human mind. Employing the model of selective synaptic growth proposed by Donald Hebb, he argues that cultural evolution produces corresponding alterations in brain function and cognition. Jean-Pierre Changeux's "epigenetic theory of brain development" (13) provides further support for his explanation of how cognition adapts to changes in the cultural environment.

In the years since Donald presented his theory, cognitive neuroscience has made considerable strides in understanding both neuroplasticity and epigenesis. In basing his evolution of human cognition on Hebb's explanation of synaptogenesis and Changeux's early model of epigenetic modulation, Donald describes changes occurring within prewired brain systems. Recent evidence increasingly suggests that altered external environments can also produce corresponding changes in the variant neuroanatomy of the brain (Quartz and Sejnowski). Although much work remains before a more comprehensive taxonomy of these brain systems can be established, preliminary findings suggest that the brain has much more flexibility in adapting to changes in the environment than previously thought and has evolved toward increased adaptability. The basic law governing this mode of brain development goes back to the late 1940s. Commonly known as Hebb's law and expressed by the axiom "neurons that fire together wire together," it gives the following basic account of brain development. At birth the brain has an overabundance of synaptic connections between neurons. Through neural pruning those synapses that are needed to process input from the environment become stronger, while those that serve little purpose die out. In this way, the nervous system of the infant is able to adapt to new patterns of sensory input provided by the environment. The technological innovations produced by each generation then reconfigure the neural architecture of the next. The main period of adaptation lasts from infancy until early adulthood, at which point the neural circuitry in an individual becomes largely fixed. When each generation reaches maturity and begins to leave its mark on the world, these changes in brain function drive the next wave of technological innovation, which then starts the subsequent cycle of generational adaptation. The new generation attains through neural pruning and synaptogenesis a mantle of neural circuitry that is needed to negotiate the technical complexities of the cultural environment it encounters.

Evidence continues to build that neural plasticity remains much more active throughout adulthood than originally predicted according to Hebb's law (Doidge). There are also increasing indications that changes in the environment not only strengthen selected synaptic connections and produce new ones but also reconfigure the body epigenetically, such that these changes are also hereditary (Tollefsbol). In particular, the central nervous system and neural processing in the brain are affected in this way. At the end of the nineteenth century Mark James Baldwin had already asserted that genetic mutations could lead to changes in the environment that then feed back into larger populations and generate epigenetic evolution. Hayles has proposed that we can now observe "a modified Baldwin effect" (2012, 100) at work in the contemporary media environment. That is, the constant development of new media that in themselves demand ever-faster response times has resulted in a continual loop of epigenetic change cycled through an information-intensive media landscape. Natural selection and genetic mutation are not the primary drivers of this evolutionary process. It is in this regard that we are to understand Theweleit's declaration: "There is no such thing as 'biological' evolution."

There is no evidence to date that changes in the neural architecture of the brain are biologically inheritable. However, this is not necessary for neural plasticity to be a driving mechanism in an evolutionary process that is not solely dependent on the inheritance of genetic mechanisms. Various challenges to a strict Darwinian view of evolution through natural selection has produced a gradually expanding version of what has been termed the "modern synthesis" of nineteenth-century theories with new perspectives. Population genetics, embryology, the adaptive landscape model, niche construction, and ecological genetics, among other areas of research, have introduced new perspectives in evolutionary biology in the second half of the twentieth century. The original concept of a modern synthesis, first formulated as such by Julian Huxley in 1942, has given way to a more complex amalgam of evolutionary dynamics that enable traits to be passed down from one generation to the next. These include among others the Baldwin effect, epigenetic inheritance, and phenotypic plasticity. When viewed in its totality, the new synthesis shifts the focus from a system of biologically inherited genetic traits to the relational entirety of the organism and the species as a whole within the environment. In arguing for the adoption of a broad-based developmental systems theory, Denis Walsh contends that adaptive phenotypic plasticity plays an essential role in evolution in conjunction with genetic inheritance. He links this functional capacity to the basic biological drive to sustain the life of the organism: "The purposiveness of organisms is manifested in their adaptive plasticity and robustness. Plasticity is the capacity of an organism to adapt to the vagaries of its conditions of existence by controlling and implementing changes to its own structures and processes" (248).

Even as the cultural environment has become an important player in evolutionary biology, most corresponding theories in the philosophy of biology continue to restrict their account of evolution too narrowly to the realm of animate organisms. The inter-disciplinary field of biosemiotics, which sees interaction with the environment as a crucial factor in the evolution of an organism and species, is good case in point. In the biosemiotic account of heredity, genetic information is only one element among other essential factors that determine how an organism adapts and evolves. "Above all, they inherit a suitable milieu or habitat (without which, such genetic material would remain inert)" (Hoffmeyer, 105). The total environment that an organism inherits presents itself as a semiosphere that poses certain constraints and requires all levels of species populations, from genes and cells to more complex organisms and cultures, to master a vast array of sensory signs in order to survive and thrive. According to this view, the evolutionary fitness of the species depends not so much on its genetic inheritance, but rather on a "semiotic competence" that governs the interaction between the organism and the environment (Hoffmeyer, 106–8). The scope of my analysis here does not allow for an explanation of biosemiotics' arguments for attributing the capacity for semiotic decoding to all living systems. Suffice it to say that according to this theory of the origin and development of living organisms, human cognition is a highly developed elaboration of physical and chemical processes that have been sustaining life since its inception.

Despite its inclusion of the natural and cultural environment as part of the relational whole involved in biological evolution, biosemiotics does not extend the cognitive capacity found in all living organisms to technical systems. By limiting the distribution of cognition in this way, it underestimates the role that the advance of technology and neural plasticity play in human evolution. As humans alter the cultural environment at an ever-increasing pace their biological system must adapt from generation to generation. Biosemiotics relies mainly on epigenetics to explain how the phenotypic plasticity needed to adapt to the perpetually altered environment can produce sustained evolutionary change incrementally over short periods of time. This is indicative of how it restricts its account of inheritance to mechanisms at work in biological organisms. Even so, other ideas advanced in connection with the theory would suggest that evolutionary adaptations occurring in technical systems produce integral changes in the human brain. Jesper Hoffmeyer argues that genetic evolution is responsible for the size and basic architectural structure of the brain but not for the more specific changes that occur through interaction with the cultural environment. He attributes the "final development of the brain," that is, the functional reorganization that enables the individual organism to adapt to particular environmental factors, to *epigenetic semiosis* (276).

Even as it limits its narrative of evolutionary change to the biological organism, biosemiotics draws parallels between the structure of the organism and technical systems in a way that points to neural plasticity as an important player in cultural evolution. Terence Deacon explains how biological *exaptation*, the recruitment of functions originally selected for one purpose to serve other purposes, is analogous to how technological innovation occurs (1997, 350–52). In both realms, the new process does not replace the original function, but rather relies on the retention of the specific original functionality. This scaffolding structure, which is key to the coevolutionary advance of the human with the cultural environment (Hoffmeyer, 138, 205–06), informs not only epigenetic inheritance but also transgenerational changes to the neural architecture of the brain. Through what biosemiotic theory calls "the constraints organizing neuronal signal dynamics" (Deacon 2012, 543) deeper structural affinities develop between ever more complex and sophisticated technologies and the neural circuits of the brain. As this occurs, each generation attains a new mantle of neural circuitry that extends the existing systems. The essential neural organization of the previous generation is retained as new networks develop on top of it to negotiate the technology of the next generation. Whether the changes to the neural architecture of the brain are inherited or not, the evolutionary chain is sustained outside the body via the persistence of and modification to technologies. The constant progress of technological innovation ensures that the neural networks required to engage with the technical world will be needed by the subsequent generation as well. Just as the advance of technology depends on the cumulative buildup of capabilities across successive generations, the neural circuitry that develops does not replace existing networks. Rather the neural systems shaped by previous iterations of technology provides the necessary foundation for the development of new systems.[3]

Deacon recognizes this dynamic in one particular, crucial area of human evolution. In countering Noam Chomsky's theory of a universal grammar that had been selected for and now resides in modules of the human brain as it developed over millennia, he argues that languages evolve by adapting to the needs of children, who would otherwise have to go through a long, burdensome process of trial-and-error language acquisition. Correcting for what would be an ineffectual process if it depended on the slower, less flexible process of changing brain function, languages evolve by becoming "user-friendly." He asserts that because we have focused on human development "we failed to notice that a flurry of adaptation has been going on *outside* the brain" (1997, 109) in the external medium (or technology) of language itself. However, Deacon and his fellow theorists remain intently focused on showing how the semiotic processes that have produced the power of the human mind to form symbolic associations have been at work in all levels of biological organisms since they first emerged. In the context of their campaign to counter vitalism on the one hand and the mechanistic computer theory of mind on the other, language stands out as the uniquely human medium that grounds symbolic thought in bios. This limited purview of *bio*semiotics inhibits its proponents from seeing the "co-evolutionary dynamic between language and its host" (112) as one particular instance of a universal process that governs all human interaction with the technology and culture it creates.

New data from a wide range of scientific disciplines suggest that human adaptations to the fast-changing environment happen more rapidly than previously assumed. Significant changes in the neural systems of the brain are occurring not only across generations, but also within the same generation and at more fundamental levels of biological organization. A quick glance at the broad timeline for human evolution over many millennia reveals a spiraling acceleration in the rate of change. For almost two million years the earliest *Homo* genus of hominids deployed a limited set of tool-making abilities, until the beginning of the Upper Paleolithic Period about 50,000 years ago. During this period *Homo sapiens* developed more advanced technologies and a greatly expanded tool set. As the maturing brain was exposed to the resulting changes in the environment, the variety and sophistication of the growing material culture and built environment developed rapidly, with distinct subcultures emerging. The next quantum leap forward came around 10,000 years ago when human societies began to practice agriculture and animal husbandry. In the more fertile areas communities began to put down permanent roots such that large and stable populations arose. The corresponding increase in population density, role specialization, social organization, and leisure time then contributed to a more flexible and adaptive relationship between the individual and the cultural environment (Wexler, 161–64). After the first writing began to appear 5,000 years ago the accumulation of knowledge began to increase exponentially, leading to the founding of the first kingdoms and civilizations that extended their dominion over large areas. From this point forward, as cultural evolution began to accelerate greatly, it becomes an arbitrary exercise to pinpoint the key junctures of cultural evolution. Recent theorists who employ the term Anthropocene to designate the current geologic-cultural era in which humans have had a global impact on the earth's ecosystems point to different starting points (8,000 years ago, the time of the Roman Empire, or much later in conjunction with the development of more powerful mechanical systems). The invention of the printing press that resulted in a rapid increase in the dissemination of writing has often been cited as a threshold event in the advance of human culture. The same is true of the industrial revolution that was spurred by a growth in scientific knowledge and mechanical technologies. And in his foundational work on cybernetics Norbert Wiener (1954) declared that the shift from a nineteenth-century epoch of power engineering to the present one of communication engineering has resulted in a dramatic increase in technological innovation and the perpetual adaptation of the human organism to the networks and flows of the modern information society.

To explain the range and depth of the bodily processes that are affected and the accelerated pace of change, it is necessary to look beyond just what is occurring in the body and to consider how diverse external influences alter epigenetic and neural processes and facilitate adaptation. Researchers in various fields have begun to search for methods of charting the coevolution of the human with the cultural environment in terms of a wide array of biological, social, and technological elements. The zoologist/psychologist Gilbert Gottlieb, for example, has developed a theory of *probabilistic epigenesis* and proposed a methodology for calculating the interlaced effects of environmental, behavioral, neural, and genetic factors.[4] While his and similar models help suggest how evolution can progress substantially within short time frames, the speed of change that has taken hold with the development of electric media has also altered the basic pattern of human evolution. It would seem that the storage of information in an interlocking network of external hardware and internal neural systems has become at least as significant for the stability and evolution of the human species as the memory fixed in DNA sequences. Moreover, we should not assume that this process is occurring in conjunction with bodily systems that have always existed. Rather, the coevolution of the human with the cultural environment creates in each successive phase new systems and a unique techno-biological pattern of adaptation.

As new media technologies have mushroomed over the last quarter century they have changed how humans experience the world even more dramatically. With the proliferation of handheld and other mobile devices (cell phone, tablet computers, laptops, and others) the screen has been liberated from its fixed position in the movie theater and travels with the user as she goes about her everyday activities. This mobility in conjunction with these devices' ability to function transparently and with increasing autonomy marks a dramatic transition from a first wave of cyborg technology (from paper and pen to electronic media) to a second, more dynamic form of biotechnological unions (Clark 2003, 25–27). In the case of moving-image media this portability is changing the way images are intertwined with the environment in which humans live and move. The moving image's proliferation and infiltration into the sphere of our active lives in the world, the ubiquity of computers and a plethora of devices run by microchips, and the speed of access to countless sources of information have created a network of fast-changing connectivity that the inhabitants of advanced technological cultures encounter at every turn. As a result, each change in the cultural environment works its effects on the human organism faster than in the case of previous technological developments. In this new media landscape the changes occurring via neural plasticity extend across broader swaths of the population and intensify the accelerated pace of change. The ever more frequent exposure to these new forms of media is altering more than how each new generation processes information. Now even within a generation there are substantial changes to the way each new wave of youth interacts with digital media. The language used to describe the cycles of technological innovation for digital devices is one indication of this new rate of change. When we speak of the next "generation" of a smart phone, for example, this reflects how digital media technology is effecting manifold neural changes in the brain and the central nervous system within the span of an individual life. Initial studies in variances in brain structure and function due to media exposure support this idea that different "media generations" exist within biological generations: "A media generation is not bound to any particular biological generation and appears to align and separate persons much more reliably in terms of media use and the information and symbolic processing habits and patterns that use entails" (MacDougall, 99).

McLuhan claimed that new technologies, and electronic media in particular, were producing substantial biological changes in the human at an ever-accelerating rate in the twentieth century. He attributes the ability to recognize that technology drives human evolution in this way to the faster speed of change: "The total-field awareness engendered by electronic media is enabling us—indeed, compelling us—to grope toward a consciousness of the unconscious, toward a realization that technology is an extension of our own bodies. We live in the first age when change occurs sufficiently rapidly to make such pattern recognition possible for society at large" (1995, 237). Asserting that any technology that creates extensions of the body is a form of media (1969, 27), he maintains that those technologies designed for the storage and dissemination of information enabled alterations in neural and epigenetic structures to proceed more quickly. From the tool as medium for archiving the steps required to manufacture it to cave paintings as the first form of visual representation, from writing to mass printing, and from the earliest production of mechanical moving images to digital graphics, advances in media technology have enabled quantum leaps forward in human mental capacity.

Although McLuhan downplays the impact film has had in this regard relative to other twentieth-century media, it follows from his basic premise that a medium that became a major factor in modern culture would alter the relation between the human and visual technologies significantly. Cinema became the key cultural deployment around which the interlaced effects of social, behavioral, and biological forces converging around film technology coalesced and through which its evolutionary impact was disseminated. The awareness that this new medium had the capacity to effect such changes can be seen in responses to it from elements of the culture that feared the repercussions. However, film has received relatively little attention in the mainstream discussion of media as prosthesis. This omission is in part, I would argue, a consequence of the halting advance of the idea that the human is constituted by an essential fusion of the biological and the technological. Inherent in all versions of this theory, from McLuhan down through contemporary accounts of technogenesis, is cybernetics' founding idea of a functional analogy between human and machine. When taken to their logical conclusion, the basic tenets of cybernetics hold that all technical systems, including the human, work according to the same fundamental laws. Breaking down the distinction between human/machine and animate/inanimate, cybernetics showed that the properties of reproduction found in the human gene were also present in such diverse organisms as computer viruses and inheritable social or cultural patterns. The human body with its powers of intelligence is then just one pattern of organization in a system of technicity that includes all organisms. Wiener recognized that cybernetic theory entailed the principle of prosthetic extension later espoused by McLuhan. In *The Human Use of Human Beings* Wiener proclaims that when humans bring their knowledge to bear on the world, they are not only exerting control, but also extending their bodies into the world in the form of the technologies that enable them to establish it: "Where a man's word goes, and where his power of perception goes, to that point his control and *in a sense* his physical existence is extended" (17, emphasis added). However, the phrase emphasized here guards against the more radical consequences of the idea that all systems, both living and nonliving, work according to the same fundamental laws. Wiener was reluctant to accept and acknowledge the radical implications of the new field of cybernetics for the liberal humanist subject. Fearing the loss of the rights and agency of the individual, rational self, he and most of the others at the forefront of the movement managed to maintain traditional humanist views as part of their system (Hayles 1999, 7–10, 112).

A more integral coupling of the technological and the biological sets McLuhan's idea of technology as prosthesis off from the view of early cybernetics. Wiener maintains an essential difference between the human and the external world that it changes through technology: "We have modified our environment so radically that we must now modify ourselves in order to exist in this new environment" (Wiener, 46). Embracing more fully the basic principle that the underlying networks of the technological and biological operate according to the same universal set of organizational structures, McLuhan asserts that advances in the operating networks distributed among technical entities mirror changes in the central control network, that is, the nervous system, of the humans who produced them. This idea remained outside the mainstream of cybernetics over the next two decades. During the second wave of cybernetics, from 1960 to 1985, Humberto Maturana and Francisco Varela's concept of autopoiesis provided a systems-theoretical basis for the separation of the human and the environment. They argued that not only biological systems but social ones as well are closed and operate according to an infrangible circularity (178–201). The principle of homeostasis, which the early proponents of cybernetics had retained to stave off the more radical consequences of their theory for traditional views of what is human, became the nucleus of a broad systems theory that encompasses all beings, whether animate or inanimate. Concurrent with its rise, the cyborg emerged as the defining cultural figure for the prosthetic relationship between the human and technology. While widely perceived to be a forward-looking conception about the fusion of the human and technology, this vision of a hybrid organism actually entailed in key respects a reversion back to humanist views of the body. In contrast to the more progressive view of technology as an interconstitutive part of the biological organism, it reinforces the view of prosthesis as a supplement to the body that is not integrally entwined with the human. The figure of the cyborg supports a structural dualism according to which the technical system underlying mechanical objects remains alien to the biological one that supports living organisms. As popular Hollywood films about cyborgs in the 1980s and early 1990s (such as *Blade Runner* [Ridley Scott, 1982], *Terminator* [James Cameron, 1984], *Cyborg* [Albert Pyun, 1989], and *Universal Soldier* [Roland Emmerich, 1992], among others) reinforced this view of technology as prosthesis, they also deflected the theoretical discussion of technogenesis away from the medium of cinema.

Another movement deriving from cybernetics would suggest that film played a significant part in the coevolution of the human with technology throughout the twentieth century. The work of roboticists in the third wave of cybernetics has played a strong part in advancing the theory of extended cognition and perception. Mirroring the artificial life model of how robotic intelligence is best distributed across its various systems that interact with the immediate environment, the concept of extended cognition does not restrict human intelligence to the mind or to the body. Rather all the media and machines we have created and surrounded ourselves with enhance our ability to remember, act, decide, solve problems, and even to dream and imagine. Thus, they are part of the cognitive machinery, part biological, part technological, that constitutes being human. Andy Clark, together with David Chalmers, and others (Daniel Dennett) began in the 1990s to challenge models of the mind that described the brain as functioning much like a computer to process internal representations of the world that were fed into it. Exposing the misconception propagated by the figure of the cyborg, Clark denies that human cognition is a process that only operates "inside [the] biological skin-bag, inside the ancient fortress of skin and skull," countering that "what is special about human brains, and what best explains the distinctive features of human intelligence, is precisely their ability to enter into deep and complex relationships with nonbiological constructs, props, and aids" (2003, 5). These "deep and complex relationships" that the human brain is able to form with technical objects occur predominantly at the subphenomenal level and are constituted by automatic modes of bodily experience that are inaccessible to consciousness. Proponents of "technical distribution," such as Clark, Hayles, and Mark Hansen, among others, take a more radical view of technogenesis than Stiegler. While he asserts merely that immediate experience with technical objects has *at least the potential* to become the content of conscious mentation, they contend that these embodied responses alter the human without ever entering into conscious thought or even consciousness per se (Hansen 2012, 57).

Because the technological dimension of human evolution is more pronounced in the digital era, recent media theory has concentrated primarily on technical distribution through digital technology. Various new impulses in the sciences and the humanities have contributed to this area of interest. The last decade of the millennium was a threshold period that introduced new conceptions of brain function and of the shared technicity of the biological and the technological. Empirical research on neural systems showed the brain to be a network of materially transmitted information flows whose structures resemble those used in computer systems. Philosophers and neuroscientists alike derived from these and related findings theories of embodied and extended cognition that challenge the classic cognitivist view of the mind.[5] At the same time as this new emphasis on embodied processes was evolving, another offshoot from cybernetics was forming a countertrend. In his 1948 *Cybernetics: Or Control and Communication in the Animal and the Machine*, the foundational text for his new science of cybernetics, Wiener had cited information as the central agent for producing and controlling energy in the computer age. In doing so, he pointed to a homologous relation between the data processing that controls computers and the neural networks of the human nervous system that regulate all bodily operations. However, under the influence of the Cartesian view of a mind-body dualism, both models became inflected with the notion that information is disembodied rather than constituted materially by neurochemical and electrical transmissions. In the 1990s a new set of cyber heroes, computer-gifted protagonists who could negotiate cyberspace, took its place alongside the muscular cyborgs of the previous decade. Picking up on themes addressed in cyberpunk literature of the 1980s, cinematic cyberthrillers began to envision the transcendence of the body through the digitization of human consciousness. Films such as *The Lawnmower Man* (Brett Leonard, 1992), *Johnny Mnemonic* (Robert Longo, 1995), *Virtuosity* (Brett Leonard, 1995), and *The Net* (Irwin Winkler, 1995) envisioned various scenarios in which simulated realities could overtake or even supplant those that our current form of consciousness generates from lived experience. These new science-fiction scenarios play out in virtual realities inhabited by living beings made up primarily of computer code and data flows. The hybrid human as an interface between the organic body and machines is replaced by the total digitization of the mind/body.

At the end of the 1990s another group of science-fiction films addresses head on the idea that virtual reality simulations could replace human consciousness with a prosthetic version that is neither grounded in nor influenced by the body and its interaction with the world. Films such as *The Thirteenth Floor,* (Josef Ruznak, 1999), *Dark City* (Alex Proyas, 1998), *eXistenZ* (David Cronenberg, 1999), *The Matrix* (Lana and Lilly Wachowski, 1999), and *Open Your Eyes* employ different versions of the body-in-the-vat motif to explore exotic visions of the post-bodied human that were circulating during this period of overlapping and irreconcilable notions of materiality. Their science-fiction scenarios generate a sense of marvel and transcendence, while also offering critical perspectives that reveal some of the fallacies inherent in fantasies of a disembodied human existence. *The Matrix* is particularly pertinent here because of its engagement of the relation between humans and machines. Subsequent chapters address the films mentioned above in greater detail. Here, a brief discussion of *The Matrix* serves to illustrate how they as a group address the issue of simulated reality in a way that affirms the imbrication of the biological human with technology. By casting machines in the role of an "alien" power that threatens to take control of humankind, the film evokes the trope of human alienation from technical culture. As the plot unfolds, the film exposes the conventional humanist attitude toward machines to be an irrational fear that stems from the unwillingness to jettison the distinction between human nature and the environment humans have created and inhabit. As it does so, it echoes a view put forward by Gilbert Simondon in his theory of technical objects: "The most powerful cause of alienation in the contemporary world resides in this misunderstanding of the machine, which is not an alienation caused by the machine, but by the non-knowledge of its nature and essence, by way of its absence from the world of significations, and its omission from the table of values and concepts that make up culture" (16). The mythical underpinning of the rebellion that is needed to fight the machines reveals the self-contradictions in the idea that they are the enemy. Machines can assume the part of the mortal enemy of humanity precisely because they are deemed to be outside of and even pitted against the domain of the human, rather than an integral part of its existence and being. When we alienate ourselves from the technologies we have created, we fetishize them, envisioning that they will turn the power with which we have endowed them against that side of life we withhold from them. With respect to digital technology, the machines in *The Matrix* are figured as *dieux trompeurs* who have produced a set of codes that can simulate human existence perfectly. Their ability to create the objects of human desire (the voluptuous blonde woman in the red dress, the taste of a juicy steak) is both the key to their success and evidence of humanity's inability to understand its relation to the technology it has created. Moreover, only because humans conceive of technology in this way do they imagine that it can produce a virtual reality (the Matrix) that supplants embodied experience and alienates them from a part of themselves.

The examination of these matters in films at the end of the twentieth century reveals an introspective investigation of how cinema nourished the fallacy of disembodied experience. At the heart of this metacinematic soul-searching is a misgiving about the classical mode of representation and its negative effect on the development of visual media. In *The Matrix* and other films explored more closely in chapter 3 the style of the image alternates radically, suggesting at times the indexicality of the film image and at other times the virtual simulations of digital imaging. As these films manipulate spectatorship in this way, they present the dichotomy between the real and the virtual as a crisis that must be overcome and raise questions about cinema's role in the coevolution of the human and technology.

The Phatic Image of Cinema—Reassessed

In *The Language of New Media* (2001) Lev Manovich argues that the film image had become the dominant cultural form of visual representation and would continue to be so in the digital age. Pondering the wide reach of the cinematic image, he asks: "Are we biologically wired to the form of visual representation of cinema?" (79). He replies definitively that "the answer is of course no" but goes on at length to declare its continued influence in the age of digital media. The subtext of his reflections about the enduring power of the cinematic image is a pervasive skepticism about its role as a prosthetic extension in the coevolutionary advance of the human and visual technology. Warren Neidich, an artist and media theorist with a background in neuroscience, addresses this matter and questions not only whether cinema has significantly altered how we process visual images but even whether film is at all capable of doing so. Citing what he calls the visual and cognitive ergonomics of classical cinema (36–37, 47), Neidich attributes cinema's effectiveness in attracting and holding the attention of the viewer to the ease with which the audience can perceive and (re)cognize film images. Drawing an analogy to how ergonomics is applied in the workplace, he explains that the film industry was able to create a cinematic image that can be processed with minimal fatigue and stress. He borrows the term "phatic image" from Virilio to characterize how cinema is closely attuned to the neural processing that produces visual mental images. A combination of technological, aesthetic, and cultural forces was able, he claims, to produce an image that "would have to undergo little transformation from its abstract code in the world to its abstract perceptual code in the brain" (89). Echoing arguments from *The Language of New Media,* he asserts that the cinematic image can compete successfully with those that represent our perception of nonartificial, "real environments" (57–59, 89–90). Assessing the politics of the phatic image, he charges that media images that function as correlates of phenomenological experience can be exploited more readily to influence and control the thoughts of viewers.

Neidich's argument illustrates the growing critique directed toward cinema in recent media theory. Warning of the regressive effects of cinema, he draws a parallel between the competition for attention (and dollars, one might add) among media in the cultural marketplace and that occurring in the body as part of natural selection. He concludes that cinema is winning on both fronts, explaining that these "more sophisticated and intense phatic signifiers . . . are pushing out their more unsophisticated progenitors from the visual landscape" as they "compete for the brain's neuronal attention" (58). It is however unclear how the process of selection that occurs as different social and cultural agents compete for space and time in the public sphere might apply to the competition taking place in the body. Neidich himself seems to waver on this. At times, he sees the competition playing out primarily with respect to pressures coming from "social, political, aesthetic, psychological, and economic relations" (89). At other times, he suggests that an aesthetics that is ergonomically attuned to the base level of neural temporalities in the brain might be able to override cultural and social factors: "An aesthetics that is ergonomically entrained may reflect these neural dispositions. Today aesthetics may in fact reflect a transhistorical discourse that concerns the construction of a visual landscape, real or imaginary, which is maximally organized to capture attention and transmit information from outside to inside the brain" (89). Most striking here is the suggestion that the proliferation of the phatic image can slow the coevolutionary advance of visual media and mind, and possibly even bring it to a halt.

Behind this suggestion of a transhistorical interaction between visual media and the mind lurks some problematic assumptions about how images are generated in the body. The idea that there can be a direct link between an "abstract code in the world" that structures material images and an "abstract perceptual code in the brain" partakes of the fallacy of disembodied information that plagued the first wave of cybernetics. It takes film viewing to be a purely spectatorial relation between the viewer and film images and implies that the brain functions like a computer in processing the visual input. This account eclipses the role of the body in the viewing experience, as if film images are conveyed to the brain through some kind of immaterial transfer of information. It claims that the technologically produced material image can be so well adapted to the neural processes underlying mental imaging that the latter are simply bypassed. There is however no such process by which external images, whether conscious or unconscious, are inserted directly into the flow of mental images: "The external images that are presented to the mind are not magically transplanted inside it as ready-made arguments. Regardless of what visual forms can be presented before the eye (diagrams, photographs, film images), they are subjected to complicated processing by the nervous system, which constructs its own internal representations" (Manovich 2006, 209). In the final analysis, Neidich's account disregards how the microtemporal properties of internal biological processes and those of external media technics are interlaced in a dynamic fashion.

This description of visual perception during film viewing runs counter to accounts of perception and cognition that have emerged out of convergent research areas since the 1990s. The 4EA model supported by this recent work in cognitive science (embodied, embedded, enacted, extended, affective cognition) counters evolutionary psychology's so-called classical sandwich (Hurley, 20) account of how the brain operates on the basis of a set of discrete modules whose structures have remained unchanged since they evolved in our Pleistocene ancestors as adaptations to their surroundings. The postcognitivist model conceives of "cognition as immanent to extended-distributed-differential bio-environmental systems in which 'real experience' is the non-representational direction of action" (Protevi, 26). It also contends that nonconscious neural processing is integrally involved not only in higher-order executive operations, but also in both the evolutionary and ontogenetic development of the human capacity for cognition. This hybrid model of how humans process lived experience rejects the traditional idea that human cognition is a process that only operates inside the body in conjunction with incorporeal thought processes. The burgeoning view of how cognition derives from the activity of a *situated living body* contradicts the notion that phatic media images can simply take the place of visual images in the mind.

Recent studies of how mental representations relate to sensorimotor functions can help explain embodied experience during film viewing. According to the principle of embodied cognition, the world that is afforded every individual at any moment arises out of the interaction of the situated living body (that originates in sensorimotor systems) with the immediate surrounding environment. On the basis of recent science, proponents of embodied cognition have also challenged the brain-centered view of how visual consciousness is formed (Wilson and Foglia). They reject the more traditional idea that certain neural structures match directly with particular content of conscious experience. Instead, they contend that conscious visual experience arises from temporary states that depend on the body's situation in a momentary environment and the potential movement and actions plotted out automatically by sensorimotor systems. From this point of view, embodied responses to frequently encountered forms of sensory input (such as that experienced during film viewing) strengthen the neural networks engaged by that experience and alter how our body produces consciousness in general, and visual consciousness in particular (Langdale, 15–18). Frequent exposure to film would produce such changes, and they would exert their effects not only during film viewing but also in real environments. Seen in this context, movies are not merely isolated external events that evoke temporary bodily responses and possible longer-lasting cognitive influence in the viewer. Rather cinema, as one of the most powerful cultural media throughout the world, is an integral piece in the extended cognitive network of individual moviegoers and the modern human.

The ability to perceive, recognize, and react to the events in a film as if they were real-life scenes is inextricably rooted in the physical (somatosensory and affective) reactions to its stream of moving images. The interrelation between movement and visual perception is a primordial component of human being-in-the-world, one that we share with many other species and cannot simply leave behind when we enter the movie theater. Only organisms that move and need to avoid or engage objects have sensory systems and are able to spatially map the world around them. The precondition for a visual world is then the possession of a body in space that is capable of self-movement in interaction with other bodies. The neural systems that produce automatic responses enable the body to pose potential movements and to relate to a virtual world. And by logical extension, the parts of the body that enable skilled spatial movement, such as eyes, hands, and legs, are also essential for the development of complex cognitive processes. Studies of the cortical and subcortical areas that produce space perception have concluded that there are not two different systems for spatial attention and for action, but rather that the same networks control both (Rizzolatti et al., 232; Noë and O'Regan, 969). Consequently, a sense of space (spatial attention) is always contingent on movement and thus also, as James J. Gibson had previously stipulated, on the present neural input for the proprioceptors. Visual imaging exists to guide our movement through the world, and spatial cognition and orientation serve to predict and plan out the results of movements. These findings have led to dramatic changes in our fundamental conception of how the mind functions. Proponents of embodied cognition, such as Clark, Rodolfo Llinás, and Varela, among others, reject the idea that mental images and thoughts are a synthesis of sensations and memories to be acted upon by cognitive faculties. Always generated in anticipation of action, they are first and foremost movements awaiting actualization. In short, our brain is an organ whose primary function is not thinking, but rather it evolved in all its complexity as a biological system designed for responding in real time to an immediate need to act.

This connection between movement, space, and visual perception has particular significance for film viewing. The movement of the images together with the construction of film space by aesthetic and technological means guides the embodied responses of the viewer. The flow of images is an essential element that produces spatial cognition in film, such that the construction of space in moving-image media is fundamentally different than in still images such as photographs (Gunning 2007, 40–44). Even when the camera is stationary and remains fixed on a still scene, what it conveys to the film viewer is not just pictorial. When there are moving objects or people in the film scene as well, they activate an additional level of sensorimotor function. As opposed to the scene depicted in a photograph, moving objects in a film elicit a dynamic response based on real-life depth perception, and spatial cognition begins to operate more proprioceptively rather than almost purely on the basis of exteroception. When there is movement our vision begins to register depth according to the kinetic occlusion among objects rather than being limited to the static form of occlusion provided in a photograph (Curtis, 254–55). More proprioceptive data is provided, and more elaborate systems of spatial mapping are automatically activated.

The typical exhibition setting in the darkened movie theater with fixed seating works to dampen the impulse to move in reaction to the movement in and of the film images. The need for such a setting is itself evidence that the moving images of cinema engage key first-order neural networks more directly than other means of representation and evoke a strong embodied reaction that must then be deterred. To the extent that the film world presents itself (or, in Gibson's terminology, "affords itself") as a resource for action, the viewer's body is automatically preparing itself to respond physically to the events in the film. The brain's ability to control the body effectively—and thus to survive—hinges on the nervous system's capacity to create a compound (that is, not just visual) image of the expected outcome of movement. In concert with the binding process that produces the continuous image flow of consciousness, the emulation circuits generate a steady stream of somatosensory (haptic) and movement (kinesthetic and proprioceptive) images (Grush). At every moment, efferent nerve signals predict the sensory data the body will receive in its next position and prepare it to take the appropriate action. This occurs even when the body is stationary (Gibson, 182–84). The brain regions and processes involved in the production of the efferent copy of movement outcomes are then also in operation during film viewing. The brain is continuously simulating and rehearsing the way the body could respond to the future scenarios enacted by the embodied engagement with film. And these systems function in the same manner as when guiding our actual movement, such that in neurological terms there is no difference between perceiving objects in the real world versus in films (Pisters, 30). In this respect, the orientation of the movie-goer to the film is much like that of the dreamer to dream scenarios (Cook 2011a). Using the same phrasing that applies to dreams, we can say that film produces in the viewer the "mental imagery of motor actions" and activates "the same motor representations and central neural mechanism that are used to generate actual actions" (Revonsuo 2003, 97). In both dreaming and film viewing the initiation of sensorimotor activity is crucial to the experience, even when stop-action mechanisms intervene to prevent execution of the commands. As the viewer becomes visually engaged with the projected screen images, the brain runs virtual scenarios whose purpose is to guide the ensuing actions and movement. With the exception of occasional minor reactions, the viewer remains of course seated and still.

The reported reaction of early film audiences to the Lumière brothers' *Arrival of a Train at La Ciotat* (*L'arrivée d'un train en gare de La Ciotat*, 1896)—along with numerous other, less-documented instances of early cinema using moving vehicles to exploit the viewer's lack of familiarity with film images (Alt, 14–16)—suggests how effectively film can activate sensorimotor impulses. The automatic activation of the sensorimotor networks that would execute the proper flight reaction to the approach of the train generated these reactions. Some first-time viewers at a time when cinema had not yet become an established cultural institution had not developed the effective stop-action mechanisms of more experienced or sophisticated moviegoers. The same automatic bodily actions that moved early audiences still play an integral role today in the film experience. The film image moves the viewer "physiologically before he is in a position to respond intellectually" and produces a "resonance effect" in the body's sensorimotor and proprioceptive systems (Kracauer 1997, 158). Embodied responses to the moving image are inevitable, such that there are "two types of motor outburst, those that escape reality testing and those that remain under its control" (Metz and Guzzetti, 76). When the reality testing fails, viewers execute limited actions, such as when they tightly grip the armrest at an impending attack in a horror film and then gasp or scream once it occurs. However, regardless of how complete the stop-action interdiction is, participation in the advancing stream of images activates the affective and perceptual networks associated with episodic memories related to similar events in the past and prepares the body for active involvement (Antunes, 47).

The strong initial reactions of early audiences demonstrate how the cinematic image engages neural substrates of the binding process at more than a purely cognitive level. These embodied responses are not merely ever-present. The initiation of sensorimotor

activity is essential to the film experience at every level. The process of rehearsing scenarios at the level of affect should not be
given secondary status, even if the aesthetic strategies and institutional constraints imposed by the film industry acted to focus the
viewer's attention on narrative scenarios that play out at the level
of phenomenal consciousness. Although these efforts may have
been able to moderate the intensity of the responses, they cannot
eliminate them. The potential narrative scenarios that are generated in the viewer are rooted in the physical (somatosensory and
affective) reactions to the stream of moving images projected onto
the film screen. Even once a film viewer has learned not to respond
to the efferent signals produced by this movement, the stop-action
mechanism operates in a nervous system already poised for action.
The coevolution of cinema and the mind began as a threshold event
with a dramatic initial impact that has moderated over time, but
not changed qualitatively.

Despite awareness of the medium's power to evoke such strong
physical responses, cinema studies has been primarily concerned
with the viewer's comprehension of the film as representation.
This is due in part to the dominance of an ocularcentric conception of spectatorship. Joseph Anderson, a cognitivist film scholar
who bases his work on Gibson's theory of visual perception, offers a prime example of this tendency. Even though in Gibson's
"ecological approach" the individual's full bodily immersion in
an environment that affords opportunities for action governs all
perception, Anderson reduces film reception to an almost exclusively visual operation. He claims, for example, that because vision
dominates the spatial cognitive system "it is possible to enter the
diegetic space of a motion picture effortlessly by way of the visual
system without the necessity of proprioceptive confirmation" (113).
His wording suggests a cleaner break between the two than ever
actually occurs. Jonathan Crary argues that the notion that it is as
if the film world is simply suspended before the eyes of the spectators is part of a cultural conception of vision that stems from
the Renaissance and is applied to film spectatorship. Stressing the
importance of tactile receptors in film viewing, he provides an important correction to Anderson's account: "Perception is always
an amalgam of information from 'immediate' tactile receptors and

'distant' optical and auditory receptors, and distinctions between the optical and the tactile cease to be significant (or could only have significance for an impossibly motionless subject with no live relation to an environment). Vision as an 'autonomous' process or exclusively optical experience becomes an improbable fiction" (1999, 352).

In the case of vision, this false sense that the internal images generated through perception stem directly from the external world is so seductive because of the way our visual system evolved. The processing of visual data is distributed across a phylogenetically older "where pathway" (the dorsal stream) and the newer "what pathway" (the ventral stream). As visual information flows along the ventral stream through the primary visual cortex into the frontal lobes and back again it is fine-tuned through interaction with the faster, "online" dorsal stream. One effect incurred along this route is that the images produced seem to issue directly from the external environment (Milner and Goodale). However, this impression leads to false assumptions about visual perception: "The notion that our perceptual experience is determined by the passive receipt of information, though seductive, is deeply misleading" (Clark 2003, 95). Vision also cannot produce spatial orientation autonomously, that is, without motor activity stimulated by the movement or potential movement of the organism through a perceived environment. It always involves both exteroception and proprioception: "Vision is kinaesthetic in that it registers movements of the body just as much as does the muscle-joint-skin system and the inner-ear system. . . . The [inherited] doctrine that vision is exteroceptive, in other words that it obtains 'external' information only, is simply false" (Gibson, 183). Even in the case of the film viewer who is seated and still, perception of the screen image entails visual processing that is intertwined with a proprioceptive sense of movement.

The audiovisual world of cinema distinguishes itself then from earlier media not in its ability to represent an external reality. Rather, the advance in moving-image technology resulted in a medium that engages the audience in the real-time embodied processes that produce a simulated reality even as that world is unfolding onscreen. Thus, the moving film image represented a momentous gain in the ability to experience technologically produced images in a more fully embodied way rather than primarily through distanced visual cognition. This gain should not be seen as exerting its influence only on some more primitive, inconsequential level. The processing of images that began as a system serving the maintenance of the biological organism is also the key to the most elaborate endeavors of humankind (Damasio 1999, 23–26). Modes of internal imaging that predate the capacity for complex episodic memory and language continue to function as part of the cognitive processing unique to humans. The narratives of cinema that require higher-order operations of thought and reasoning are grounded in physical responses to film at the somatosensory and affective level. Given the proliferation of film images throughout global culture we can only assume that cinema has augmented our faculties of perception-cognition at this automatic level as well. Much as humans' visual and motor occupation with early tools fostered both sensorimotor systems and mental representations that enabled the reproduction and improvement of these tools, film images exercise and enhance not only the cognitive faculties required to process complex narratives but also the affective and motor systems that guide our body's interaction with the immediate environment.

"Consciousness Is an Epiphenomenon"

In its path to a standard film form and the classical style, cinema became efficient as a prosthetic medium that has augmented our ability to process narrative information, such as memories, episodic events, and various other conscious as well as subconscious scenarios. To a certain extent this enhancement with respect to information that is conveyed to a viewing subject has come at the expense of film's ability to engage the viewer at the subphenomenal level and to activate data flows that construct the organism. The suppression of sensorimotor and affective effects is however not, and has never been, absolute—nor could it ever be so. Nor should we conclude that cinema's ability to engage narratively and work with our conscious grasp of reality has exerted a retrogressive influence on the coevolution of humans with technology. To suggest that the assimilation of the cinematic image to the image streaming of consciousness could disrupt or impede the technogenetic interrelation between the body and film misrepresents the fundamental relation between the mind and media. Indeed, I would contend that cinema has had a greater effect on the embodied processes that underlie cognition than on the cognitive processing of higher-level narrative scenarios.

At the same time, one must guard against the inclination to dismiss the effects cinema has had as a prosthetic extension of consciousness. In the classic cognitivist view consciousness and perception are privileged over sensory experience. As the pendulum is now swinging away from this traditional Cartesian model of the mind toward the idea of embodied and extended cognition, some have begun to question the importance of consciousness. This tendency has gained traction primarily among roboticists associated with the third wave of cybernetics who were most successful when they designed robots that did not simply follow comprehensive preprogrammed instructions, but rather learned via feedback from distributed systems that interact directly with the environment. On the basis of this work these scientists and engineers learned to downplay the importance of central processing units that guide the actions of arms and other extended systems according to a set of preprogrammed criteria. When roboticists applied these discoveries to humans, they concluded that too much emphasis has been placed on consciousness and the role it plays in determining our actions and decisions. In particular, the representational self-awareness provided by consciousness is seen by some as largely a by-product of the more essential bodily systems that enable humans to survive in the world and evolve in response to our experiences. Those involved in this research have even suggested that "consciousness is an epiphenomenon" (Hayles 1999, 237–38). The result has been either to downplay its importance or to repudiate it more summarily as a misconception that distorts how we experience, learn, and evolve.

Roboticists have deemphasized higher-order consciousness because operational models based on this relatively recent product of evolution have not contributed much to their efforts to create robots that can perform basic human functions. However, such inferences made in a discipline that builds machines through deliberate stages of production may not be so directly applicable to human evolution. Our evolutionary history reveals a cumulative expansion of biological and cultural capabilities that build reciprocally upon earlier developments in the prosthetic relation between our bodies and technology. And these past states do not simply dissipate and pass away, but rather they remain functioning alongside or assimilated into more recent systems. To call any aspect of our mental operations an epiphenomenon seems to merely indicate that we do not understand how it underlies, is enmeshed in, or converges with other processes that are considered more fundamental.

In contrast to these proponents of artificial life in the field of robotics, most cognitive neuroscientists who have focused on consciousness explain how our sensorimotor systems work in conjunction with the higher-order processes that produce conscious mental representations. Considering our conscious mental functions a product of selection for heritable advantage, they describe how the ability to process images as distinct and visually observable mental representations enables us to sort through and act on them according to a higher-order process of selection and decision-making. The mental scenes of consciousness are important in this respect because they provide an essential link between the basic structural states of the nervous system and processing that takes place in the frontal cortex. Antonio Damasio, one of the leading neuroscientists to speculate about what brain research tells us about consciousness, bases the selection of consciousness in human evolution on this function: "As a device for manipulating images in service of maintaining the body/organism, [consciousness connects] the inner sanctum of life regulation with the processing of images" (1999, 24).[6]

In this vein, the 4EA account of cognition proposes a hybrid model whereby embodied or enacted modes of processing experience are tightly interlaced with the higher-order cognitive processes that require attention be paid to the mental images produced for conscious deliberation. Evaluation of cinema's efficiency as a prosthetic medium that has expanded and advanced human technics must then consider how film has engaged the biological/technological interface between the body's subphenomenal responses to moving screen images and the cognitive operations they generate. This is no easy task. Borrowing a term from analytical philosophy, we might say that the "hard problem" facing media theory and the arts today—as well as neuroscience—is how to understand the gap between the microconscious and consciousness, or between affect and cognition. Part of what makes this question so difficult is its formulation. The idea that there is a gap between the two misrepresents what recent neuroscience tells us about brain function. It is a carry-over from the classic cognitivist view that there is an essential difference between discrete modules dedicated to lower-level activity such as sensory processing and higher-order cognitive systems.[7] As neuroscientists seek to understand how widely distributed circuits can interact synchronously to produce the neural correlates of consciousness, they address some of the related philosophical issues. For example, Gerald Edelman has joined forces with Bernard Baars at the Neurosciences Institute in La Jolla, California, combining his dynamic core theory with Baars's concept of the global workspace to pursue these questions. In the case of qualia, which serves as the "hard problem" for analytical philosophers, they have reached a conclusion similar to the one I suggest for the relation between affect and cognition. When qualia are recognized as what they are, "reliable correlates of underlying causal neural mechanisms," the problem melts away by itself. From the perspective of a biologically based view of consciousness, "the hard problem does not require a solution, but rather a cure" (Edelman et al. 2011, 5).

The cure they propose, and the one I want to apply to film reception, describes the "gap" between microconscious processing and consciousness as a difference in temporality. Edelman's theory of the dynamic core describes a pattern of brain activity where the neural maps for sensorimotor, affective, memory, and cognitive selection all operate according to the same basic pattern of *reentry*. Multiple and redundant processes are continuously occurring simultaneously, providing a vast offering of potential components for the combinations that will determine courses of action. At any one moment, the great majority of the currently active neural processes are not included in the consolidation of selected circuits (the dynamic core) that gives rise to conscious mental images. The higher-order systems that have evolved to deal with the unforeseen and

novel situations that continually present themselves as the body interacts with the world must sort through the signals received from
all the diverse neural circuits in order to cope with complex, am-
biguous, and unpredictable sets of "information" (neural patterns).
This takes more time than the automatic selective processes that
provide sensorimotor and affective input. Cognitive operations
that perform long-term planning and decision-making are more
laborious and take even longer. In particular, those operations that
require that the brain "speaks to itself" (Edelman et al. 2011, 2)—
the formation of long-term episodic memories and the combination of such memories into the complex narratives that comprise
our sense of identity—require yet slower cognitive processing over
extended periods of time.

Other recent research in neuroscience has suggested how these
temporal differences do not mean that there is a distinction in kind
between the microtemporal versus the phenomenal level of mental
processing. According to the synchronization theory of binding
initially proposed by Francis Crick and Christof Koch, 40-Hz os-
cillation supports the binding of neurons into a synchronized pattern (Edelman's dynamic core) that produces the coherent percepts
of discrete objects and the mental images of consciousness.[8] In a
series of studies on feedback loops between the thalamus and the
cortex, Llinás has shown how two sets of 40-Hz oscillators interact
in the cortex.[9] One stems from connections between the thalamus
and specialized cortical areas dedicated to more narrow sets of
data, including, for example, visual information conveyed from the
retina. These are the microprocesses that produce subphenomenal images such as those expressing color, motion, or orientation.
The other, produced by diffuse projections from the thalamus, creates a basic context in the cortex for conscious perceptions bound
at 40 Hz. These studies link 40-Hz oscillations not merely to the
binding of neural networks dedicated to specialized attributes of
objects, but also to the cognitive processing of this information in
the cortex. Neural assemblies synchronized by oscillations at 40
Hz are responsible for the binding of specific sensory information
as well as the cycles that are spread more widely throughout the
cortex and determine higher-order responses, such as triggering
and directing conscious attention. In other words, this study shows

that the macrotemporality of consciousness, which some theorists have linked to the reductive phatic image and set in opposition to the microtemporality of digital media, is actually grounded in patterns of 40-Hz oscillations similar to those involved in the binding of sensory input.

This evidence that neural binding synchronized at 40 Hz extends from the thalamus to the cortex challenges some of the underlying assumptions about the phatic image of cinema. A case in point is Hansen's historical account of how media images became geared to phenomenal consciousness in a limiting fashion. He attributes the limited range of external media images to a long historical process that goes back to cave paintings. In his view, these pictorial representations at the dawn of human history were attuned to higher-order consciousness in such a way that internal mental images became fixed in external media according to a reductive paradigm. As a result, the more dynamic processes of internal imaging at the microconscious level and the microtemporal neural properties associated with them are eclipsed (2011, 84–87). With respect to visual media, he argues that since its introduction in cave painting the reductive phatic image has remained dominant across all media down to the present. Cinema is then for Hansen a latter-day instance of an enduring visual culture that follows this reductive model: "This remains true, I want to argue, even in the case of cinema, where static phonograms are animated in a manner that makes them temporally dynamic for a perceiving consciousness" (2011, 89).[10]

In tracing the technogenetic properties and history of the cinematic image, my analysis offers a somewhat different view. For Hansen, the temporal correspondence between media technologies and the neural activities underlying mental imaging determines how a material image engages the plasticity of the brain. He distinguishes between the microtemporality of digital media that are able to engage and alter the sensory networks directly and "the technical media characteristic of the nineteenth and twentieth centuries, for example, photography and cinema, [that] primarily address human sense perception and experiential memory" (2015, 38). Because digital media systems no longer privilege consciousness and perception over sensation, he argues, they have a greater potential to disrupt habituated correspondences between neural processing and external images. They "operate both micro- and macrotemporally, directly on microsensory experience and, by way of various *aesthetic* mediations, indirectly on higher-order sense perception and consciousness" (2015, 38). Operating in this hybrid fashion, they can expand how humans interact with the technically distributed systems that mediate our interaction with the external world.

I agree with Hansen's basic claim that the microtemporal correspondences between neural processing and visual technologies restores materiality to the image across both the internal biological and the external technological medium. Also, I concur when he attributes particular significance to digital technologies, and new media in particular, explaining how they are triggering "a massive expansion in . . . the interface between human being and sensory environment" (2015, 46), and arguing that this constitutes a correction to what has been a detrimental bias in favor of consciousness. However, the hybridity he attributes to digital media also applies to cinema, I would argue, and indeed to all our interactions with the environment. The research by Llinás cited above bears this out. It indicates that slower, more comprehensive operations in the cortex may overcode the faster micro-operations that process specific pieces of data, but that they are also subject to the temporal modalities of these subphenomenal networks. This finding suggests that aesthetic strategies designed to engage and promote plasticity should target a complex network across a broad spectrum of interlocking temporalities rather than concentrating more singularly on microtemporal processes occurring in specialized neural assemblies. They should not abandon traditional media and only focus on new technologies that engage neural plasticity at the synaptic level. At the same time, the answer is not to resort back to traditional film aesthetics. Rather, hybrid forms are needed that mirror the kind of feedback loops Llinás discovered between faster processing of specific sensory data in the thalamus and slower, higher-order operations in the cortex. Such strategies would integrate conceptual and affective responses in an act of viewing that can disrupt habituated modes of experience via technics and generate discursive reflection at the same time. This approach would engage the multiple temporalities involved in biological systems on the one hand and technical processing on the other to show how complex narrative texts can engage plasticity across a whole range of conscious, unconscious, and nonconscious mental operations.

In *How We Think* Hayles makes a similar case in her analysis of the new literary form of electronic/print hybrid "technotexts." Her study addresses electronic and print literatures, but the lessons she draws from recent models of brain function also apply to cinema. She employs Daniel Dennett's analogies between computer and brain in *Consciousness Explained* to explain how the hardware/software interface of computer technology reflects the multiple temporalities at work in mental operations that are distributed across diverse brain regions. Dennett draws the parallel between computer and mental processing to counter the classic cognitivist view that depicts the brain as a central control module and cognitive processing as a combination of bottom-up and top-down sequences organized in a neat linear pattern. In both computers and the human body, he argues, the slower, more laborious work of processing data into meaningful narrative involves a complex network of simultaneous overlapping and recursive operations of various durations. The sequences of mental imaging that make up consciousness crystallize out of "multiple drafts" that are circulating across many neural networks while undergoing constant alterations (Dennett, 111–43). Edelman's theory of how the synchronous, recursive interchange in the brain between large numbers of diverse neuronal maps serves as the dynamic for higher-order selection also suggests correspondences between the plasticity of computers as high-level memory-processing machines and that of event-oriented cognitive processing in the brain (Edelman 1990). Both Dennett's drafts and Edelman's recursive neural processes are in most cases not considered consciously for selection by some kind of central executive system. Nonetheless, according to these models, cognitive systems operate on the basis of choice, at least in the limited sense of higher-order neural selection, while the drafts are produced, have a potential for actualization, and are selected for at all levels of microtemporal processing.

Dual Temporalities of Media and the Mind

This account of the network of multiple temporalities at work in both complex technical objects, such as a film, and in the brain admonishes against writing off cinema as a medium that produces exclusively phatic images. To be sure, after its basic technology became standardized the film industry marshaled its resources to create a cinematic image that engaged the viewer predominantly at the level of phenomenal consciousness. The ensemble of its commercial infrastructure, assimilation of new technology, and aesthetic adaptations has promoted a spectatorial mode of film viewing. As narrative integration became the aesthetic standard, the act of piecing together the events of a film into a cohesive narrative dominated the viewing process and overshadowed the faster affective responses to the film image. The stronger narrative code written into the media object (the feature film) elicited a viewing experience dominated by the cerebral code of cognitive processing. Even so, media technologies can never bypass the complex interplay of cognitive and affective processes that generate conscious mental images. External images always interact with both the fasttrack processes of microconsciousness and the slower cognitive processing that selects and organizes them. With respect to the developments that led to classical cinema, they may have slowed or even stalled the technogenetic dynamic between film images and subcortical neural networks, but they could never eliminate it.

At the same time, cinema has made its impact felt at the level of conscious reflection and thought as well. Although some may want to write the cinematic image off as a phatic image, it has boosted our cognitive powers in a similar fashion to writing. Human thought and cognition evolved out of and have advanced with our faculty for language. However, without the invention of symbolic systems for representing spoken language and recording it in external media our cognitive skills would not have attained the highlevel theoretical ability we have to generate, refine, and support or reject sophisticated ideas. In writing we can grasp and fix fleeting phrases and sentences in an extended cognitive space such that they become a stable object for critical review. This has resulted in a complex system of scaffolded thinking that has enabled the expansion of human mental powers far beyond what our brains could produce using only biological systems (Clark 2003, 73–83). The space writing opens up for critical reflection is an external expansion of the workspace in working memory that is dedicated to speech-based information (the phonological loop). Film serves in a similar fashion as an external medium that supplements the biological workspace for processing visual information in working memory (below, in a different context, the two different workspaces of working memory—the visuospatial sketchpad and the phonological loop—are discussed in more detail). Just as writing enhances the functionality of language and has greatly increased the collective human powers of cognition, so too has film expanded our ability to visualize alternative scenarios both physically and cognitively. It has done so because the capture and projection of moving film images made a qualitatively different kind of visual image available for higher-order processing and expanded the field for the "second-order cognitive dynamics" that drive critical reasoning and theoretical thought (Clark 2003, 78–79).

My argument here parts company with other theories of media and evolution that tend to focus more on linguistic modes of representation at the expense of visual imaging. Donald's account of the origins of the human mind offers a case in point. He excludes the earliest pictorial representations from his explanation of how the external storage of memory initiated human evolution and produced a hardware change in cognitive processing. He maintains that the appearance of cave paintings constituted a major step forward in that they were located in external media rather than in visual memory, but then denies that they enabled any new "biological capacities" (283–84). According to Donald, it is only with the advent of writing that visuosymbolic representations were able to effect material changes in the body. In an account that discounts the technogenetic effects of external visual images, he suggests merely that "pictorial invention might have signaled the start of a new cognitive structure" (284). He does not however consider early pictorial representations to be a significant part of feedback loops that alter the human mind.[11] As embodied cognition has mounted a strong challenge to the classic cognitivist view of the mind, an alternative view has emerged. It maintains that sensorimotor

representations, including visual images, are integrally involved at
all levels of mental processing, including in the most complex operations of symbolic thought. Patricia Pisters draws on the work of
the neuroscientists Victor Lamme and Pieter Roelfsema to provide
an account of how visual perception functions in this manner in
film viewing. She employs their description of the "feed-forward
sweep" of automatically processed visual data that identify attributes such as form, color, shape, and movement, among others, to
distinguish between the restricted processing that establishes (not
yet conscious) *attention* and the more elaborate processing that
produces *awareness.* Building off Deleuze's claim that the brain
is the screen, she argues that the "neuro-image" of cinema works
primarily at the level of subphenomenal consciousness and that
this initial automatic processing prefigures the salient features of
the discrete image that presents itself to the higher-order process
of critical assessment.

   In this regard, film provided a visual technology well suited for
projecting our psychological and cultural experience in much the
same mode as literature. It also expanded on literature's potential
to represent and examine the mental and psychological calcula-
tions that guide our decision-making. With the invention of continuous moving-image media there was a quantum leap forward
in the ability to involve sensory experience in the telling of stories.
This intensification of the diegetic effect also endows the viewing experience with a stronger sense of immediacy than can be
generated by literature. Commenting on how film extends visual
media in a qualitative manner that complements literary writing,
Virginia Woolf says of the images that are presented in movies:
"They have become not more beautiful in the sense in which pictures are beautiful, but shall we call it (our vocabulary is miserably
insufficient) more real, or real with a different reality from that
which we perceive in daily life? We behold them as they are when
we are not there. We see life as it is when we have no part in it"
(269). Her description suggests how the moving image both draws
us into affective engagement in the present while at the same time
providing a distance to the flow of images as they are projected
onto a screen in front of the viewer. The novelty of the experience
she is attempting to put into words stems from the way the viewer

is exposed simultaneously to the affect of the image and to the subjective vision that this sensory input creates. That is, film "projected and made visible *for the very first time* not just the subjective world but the very structure and process of subjective, embodied vision" (Sobchack 2004a, 149). The remediation of individuated human perception—and in this case, of a particular dynamic of operative vision—into the technical and aesthetic production of the cinematic image represents a radically new prosthetic extension of our mental universe.

This dual effect mirrors key aspects of the dream experience. It does so because film engages the viewer at the subphenomenal level of bodily responses much as dreams produce moments of strong affect that are inextricably tied to the dream vision. The moving-image camera and projector enabled the display of causal links between images, sequences, and scenes according to what we perceive to be a natural order. What is novel about the medium is not its ability to reenact causal linkage at the level of conscious thought. Various types of representational art had long done this, employing narrative as a structural device for conveying causality. These traditional forms of media have also always engaged to some extent the sensorimotor systems of the participant, user, or viewer in the process. But none had been able to present an external manifestation of causality at this neural level with the same sense of immediacy as generated by the moving image of film.

In his 1906 novel *The Confusions of the Young Törless* [*Die Verwirrungen des Zöglings Törless*], Austrian writer Robert Musil reflects on the way film engages the mind in this way at a subphenomenal level. The novel's one reference to film viewing comes as the protagonist is grappling with the feeling of being overwhelmed by a flood of sensations in modernity, of losing the ability, or least the presumed ability, to identify and grasp all these impulses with the conscious mind. In a futile attempt to fix in his mind a firm image of one of his classmates, Törless senses that "he constantly felt a restless unease within, like the feeling you have watching a movie, when despite the illusion of an intact, seamless presence you cannot shake the vague sense that behind the perceived film image hundreds of other distinct, yet fleeting images are scurrying past" (128–29; translation is my own). This passage's reflection on how film engages the mind of the viewer runs counter to the more common fascination at the time with the question of motion perception. Early film devotees were intent on understanding how still photos fed through a projector at twenty-four frames per second could produce a continuous moving image. This was originally explained on the basis of the theory of persistence of vision,[12] but enthusiasts still marveled at how a limited set of distinct images could perform the work of what would seemingly require many more. Törless's allusion to film viewing expresses however the sense that something like the reverse is happening. There are many moving images, only a few of which can be gathered into the flow that becomes visible to the spectator.

The film effect described in Musil's novel refers not to moving-image technology, but rather to the biological system of mental processing that produces consciousness. While many questions remain about how the neural circuits that process information are synchronized so as to generate consciousness, the evidence increasingly points to a dynamic whereby a surplus of mental representations are generated, many of which remain beneath the threshold of phenomenal consciousness. We are aware of these images, sometimes detecting their presence much like when we know we have dreamed but cannot restore the images to consciousness. These images are not only visual. They include other kinds of mental representations, such as aural, tactile, olfactory, proprioceptive, kinesthetic, and verbal ones. As with visual images, there is also an abundant surplus of these others as well, such that parallel to the stream of images that constitute consciousness there is a constant circulation of many others that become mental representations, but are not selected for consciousness. Those that are selected but do not necessarily attract our attention comprise one part of what William James famously recognized as the different kinds of consciousness that, largely unbeknownst to us, exist alongside one another at every moment. His account of the composite makeup of consciousness resonates with the experience described by Törless:

> Our normal waking consciousness, rational consciousness
> as we call it, is but one special type of consciousness, whilst
> about, parted from it by the flimsiest of screens, there lie

potential forms of consciousness entirely different. We
may go through life without suspecting their existence:
but apply the requisite stimulus, and at a touch they are
there in all their completeness, definite types of mentality
which probably somewhere have their field of application
and adaptation. No account of the universe in its totality
can be final which leaves these other forms of consciousness
quite disregarded. (James, 305)

The oblique reference to movies in *The Confusions of the Young
Törless* suggests how film mirrors the stream of visual images
that comprise consciousness and, in doing so, arouses awareness
of those other images lying just behind "the flimsiest of screens."
Watching externally projected moving images seemingly flow by in
front of our eyes evokes the sense that there must also be accompanying nonconscious images. Film viewing triggers this response
because the moving images form a continuous stream that effectively simulates our experience of a unitary consciousness. The
film apparatus strings together individual images in a way that corresponds to how the mind collates perceptions, memories, emotional impulses, and sensorimotor input into a stream of images
that is made available for metacognitive appraisal. Looking at this
from the reverse perspective, we would say that the mind works
like the camera and projector. It perceives, processes, and archives
experiences as categorical memories that can then be accessed and
employed to process later engagements with the world around us.
Mental faculties are continuously selecting stored memories and
calling them into consciousness in a process that mirrors the mechanical operation of the projector. In *Creative Evolution* (1907), a
work written at the same time as *The Confusions of the Young Törless*, Henri Bergson compares the mind's mechanism for creating
"ordinary knowledge" (306), his term for what more recently neuroscientists have termed "primary consciousness" (Edelman 2006,
36–39) or "core consciousness" (Damasio 1999, 82–106), to the
film projector. He refers to the mental process that generates consciousness as an "inner film projector" that arranges and places the
individual "snapshots . . . of the passing reality" (perceptions and
memories) before us and in motion: "We place ourselves outside

[the inner becoming of things] in order to recompose their becoming artificially" (306).

Musil's passage and Bergson's concept of the *cinèmatographe intèrieur* reflect how film is a prosthetic extension of consciousness. The moving images projected onto the movie screen mirror not only the stream of internal images that constitute consciousness, but also the process by which they are produced. Törless's musings about his film experiences suggest how the correlation between the mental production of consciousness and its prosthetic extension in film functions at two levels. The invention of the camera and projector replicated on a mechanical level the mental networks that bind a myriad of simultaneously firing neural circuits into images (mental representations). The technical systems for film capture and projection were so designed that they simulate the temporal and spatial constructs of consciousness. To some extent then, the affective-cognitive operations that select and order images to produce consciousness were built into the medium itself. Thus, in its earliest instantiation, even before narrative film became the standard form, film was simulating the unitary experience of consciousness, such that it created, in Törless's words, "the illusion of an intact, seamless presence." At the same time, the new moving-image technology of film engages the viewer at the subphenomenal level more directly than not only literary media, but also previous visual media. Drawing the viewer into affective participation with the presence generated by its moving images, film exerts its influence directly on tactile and sensorimotor systems. As it produces embodied responses that normally remain below the threshold of consciousness, film stirs the kind of fleeting images whose presence Törless sensed but was not able to grasp and observe, like snapshots of a passing reality.

This dual effect that the moving film image produced in the viewer has contributed to divergent views of cinema's role in the coevolution of visual media and the mind. An understanding of the synergy underlying what we perceive as two distinct forms of information is needed to resolve the seeming disparity involved in film viewing. Damasio's description of how consciousness arises helps explain how film functions as a prosthetic extension of neural circuits at both levels. In *The Feeling of What Happens* he describes how a dual system of neural mappings in the brain underlies the process by which consciousness and a sense of self arise simultaneously. Second-order neural processes are mapped onto first-order neural patterns activated by the interaction between the body and an external environment. To enable us to comprehend this process, he describes what is in actuality a much more fluid and overlapping complex of first and second-order maps as a clearly sequenced two-stage process. To represent how the self comes into being—how it becomes revealed in our consciousness—Damasio depicts it as a retroactive capturing of a past moment: "Looking back, with the license of metaphor, one might say that the swift, second-order nonverbal account narrates a story: *that of the organism caught in the act of representing its own changing state as it goes about the representing something else.* But the astonishing fact is that the knowable entity of the catcher has just been created in the narrative of the catching process" (1999, 170).

On one hand, this account suggests how film could reinforce traditional humanist notions about the self and its relation to the world around it. Chief among these is the idea of the persistence of the self as a coherent subject set off from a reality that, as its other, is similarly pre-given and permanent. In this effort to explain how the mental processes that generate consciousness present images as being set apart from and put on display for an attentive self, Damasio employs film as a metaphor. What James termed stream of consciousness he calls the "movie-in-the-brain" (1999, 11). While skirting the trap of positing an internal subject within the brain that perceives this "movie," the so-called Homunculus, or little man inside the head, he nonetheless grants that this process occurs in a way that generates "*the sense* that there is an owner and observer for that movie" (1999, 11, emphasis added). The similarity Damasio posits here between the moving images of film and consciousness underlies certain ontological assumptions that have shaped our understanding of film viewing. Cinematographic images are so palpable, so seductive, some critics would assert, because of their affinity with the "movie-in-the-brain" and the way we situate ourselves with respect to images in that scenario. The viewing subject of cinema and the internally imagined self that must be assumed as the subject for whom consciousness presents its picture of the world would tend to lead us to posit an autonomous self that exists independently of the world outside it. A sense of a division between the internal seeing subject and what is seen (the image stream of consciousness) creates the impression that the images themselves exist autonomously outside the body. Thus, both consciousness and cinema give the impression that their images issue directly from this world. This masks the constitutive role the body plays in producing a world from within.

In this way film offers another dimension to the constitution of the subject in literary fiction. It awakens those phantoms that have been the providence of imaginative fiction since the Romantic period, even as the moving image arouses the sensations whose exclusion gives rise to such ghostly visions. The film experience exposes the duplicitous nature of our mental world not merely through philosophical reflection, but directly through affective impulses that are produced by our embodied interaction with the image. Ultimately, the phantom it conjures up is that of a self that has been constituted as if it can bypass the body's technically mediated interaction with the cultural environment altogether.

Film possesses the power to generate this effect in the viewer because the moving image exerts its influence as prosthetic extension in direct fashion as well. In his account of how consciousness and the self co-arise Damasio accounts for this effect as well. He argues that the perception of the self as an enduring entity set apart from the stream of images that constitute consciousness evolved in conjunction with the adaptations that produced conscious mental processing. We are compelled to conceive of the unitary process that produces consciousness as happening in stages precisely because it produces the sense of a self that persists over time. Moreover, the sense of the knowing self that emerges along with the mental images is not merely an epiphenomenon. It plays a vital role in the operational organization of the human organism. Damasio explains its function in this way: "Those [unified mental] scenes do not exist in a vacuum. I believe they are integrated and unified because of the singularity of the organism and for the benefit of that single organism. . . . The biological state we describe as sense of self and the biological machinery responsible for engendering it may well have a hand in optimizing the processing of the objects to be known—having a sense of self is not only required for knowing, in the proper sense, but may influence the processing of whatever gets to be known" (1999, 19). According to this view, both consciousness and the self that arises along with it are epiphenomena in the sense that they are constructed on top of the body's basic system that orients it in the world, enabling it to move, interact, and survive. However, in describing this process that produces a more permanent sense of a self that is in actuality always in flux, Damasio takes care to specify that these memories include both conscious ones (explicit memory) as well as those that have never attained conscious re-cognition (implicit memory). Thus, he firmly roots extended consciousness in the whole range of automatic bodily interactions with the world around us.

Cognitive scientists working in the new field of neurocinematics have speculated about cinema's influence on these mental operations and designed experiments using advanced brain-imaging technology to test their theories.[13] They apply current models of mental processing to film viewing to explain how cinema attracts and holds the viewer's attention, establishes spatial orientation, or generates coherent mental narratives. These studies have concentrated mainly on conscious cognitive operations, in part because the cinematic image is constructed to appeal to phenomenal consciousness and the way it entertains and manipulates images. In doing so, they have argued that film, as a prosthetic extension of the stream of conscious mental images, alters and enhances certain related brain functions. In "Enslaving Central Executives: Toward a Brain Theory of Cinema," neurobiologist Yadin Dudai applies Alan Baddeley's widely accepted model of working memory, first proposed in 1974, to film viewing. Assessing how narrative film engages this mental mechanism, he argues that cinema augments the brain's system for activating and manipulating memory in the service of goal-oriented actions. As it conducts operations, working memory encodes information from the body's current activity and re-encodes information from past experiences into long-term memories that can be used by the executive center to envision future scenarios and choose between possible courses of action. A key to understanding how cinema can exercise and influence this system is its functional division into automatic sensorimotor input and higher-order cognitive processing. The *content-dedicated workspaces* of working memory divide input for the most part between sensorimotor data that is primarily automatically encoded (in the *visuospatial sketchpad*) and speech-based information that requires greater cognitive intervention (via the *phonological loop*). Focusing on the buffering of episodic memory, Dudai argues that the production of audiovisual narratives in cinema simulates how memories are generated in the episodic buffer and then stored in long-term memory. He claims that the simulation of these processes in a moving-image medium has enabled us to create narratives with more complex temporal structures. Trained by cinema's manipulation of the relations between past, present, and future events, we become more adept at "running scenarios" that are not limited to chronologically sequenced events in time. And when he explains that audiovisual media, and cinema in particular, "provide an extra-corporal audiovisual space" (36) that expands the brain's ability to generate and store episodic long-term memory, Dudai marks film viewing as an instance of distributed cognition that augments our mental faculties by extending them into the external world.

In another study, Daniel Levin and Caryn Wang (2009) provide an equally compelling case for applying scientific knowledge of the visuospatial sketchpad to the analysis of the cinematic construction of space. Although they do not work explicitly with the working memory model, their account of how the body's innate systems for spatial mapping work in film reception complements Dudai's work on the temporal correspondences between cinema and the brain. Their study also centers on the differences between acts of spatial cognition that require mental cognizance and automatic information processing that does not require conscious intervention. Mainstream cinema has, they argue, developed a system of spatial continuity such that the spectator can remain oriented primarily via habituated, mechanical means for deciphering spatial geography and the structured network of human gazes. They then analyze scenes where filmmakers consciously break the classical continuity rules, but maintain the same level of spatial orientation through more complex techniques. In the examples they explore, spatial cues that require mental recognition, although not necessarily conscious awareness of it, compensate for the disruption of

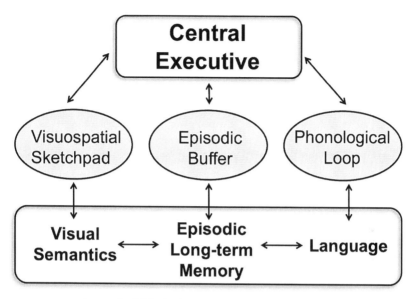

FIGURE 1. *Aaron Baddeley's classic model of working memory.*

the conventional cinematic dependence on automatically encoded spatial information. Although Levin and Wang do not address the question of changes to or enhancement of brain function, their study offers another piece of evidence to support Dudai's claim.

Dudai argues that cinema's ability to actively engage the viewer in an external reenactment of what occurs in the episodic visual buffer has improved this cognitive function in individual movie-goers and across the broader population (36). He contends that the refinement of moving-image technology and its cultural dissemination have enhanced our biological capabilities in important ways: "Film is a subset of the audiovisual media that allow humans to expand their natural capability to simulate and rehearse the world." Here I think he puts his finger on a key dynamic that can help explain cinema's meteoric rise as a globally successful cultural form. In particular, he emphasizes the influence that cinema has had on the brain's visual and cognitive capacity to run scenarios. In accounting for this effect, he puts forward an argument that Jean Mitry had made in his 2000 study *The Aesthetics and Psychology of the Cinema*: that cinema creates out of its images and sounds a narrative that is more coherently and economically constructed than those internal scenarios produced by consciousness.[14] Dudai's account of the correspondence between cinema and working memory focuses mainly on its effects at a high level of narrative and explains how film offers models for mapping potential paths through social and cultural situations that shape our lives. By constructing potential life narratives on screen, cinema has enhanced our ability to play out these potentialities in self-generated, individuated virtual worlds. In doing so, it has enabled novel patterns for structuring time and space and expanded our capacity to combine memories, thoughts, and emotion.[15] It is then only logical to assume that this prominent cultural vehicle for producing virtual worlds has altered the way our mind generates both spontaneous fantasies as well as consciously constructed narratives of what our life is or could be. And as I have argued in "Correspondences in Visual Imaging and Spatial Orientation in Dreaming and Film Viewing," it has had a similar effect on our dreams as well (Cook 2011a).

Dudai concentrates mainly on this influence at the phenomenal level of stories revolving around a narrative self. At the same time, his account of how this is initiated at the level of working memory indicates that cinema has a similar effect on the brain's ability to process automatically encoded information in the episodic buffer and to store an account of that process in long-term memory. Because the brain also runs virtual scenarios that guide the selection of automatic actions and movement, the externally produced moving images of cinema extend and enhance our faculties of perception-cognition at the level of physical realism as well. That is, his explanation of how cinema trains our ability to run scenarios as options for selecting actions cuts across both the processing of sensorimotor information and conscious or potentially conscious decision-making. In the previous section, we observed how neuroscientists have proposed neural models of consciousness that describe how the body is constantly producing what Dennett called "draft models" at all levels of brain activity. Comparing "the current state of the world with a predicted state" (Gray, 659), the brain operates universally according to this principle, whether it is involved in sensorimotor control or theorizing and planning: "It is clear that prediction and mismatch are important parts of the machinery of the mind, with mismatches being both at automatic level (as certain EEG signals observed in audition show) and at the level of conscious thought" (Taylor, 116). In the same vein, Finnish neuroscientist Antti Revonsuo describes our conscious correlates of the events and objects we encounter in the world as "transparent surrogates constructed in the brain." That is, "the brain creates for us *only virtual presence* or telepresence in the surrounding world" (2006, 109; emphasis added). This account of what he calls *world simulation* indicates a close correspondence between the sense of presence experienced in film viewing, what Deleuze termed "camera-consciousness" (1986b, 74), and our real-life experience of being immersed in a surrounding world. In other words, all the virtual events and objects represented onscreen have the same ontological status as the phenomena that produce consciousness outside the theater.

Approaching this mode of mental processing from the perspective of computer science, computational learning theory has framed the evolutionary dynamic of "prediction and mismatch" in terms of mathematical analysis. Leslie Valiant has proposed that algorithms guide organisms' interaction with the environment. Calling these computational procedures "ecorithms," he describes how algorithms accounting for an encountered object are formed as hypothetical approximations that then get slowly adjusted as more knowledge about the object is acquired. This is happening automatically, he asserts, throughout the nervous system—not only in humans, but in other organisms as well—as neural circuits are formed and maintained without cognitive input. Ute Holl provides support for this claim in a media-theoretical analysis of German neuropsychological studies related to *gestalt* theory. Citing the work of the former director of the Max Planck Institute for Brain Research in Frankfurt, Wolf Singer, she describes how the process of producing draft models based on rhythmic vibrations functions for the mental "representation of both composite perceptual objects and composite movement trajectories" (Wolf Singer, 162; quoted in Holl, 168). Here, Holl explains how the brain runs scenarios as it works to identify visual information: "Rhythmic and vibrational processes establish a perceptual structure, which lasts over a period of time until perception makes up its mind to find another vibrating or vibrant correspondence that is more probable." She employs these scientific findings to analyze how the digital image alters the relational states between the neuronal assemblies that produce draft perceptual structures and how the changes in these subperceptual operations affect behavior and psychology.

The upshot of these various models of neural processing for film is that cinema runs scenarios that also engage and expand our patterns of interacting with the world on the subphenomenal basis of automatically encoded memories. Through embodied film reception changes are occurring at the cellular level where implicit learning takes place and is retained via the plasticity of neural circuits (LeDoux, 116–19). Given our present knowledge of brain function, we may not be able to precisely pinpoint the specific nature of changes to the neural circuits that process automatically encoded information. Nonetheless, we can make a strong case that there are such effects and that they promote technogenesis. The most directly affected regions are located primarily in areas of the brain that predate the neocortex and the development of humans' most sophisticated mental faculties. Not enough is known about the intermediary steps between fast-track, subcortical activity and the neural maps of high-level mental patterns to be able to trace exactly how they interact. Still, work in cognitive neuroscience indicates that even the lowest order of neural processing plays a constitutive role all the way up the ladder to the most intricate cognitive operations conducted by the human mind (Panksepp 306–13). What closely links the two levels of processing is the body's ability to produce a constant stream of not only visual, but also auditory, somatosensory, kinesthetic, and other types of images. This capacity to generate internal images is the core processing operation for both basic survival (in this respect, not only for humans but for other mammals and apparently other species as well) and for higher-order cognitive functions that enable longer-range planning.

The running of scenarios described by Dudai occurs automatically and primarily without the awareness of the viewer. However, these scenarios are mental representations that are potentially accessible to our conscious mind. During film viewing the viewer's body is also running scenarios at the subphenomenal level, prior to the process of synchronization that gathers them into a higher-order neural network and produces the content of consciousness. As the body reacts to the cinematic image at this basic level of affect, the visual medium is working its prosthetic effect on these neural networks and altering both the individual viewer and the distributed media network of the collective film public in crucial ways. In this regard cinema is part of a complex media landscape that is constantly evolving and altering how the pre-individual engages with the cultural environment at the level of body technics. At this level, human capabilities and sensibilities interact with a technically distributed network that not only shapes our internal milieu, but is also an integral part of it. As this system "engineers" new relations between the pre-individual and the world we inhabit, the process remains closed to consciousness (Hansen 2012, 33–34). The embodied responses to the film image have a direct impact on the central nervous system and belong to a broad and versatile system capable of performing many functions that have previously been thought to require awareness and attention. Cognitive scientists have taken to calling this network of unconscious neural processes that are integral to all human activity, from the maintenance of the autonomic nervous system to intentional actions and from automatic affective signals to attentive thought processes, the "new unconscious" (Uleman). Structured by the complex and pervasive interconnection between the human and technology, this technological unconscious is more adaptive than higher-order consciousness. The neural subsystems underlying its functions dovetail with the external environment in a transparent manner to extend our affective-cognitive resources and enhance mental processing at all levels (Clark 2003, 28–34).

Postcinematic Reflections on Spectatorship

When the process of second-order cognitive assessment occurs in an artistic domain such as cinema, aesthetic strategies perform a crucial part of the critical work and become an object of it as well. In particular, the status of the medium within the broader landscape of contemporary culture becomes a key theme. The convergence of film and digital technology has spurred the kind of crisis in cinema that leads to such self-reflective critique. A few films appearing at the end of the last century reflect on the effect that the dominant film style of conventional cinema has had in this regard, even as they employ digital technologies to break its hold. On neither count do they take a purely thematic, representationalist approach. Foregrounding their hybrid construction, they combine traditional narrative film with the digital image, employing its ability to engage the body at the microtemporal level as an antidote to the conventional cinematic image. The result is a multidimensional cinematic experience that disrupts conventional patterns of reception while spurring deliberations about the effects of the classical mode of spectatorship on human cognition and perception.

One example of a film that preforms such a metacritique of cinematic representation is Kathryn Bigelow's 1995 neo-noir crime thriller *Strange Days.* It envisions how digital technologies might be applied to the specific technique of POV filming to commandeer the conscious mind of the viewer/user for a single, continuous sequence. Set only four years into the future, and coincidentally in the same year that *Dark City, The Matrix,* and *eXistenZ* all appeared, the story involves a new recording device called SQUID, or Superconducting Quantum Interference Device, that records the full sensorimotor experience of the wearer. The fully embodied memory of the recorded experience can be transferred to a minidisk and played back on a deck that enables the user to have the same experience as the original participant. The SQUID apparatus functions much like a camera, but it can record and present during playback a more immersive experience than is possible with cinema. It also increases the likelihood that people will be harmed and even killed to make recordings that appeal to the most sordid urges of the users. Originally developed to aid law enforcement in the gathering of evidence, the making and selling of disks for private use is illegal. The central character, the former LAPD vice detective Lenny Nero (Ralph Fiennes), deals in SQUID recordings. He refuses however to sell "blackjack" clips in which the person whose experience was recorded dies at the end. The crime story revolves around a disk given to Lenny by one of his contacts that plays back a brutal rape and murder recorded from the perspective of the perpetrator. This "playback" is particularly harrowing because the murderer straps a SQUID onto his victim before he rapes and kills her. The woman was a friend of Lenny's former lover, Faith Justin (Juliette Lewis). Worried that she is in danger as well, Lenny sets out to find the disk with the victim's recording, which will reveal the identity of the murderer.

As the story unfolds, parallels between the playback of SQUID recordings and cinema offer a cinematic critique of conventional Hollywood film. Bigelow's film features many elements typical of classic noir, both in plot and characters (a crime investigation, an alienated hero with dubious ethics, false accusations, betrayal and double cross, police corruption and general moral degeneracy, a fall guy, and a femme fatale) and in style and structure (convoluted plot twists, dark and foreboding settings, scenes set in bars, lounges, and cheap hotels, and fast dialogue full of crime jargon, sexual innuendo, and sharp repartees). Subjective sequences of playback clips also emulate the narrative function of flashbacks that were common in film noir and highlight the parallels between "jacking in" to SQUID recordings and film viewing. The continual metacinematic references in *Strange Days* clearly draw comparisons between SQUID playback and other moving-image media. Early in the film, when Lenny is haggling with his dealer, Tick (Richard Edson), he complains about the mundane, uninteresting recordings he has to offer, referring to them as "the usual soaps you bring me." Tick responds by repeating something Lenny had said in a previous bargaining session: "Bring me real life. Bring me street life. And, like, one man's mundane and desperate existence is another man's Technicolor." This allusion to the reality effect of film suggests that mainstream narrative cinema's pursuit of a total diegetic reality had subjugated the technological capabilities of the medium to this single effect. In trying to make a sale to a potential client, Lenny declares there is no comparison between television and playback: "Look, I want you to know what we're talking about here. This isn't like TV only better. This is life. It's a piece of somebody's life. Pure and uncut, straight from the cerebral cortex. You're there. You're doing it, seeing it, hearing it . . . feeling it." Here too the film is implying that SQUID playback, with its ability to convey a fully embodied experience associated with the visual stream of images, has finally achieved the goal of full diegetic reality that the film industry had long been pursuing.

The dealers of SQUID technology claim that by adding affective and sensorimotor elements to POV footage it can transform the distanced, spectatorial experience of cinema into a full-fledged embodied reality. However, the film puts the viewer in the position of the user and, in doing so, lets the audience experience directly the inability of playback to completely supplant bodily presence and assume the subjectivity of another. The opening sequence of *Strange Days* primes the viewer to respond like the player in an interactive video game, even though the viewer lacks the ability to intervene and change the outcome. It begins with a playback episode. It opens with "You ready?" in voiceover against a blank, black screen, followed by the close-up of an eye and the response, "Yeah, boot it." The screen then turns to audiovisual static that quickly comes into focus as the playback of a Chinese restaurant hold-up recorded through the body of one of the three armed robbers. A typical crime-film action scene unfolds, but the playback mode situates the viewer directly as an active participant rather than merely as a spectator. Shot strictly from the point of view of the robber, without any cuts, the three-plus minutes of frenzied kinetic action and intense nervous energy has the viewer immersed as an active participant in the robbery.

In this sequence the film viewer experiences firsthand the distress the user feels when her subjectivity is not totally subsumed by the vicarious participation in the playback episode. The ensuing dissonance reveals the innate limitations of the fictional SQUID technology. Regardless of how completely playback can envelop the user's stream of consciousness, it cannot quell the flow of embodied input into that experience. The body feeds a wide array of implicit memory, ranging from emotional associations to muscle memory, into the mental stream of playback. Emotional and evaluative associations based on one's own past intrude, often conflicting with the recorded experience. When the recorded experience conflicts with one's own embodied desires there can be no smooth experience, must less enjoyment, of the simulated consciousness. SQUID technology must ultimately fail to deliver on its promise of a total spec-

FIGURE 2. *A shot from the point of view of one of the bank robbers in the opening sequence of* Strange Days.

tatorial immersion.[16] In attempting to create this effect, it intrudes into the viewing experience in a more disruptive manner than cinema. The enticing illusion created by cinema engages the viewing subject as constituted by memories, expectations, and emotions, and this negotiation between the simulated world of the film and the real world is always at work. But there is also a lesson here for cinema. Its production of a spectatorial prosthetic consciousness based on the idea of total immersion must be rejected in favor of a film experience that better channels the reality of our embodied existence in the world. Ultimately, *Strange Days* suggests that a technology capable of doing this can never supplant lived experience and will also inflict lasting damage. This warning to cinema is implied obliquely when Faith, exasperated at Lenny's determination to win her back, quips: "You know one of the ways movies are still better than playback? The music comes up, there's credits, and you always know when it's over."

Alejandro Amenábar's 1997 film *Abre los ojos* (Open your eyes) also exploits digital technology to provide a critical lens for assessing the diegetic effect produced by narrative film. Like other sci-fi films at the end of the century, it alludes to conventional genre patterns and film styles to link the diegetic cyberreality of its plot to the virtual film realities of mainstream cinema. An automobile accident that leaves the film's attractive and wealthy protagonist, César (Eduardo Noriega), horribly disfigured leads him to seek out the virtual existence offered by the Life Extension corporation. César chooses an option called Clause 14 that allows the client to live in the future in a virtual reality that has been implanted into the brain. Those who choose this alternative continue the life they have been living, shaping it according to desires that emanate from their own unconscious and without any recollection of unpleasant or traumatic events of the past or awareness that they are in a virtual reality. César buys into Clause 14 despite the company's warning that it is not yet fully developed. In the narrative present of the film story César is incarcerated in the psychiatric ward of a prison after the Life Extension program had failed to provide him with the ideal virtual life that he desired. As he talks about the past with the prison psychiatrist in an attempt to sort out what has happened to him, it is difficult for the viewer to distinguish between his actual lived past and the jumbled recall of episodes in his new virtual existence. Interspersed among his narration of the events leading up to his arrest are scenes that return to the diegetic present of him in prison and his conversations with the psychiatrist. Memories from his previous life intrude into his virtual reality, creating nightmarish episodes that the Clause 14 program should have blocked, including the scenario that he is now imprisoned because he killed an ex-lover. In the course of their conversations he manifests his desires, fears, and insecurities in a retelling of his past in which he is not able to distinguish what really happened from dreamlike fantasies and hallucinations. As he is unable to construct a consistent narrative self out of this chaotic set of episodic experiences, the film's jumbled chronology and fusing of lived experience with virtual reality enables the viewer to share in his tortured state of mind.

As a fantasy life that meshes with memories from an individual's past and forms a virtual continuation of it according to one's wishes, the "artificial perception" created by Clause 14 reflects key aspects of the cinematic experience. Film theories have posited in various ways that film reality is at once foreign to and inseparable from the viewer's individual history and thus tends to construct the viewing subject as a tortured phantom that gravitates between real and virtual experience (Schefer, 112–15). César's inability to assimilate his embodied memories into the virtual scenarios offered by Clause 14 mirrors this facet of spectatorship. This metacine-matic reference is reinforced via the narratives César creates as he struggles to make sense of his virtual existence. Each of the three scenarios he generates in his conversations with the psychiatrist (which is also a self-generated virtual episode) is a generic film nar-rative. When he first starts living out his own personal virtual real-ity it takes the form of a happy love story. In this version, the plastic surgeons are able to use an innovative new technique on him and reconstruct his face, restoring his Hollywood good looks. He then revives his fledgling romance with the beautiful Sofia (Penélope Cruz), but is not able to sustain this ideal version of his life. During sex Sofia suddenly transmutes into his former occasional sex part-ner Nuria (Najwa Nimri). He imagines that she is preventing him from having a relationship with Sofia and murders her. This leads to the second strand of personal narrative, and again it plays out in the mold of a Hollywood genre film, that of a criminal detective story. Accused now of murdering Sofia, he sets out to discover why everyone thinks that the woman he murdered, Nuria, was actually Sofia. As his sanity is challenged, his life becomes even more frac-tured. The representative of Life Extension approaches him at a bar and attempts to explain to him that he is in control of his own story and can choose to experience pleasure and happiness rather than the torment he is suffering. However, he does not heed this advice. Instead, he now becomes obsessed with discovering what part of his life is real and what is merely a cyber-induced fantasy. From this point on César's virtual life takes a different tack, one that coincides with the actual genre of *Open Your Eyes*. In its third and final manifestation, his life story becomes a cyberthriller in which he is trying to discover what is real and what is illusion. César now finds himself playing a role like that of the protagonists in classic cyber-fiction films, such as *Blade Runner* or *Total Recall* (Paul Verhoeven, 1990). These three strands of cinematic narrative allude to the way the Hollywood dream factory offers the viewer a prosthetic life story that lacks embodied grounding in the world. In this respect, Amenábar employs a tactic similar to the one David Lynch used in *Mulholland Drive* (2001). In that case, the cinematic scenarios that percolate through the protagonist's feverish dream state reveal how visions of stardom that were both induced and created by Hollywood have infiltrated her unconscious and fractured the boundaries between fantasy and reality (Cook 2011b).

Open Your Eyes attends to its metacinematic reflections not only thematically but also somatically by evoking embodied responses in the viewer that correspond to César's experiences. The Clause 14 alternative offered by Life Extension successfully enables him to create a virtual life for himself that is completely lifelike and convincing. However, the prosthetic consciousness that supports the new autobiographical self lacks grounding in embodied memories. As part of his new virtual life César can generate simulations of people from his past and determine the image they have of him. But the program cannot produce their physical responses to him when in his presence. The discovery of mirror neurons and the determination of their role in the embodied production of social cognition (Gallese 2005; Spaulding) has shown that our conception of self is not highly independent and private, even in its relation to the biological systems of the body. Rather it emerges from a reciprocity of physical interactions with other individuals. As a result of mirroring mechanisms, we share a multiplicity of bodily states with others and a uniquely human form of intersubjectivity (Gallese 2009, 171–73). Lacking input at this subpersonal level of automatic responses, César is caught up in a loop where the only feedback he receives is produced by himself.[17] This idea is conveyed in the recurring scenes of César looking in the mirror alternatively at either his beautiful or his horribly disfigured face. Neither the mirror nor the virtual faces of those who people his virtual world—and are thus projections of his own imagination—can evoke the embodied social cognition needed for a stable sense of self.[18] In his conversations with the prison psychiatrist Antonio (Chete Lera), César wears a mask and cowers on the floor or slumps in his chair in abject disconnection from the world around him. This also manifests his lack of embodied interaction with others. The virtual Antonio has no mirror neuron system to read César's emotions and intentions on his body and reflect them back in a reverberating interplay of physical cues between self and the other. The mask and posture also create a somatic resonance between César and the viewer. Deprived of the facial expressions and bodily movements that could provide a direct physical link to César's subjective world, the viewer's only access is through his secondary projections of himself in the scenarios he imagines in his talks with Antonio. In this way, the viewer, like César, is cut off from key physical signals needed for integration into a sphere of social or cultural interaction. In the film story, César lacks the embodied substrata necessary to give his virtual life affective grounding. In the case of the viewer, mirroring mechanisms lack access to the synchronized audiovisual information needed to assess César's situation and to be sutured securely into the diegetic film world. Thus, the viewer experiences a disassociation from the affective dimension of the film world analogous to that César suffers in the Clause 14 construction of a virtual continuation of his life.

However, *Open Your Eyes* does not simply dismiss classical cinema as a purveyor of illusions that must be recognized as such and abandoned. Rather, the film's dramatic ending suggests that the filmic episodes that have disrupted César's ability to assume the virtual subjective-being-in-the-world offered by Clause 14 have helped him understand and accept an alternative path. He ultimately chooses his own flawed history over the Clause 14 existence that was supposed to free him up from the vagaries of human existence. Offered the chance to have his dream restarted so that he

FIGURE 3. *César wearing a mask in his session with the psychiatrist in* Open Your Eyes.

can now create an ideal virtual life for himself, he declines and decides to commit (virtual) suicide, knowing that he will awaken to begin an actual life anew in the year 2045. He leaps off a skyscraper, and the screen goes black when he hits the ground. The film ends with guttural sounds of him waking up over the black screen, while a soothing female voice says softly, "Relax, relax. Open your eyes." He opens himself up to an unknown future, one where he must seek out a new life for himself in a world where the narrative constructs of the old visual culture hit up against the virtual realities of digitized media. Addressed as much to the viewer as to the visually absent César, the final words of the film admonish that the great cinematic accomplishments of the twentieth century have not passed away. In the postcinematic world, they no longer are the dominant force they once were, but they continue to influence how we construct reality and give meaning to it in the digital age: "Among the meanings that are made for creatures like us are meanings of worldness, in which possibilities for future worlds are entertained, thought and felt, played and worked with, responded to and realized. Cinema is the making of worlds and the taking on of those worlds, in limited ways but in ways that allow us to change the shared worlds we create together" (Ivakhiv 2016, 744).

What César must shed when he awakens in the year 2045 is not those worlds that cinema has created, but rather the illusion that its images exist independently outside the body. This misconception enabled those subjective identities that plagued both his real life before the accident and the failed attempt to assume a Clause 14 existence. Rather, the key to successfully blending his old form of consciousness with the new media environment of the future hinges on understanding how the self is always changing, being constructed anew at every moment as our body/mind engages a cultural environment that is in constant flux. This is a key tenet of Mahayana Buddhism that Varela and his coauthors tout in *The Embodied Mind* to bring the idea of autopoiesis formulated in his earlier work into harmony with recent scientific discoveries about the biological substrates of consciousness. The principle of *codependent arising* maintains not only that there is no independently existing subject, "no truly existing subject (a self) continuing unchangingly through a series of moments" (Varela et al., 221), but also that neither the external world of objects nor the relations between subjects and objects can exist in any such independent manner. It articulates an idea that has gained currency in recent media theory via a revival of interest in the philosophy of Alfred North Whitehead,[19] namely that subject, object, and the relation between them exist only in the state of codependent arising, always codetermined according to the contingencies of a particular moment.[20]

However, even if the world-as-given never exists independent of the particular moment with its new and unique set of relations, the potential forms it can assume are mediated by a set of historically determined variables. In the case of cinema these include the technological means for moving-image media, the commercial and cultural infrastructure for production and exhibition, film grammar, genres and narrative tropes, the mode of spectatorship these elements promote, as well as those classic cinematic worlds that continue to inhabit our collective memory. In all these respects, postcinema carries this past forward as the basis for the new worlds it brings into being. As argued earlier with respect to technology writ large, this structural dependence on cinema's past mirrors the way the neural architecture of our brains evolves along with the medium. The constellation of neural networks that come into being as cinema is reshaped by digital technology is built on top of a stratified accumulation of past configurations that correspond to prior film experience. In the case of a medium that engages the viewer actively in an external process of codependent arising, this evolutionary process entails both new bodily dispositions toward the film world and new meanings of worldness.

The films I have discussed here are but two examples of how at the end of the last century filmmakers were grappling self-reflectively with the mode of spectatorship fostered by mainstream cinema. The explosion of new media generated by digital technology spurred cinema to reassess its conventions and to search for novel forms of address. Second-order narratives of the kind found in *Strange Days* and *Open Your Eyes* question the prospect that the viewer of a postmodern, digital cinema might be (re-)constituted as a latter-day version of the disembodied spectator of classical cinema. In chapter 3 I analyze other films from the last few years of the previous century that also probe alternative realities as a way of critiquing mainstream film culture: *eXistenZ, The Thirteenth Floor, Dark City,* and *The Matrix.* In contrast to earlier movies with similar themes, these films employ digital technology to create their diegetic simulations as cyber worlds. By reproducing cinema's traditional mode of representing reality in a medium altered by new technologies, they offer what one critic calls, in reference to *eXistenZ,* an "intermedial filmic presentation of cyberspace's virtual realities" (Hotchkiss, 28). They reconfigure spectatorship and provide new perspectives on how the changes to the medium and to contemporary narrative film precipitated by digital imaging have substantially altered the relation between the viewer and the moving images of cinema. In this way, these films illuminate the role cinema has played mediating between the body and technology and explore the cultural fantasies it has generated about the relationship between representation and reality. Even as these films offer such metacritical reflection on the way cinema has reinforced the dominant spectatorial relation to visual media, they engage the battle for the body and mind of the movie-goer in the digital age.

Their intervention is itself a sign of how cinema contributes to the steady march toward more flexible and productive interfacing with media images. It is part of a dynamic trajectory of alternating stasis and disorder that marks the evolution of media. Standard forms are established, but then become dislodged, leading to chaotic situations out of which new patterns form. With the establishment of classical cinema, film temporarily ceded much of its power to generate alternative patterns of embodied spectatorship that foster creativity and plasticity. Nonetheless, alternative impulses have continually intervened in the fixed patterns of dominant cinema, shaking them up and generating new patterns that revive the coevolutionary advance of the medium with the human biological organism. In keeping with this view, the idea that cinema produced a phatic image that has remained static over the course of its subsequent history is a fiction. Even when the prevailing economic and cultural forces push toward coalescence around a new pattern that maintains the same basic features as the traditional model, it contains impurities. These channel energies back toward the offending microsystems that produced the irregularities and infuse them with more, not less agency. The result is innovation and the accumulation of resources around the anomalies. There are always filmmakers who enter uncharted territories where the possibilities for selecting and combining film images are relatively open and empower new ways of constituting and giving birth to the world. Forms of cinema that are more participatory in relation to the viewer support the fusion of the human with emerging media technologies and the new environments produced by them. This enhances and expands higher-order cognitive processing by promoting the plasticity of the action circuits that support it. When cinema functions as prosthetic consciousness in this manner it opens up new modes of information exchange and pushes toward new stages of the human. Above all, in this progressive mode cinema works to establish modes of spectatorship that no longer situate the viewer as a disembodied subject set off against an intact material reality that exists apart from it.

2

1900

Film Transforms the Media Landscape

Film as Prosthetic Visual Consciousness

The invention of film capture and projection was a culmination of a gradual process that goes back at least to the invention of the magic lantern in the middle of the seventeenth century. It involved advances in technology that were applied to visual media and led to new mechanical means of projecting moving images. The development of these devices, together with the cultural practices and aesthetic techniques that determined how the images were exhibited, constituted a prosthetic extension of human visual consciousness into external media. Existing bodily networks for processing both internal and external images were incorporated in the technology, thus producing more sophisticated technical systems for producing moving media images. The experiences offered by various exhibition mediators then trained the viewing public to process external images in ways that produced new modes of visual consciousness. As the viewer became situated differently with respect to both the mechanical apparatus and the projected images, spectatorship evolved to include more fully embodied participation in the viewing experience. As a result, neural networks formed in the spectator that enhanced the human capacity to process not only external media images but also internal images generated by the five senses of perception as well as sensorimotor functions (kinesthetic and proprioceptive, among others).

As always happens when technological innovation disrupts the existing constellation of media, established aesthetic elements and cultural conventions are remediated into the new artistic ventures. This entails a collaborative interchange, but combative confrontations also erupt between those promoting the innovative potential and others whose interests are best served by the status quo. In the case of visual media, the way the spectator is situated toward the image in terms of both nonconscious bodily engagement and mental contemplation is a key aspect of the clash between the old and the new. As new devices for projecting moving images appeared in the course of the nineteenth century they fostered increased attention to the mechanical apparatus and, in concert with it, stronger physical engagement in the viewing experience. This trend encountered popular exhibition practices that tended to limit the influence of nonconscious sensorimotor processes in favor of a phantasmagoric relation to the image. The competing push toward these two opposing modes of spectatorship was a pivotal factor in the evolution of moving-image media from the magic lantern until film burst onto the scene around 1900 and sparked a more intense conflict between the new visual medium and those it threatened to diminish. However, analysis of the gradual evolution of moving-image devices reveals that film posed less of a threat to other visual media than to the long-dominant medium that was driving human cultural evolution—writing.

When the first exhibitions of the magic lantern began traveling through the capitals of Europe in the 1660s these shows evoked marvel at the scientific discoveries of the time and the technological innovations they enabled (Ndalianis, 28). At the same time, the new powers unleashed by these advances produced both awe and, depending on the presenter, possibly terror in the spectator: "From the outset when the device [the magic lantern] was in less scrupulous hands, it was employed to deceive, terrify and manipulate naïve spectators" (Grau, 142–43). As Arthur C. Clarke famously asserted in his third basic law of prediction, "any sufficiently advanced technology is indistinguishable from magic" (21). In particular, technologies that enable new modes of visual representation invoke awe at their seemingly magical powers. As new technologies appear to defy the laws of nature, they also alter and advance our understanding of what is real. Because human culture is ocularcentric our conceptions of the mind and how we interact with the world are largely defined by what we see and how we see it.

Thus, visual media play a pivotal role in periods of cultural transformation that challenge how we conceive the world.

During the first hundred years of its existence, the fantastic images projected by the magic lantern aroused wonder at the new conceptions of the universe spawned by the burgeoning science of the time. As a result, the attention of the spectator was trained largely on the workings of the apparatus, and this generated increased interest in developing more advanced means of projecting moving images. The fascination with technology and the development of new moving-image devices fostered more extensive bodily involvement in the viewing experience. At the same time, another cultural tendency was pushing in a different direction. At the end of the eighteenth century, after a long, gradual rollout to a larger public, magic lantern shows staged first for the emergent bourgeoisie in France and then more widely to the new middle class throughout Europe introduced a new paradigm of scopic pleasure. With his "phantasmagoria" presentations in Paris in 1799, Belgian physicist and stage magician Ètienne-Gaspard Roberts, who went by the stage name of Robertson, set a trend that would hold strong throughout the nineteenth century even as new moving-image technologies appeared at an increasingly accelerated rate. He characterized his magic lantern illusions as "Phantoms, or Apparitions of the Dead and Absent," which had terrorized individuals in the preceding age of superstition and prejudice and still held some of the same power in his current audience's enlightened age (Musser 1990, 24–25). As a well-known Parisian critic noted in 1800 about Robertson's shows, the creation of fantastic illusions curtails embodied participation in the viewing experience: "Everything is arranged to impress the imagination and conquer the senses" (Grau, 147). To a certain extent, increased familiarity with the mechanics of the device was a reason that interest shifted from fascination with the apparatus to the fantastic visions it projected. Still, as these shows presented illusions that we know to be such but perceive as real, the interest in the scientific knowledge that made them possible did not totally disappear. As part of his phantasmagoria exhibitions Robertson often gave instructional demonstrations that exhibited the technical principles at work in his device (Musser 1990, 27). As part of his show he also produced electrical sparks that created the illusion of dead bodies coming alive and linked recent advances in technology and science with the supernatural: "the new medium of electricity with its utopian connotations was linked with sensory illusions so that the audience was in the right scientific and magical frame of mind as they entered the projection room" (Grau, 146–47). The dual nature of these phantasmagoria exhibitions as both technological achievement and as novel visual representations of a mysterious world that defies comprehension reflects two opposing tendencies at work in the development of moving-image technology that culminated in film at the end of the century.

A series of short-lived moving-image devices invented in the course of the nineteenth century (stereoscope, zoetrope, phenakistoscope, and related mechanisms) fostered a more intense relation between the viewer and the apparatus. In contrast to the magic lantern, which conceals the device, these machines brought attention to their mechanics and established the observer as a more embodied participant. The stereoscope stirred scientific exchanges about how the new medium rendered vision tactile and produced a reorganization of the senses (Plunkett). As the trend moved increasingly toward the kinetic movement of partial or serial images, these inventions became the technical forerunners of film. They also advanced the gradual extension of the nonconscious cognitive processes that produce visual consciousness in the body into technical systems.

Following in the tradition of the devices that preceded it, film was a breakthrough technology that did not merely survive, but enjoyed spectacular success due to its more sophisticated ability to capture and exhibit moving images. Its ascendancy at the turn of the century as the new standard for moving-image production and exhibition was due in large part to improvements in the mechanisms for capturing successive still images with the camera and then running them through a projector. Most importantly, this new moving-image medium could project the sequence of moving images with a temporal consistency that mirrors the flow of images in visual consciousness. At the base level, this is a correspondence between the machinic process of film capture and exhibition

and the complex network of perceptual processing that produces
the internal images of consciousness. The bodily binding process
that produces an internal stream of mental images precedes the
higher-order processing that provides a conscious temporal structure to visual input in the visuospatial sector of working memory
(as discussed in chapter 1). In their theory of visual consciousness,
Andreas Bartels and Semir Zeki argue that autonomous, specialized visual processing systems in the brain create perceptually
explicit content (percepts) for different modalities of vision (252).
These include correlates (microconsciousnesses) for color, shape,
and motion among other properties that are then consolidated into
the perceptual objects that comprise consciousness. The temporal consistency gained with the refinement of the film camera and
projector simulated how the brain binds the percepts produced in
multimodal, asynchronous microconscious processes into a temporally and perceptually integrated stream of conscious images. In
this way, the prosthetic extension of visual consciousness through
the medium of film expanded the human ability to "see" the world
in the form of a temporally structured conscious vision.

As sequences of moving film images projected onto screens corresponded more closely to those that comprise visual consciousness, this created the sense that the viewer was afforded a window
onto the real world. In addition, film remediated the basic photographic method of capturing a still image on film into a moving-
image medium and, in doing so, inherited the nineteenth-century
idea of realism associated with the photograph. Consequently, film
was seen as an advance in the human ability to grasp and show the
external world as a real, existing object-of-perception. In the nineteenth century, one of the precursors to film had already prepared
spectators to embrace this notion of realism. As photographic
slides were developed for use in a special lantern projector (the
stereopticon, so called because it was usually deployed with dual
images that offered a stereoscopic view), the exhibitors generally
dispensed with the fantastic elements that were common in magic
lantern shows. Instead, they highlighted the photographic projection's ability to produce a heightened reproduction of the thing itself as a new display of technological magic. Images of the recent
past (e.g., Civil War figures and events) and distant places (famous

landscapes and architectural structures) appeared before the viewer as if they were present. Publicists for the traveling stereopticon shows touted their unmediated realism, their ability to offer "a literal transcription of the actual" (Musser 1990, 31). In the last half of the nineteenth century, a few exhibitors presented their travel lectures to audiences in America's larger cities with some success. In the 1890s, others developed a style of social realism that showed scenes of everyday life and struggles of ordinary people rather than views of faraway glamorous locations.

The rapid success of the first film cameras and projectors in the mid-1890s quickly rendered these photographic slide projection shows obsolete. The earliest film screenings adhered to the same basic formula as the stereopticon shows. The so-called actuality films of 1895–1897, most notably the first film exhibited by the Lumière brothers, a one-minute shot of workers leaving their factory called *La sortie de l'usine Lumière à Lyon* (Workers leaving the Lumière factory in Lyon; Louis Lumière, 1895), featured film's ability to capture and present real-time episodes of actual events. Fascination with the new moving-image technology captivated the first film audiences and created a public sensation that drew new viewers into the screening venues in large numbers. Neither the exotic and unfamiliar scenes displayed in the stereopticon presentations nor the fantastic visions typical of magical lantern shows were necessary for film to establish itself as a vibrant new medium.

After the breakout novelty year of the 1896–1897 theatrical season, the fledgling motion-picture companies could no longer depend on fascination with the new medium to sustain or expand their commercial enterprise. They turned to narrative, initially in the form of short, usually comedic skits, to lure spectators back for repeat visits. As storytelling gradually replaced unvarnished recordings of actual events, the screening process changed accordingly. Actuality films were recorded on a single continuous strip of film that ran repeatedly through the projector. The narrative shorts consisted of multiple shots edited together in a sequence that would be shown only once. Emphasis on the indexical capture of reality faded quickly in commercial screenings, but the idea that the medium could lead to an enhanced mode of realism remained at least latently inherent in film theory. When Italian neorealism flourished in the period following World War II, the idea of cinematic realism resurfaced along with it. Most notably, André Bazin's writings gave the concept new life and, in doing so, led to conflicting ideas about realism that have continued to spark controversy in recent film criticism.[1]

The staying power of the notion that film endows cinema with an intrinsic realism effect derives in part from the mode of spectatorship associated with Renaissance painting. In this model, the spectator is oriented toward media images in a largely fixed position and vision is figured as a window onto the world. The observer in this scheme is not a participant in the modern sense but rather a fixed biological system that visually registers an objectively given external reality as it is. Immobilized by the system of linear perspective, she operates as a disembodied Cartesian subject situated outside the world. The dominant view in film theory has asserted that this fixity not only remains a key aspect of cinematic spectatorship but has also been reinforced by the exhibition settings and aesthetic strategies of classical cinema. Describing how "the mobility of the gaze became more 'virtual,'" Anne Friedberg maintains that as a result "the observer became more immobile, passive, ready to receive the constructions of a virtual reality placed in front of his or her unmoving body" (1994, 28).[2] Assessing the fixed position of the spectator in the movie theater together with the confinement of movement to the framed image, she declares that the "bodily, haptic, phenomenological perception" of the viewer plays a minimal role in a largely immaterial film experience (2006, 173).

While not contesting this general account of how the viewer is situated with respect to the screen, I believe Friedberg's characterization, as well as the account of cinematic spectatorship in apparatus theory more generally, conflates two aspects of the viewing experience prior to film. In doing so, she discounts how the mechanical means of extending the human ability to think visually also enhanced areas of human sensory and nonconscious cognitive processing that contribute to visual consciousness. To be sure, the Renaissance perspective excludes the body from the visual field that frames the external object being observed. However, this absence does not render the sensorimotor and tactile systems of the observer inactive. The body is ubiquitous in the human field of vision in everyday situations, yet ordinarily left out of the visual field as constituted by the act of visual perception (Mach, 122–42). Nonetheless, all the sensory processing associated with all parts of the body continues to operate and provide the situational information needed to direct movement and chart potential movement through the current environment. This includes the kinesthetic and proprioceptive information associated with the extremities that are visible but left out of visual perception. The evacuation of the body from the visual field may have become more comprehensive after the Renaissance, in part perhaps because of the increasing exposure to perspective in painting and other visual media. However, the full set of sensorimotor systems remains operational and attuned to the potential need for bodily action even when the body is at rest and viewing external media images. When exposed to moving media images, as in the case of film viewing, these systems operate at a higher level of activation and preparedness.

The cultural traditions surrounding visual media generate another form of absence or lack that has figured into the dominant modes of spectatorship. It pertains to the construct of a disembodied viewing subject. In this regard, the Renaissance perspective acts to situate the viewer as a "'pure,' 'disembodied intellect'" (Merleau-Ponty 2004, 70–73), although again, the idea that this could ever actually happen is a fiction based on the Cartesian idea of a mind/body dualism. As moving-image media began to reach the general public in a limited fashion around 1800, the exhibitions or screenings were designed to appeal to a different kind of disembodied viewer. For example, by presenting illusions as "Phantoms, or Apparitions of the Dead and Absent," Robertson's magic lantern shows exploited the sense of dread aroused by the lurking awareness that the self is a hollow fiction. This phantasmagoric relation to the visual image is an early instance of what Crary (1990), Martin Jay, and others have called the scopic regime of modernity. This mode of spectatorship hinges on a modern sense of longing that is rooted in the absence of the body and the insubstantial nature of the individual self. It situates the viewer not as a "disembodied intellect," but rather as a "disembodied ego or subject" (Burch, 22). This notion of a subject shaped by a scopic regime designed to give agency to individual desire is at the core of apparatus theory and psychoanalytic theories of cinema that proclaim, "The experience of the classic film interpellates us solely as *incorporeal individuals*" (Burch, 22).

As a fusion of these two aspects of the viewing experience, the assumed subject position of classical cinema is a throwback to the early nineteenth century. The shift in emphasis to the spectatorial experience offered by the magic lantern coincided with the Romantic movement in literature and art away from intellectual thought and toward lyrical language and the visual imaginary. The paintings of Caspar David Friedrich provide insight into how the establishment of this viewing position in narrative film rehearses a similar development in Romantic art. Friedrich's landscape paintings contain subjective elements in the scene that evoke an emotionally charged contemplation of nature. Conversely, the traditional presentation of the scene as a framed painting that cuts all closer peripheral elements out of the field of vision conforms to the Renaissance model that constructs the observer's point of view as if it were a window onto the world. In *Woman at a Window* Friedrich draws back from the standpoint of the classical observer and lets us see the scene being observed with the figure of the viewer included in it. Thus, the observer of the painting is drawn into the space of the painting as an invisible avatar who shares in the feelings of the painting's subject even while situated as the classical observer. In the course of the nineteenth century, the objective spectator in the classical paradigm continues to acquire subjective traits like those manifested in *Woman at a Window*. The biological becomes more intricately interlaced with the psychological, such that the viewer becomes an observer endowed with agency but also shaped by the alterity of that which is observed.

The depiction of the Romantic mode of spectatorship in Friedrich's painting also offers insight into the process of remediation occurring between writing and visual media at the time. The flourishing of the Romantic sensibility in the arts provided an advantage to literature over the major visual media. *Woman at a Window* captures the psychological complex that sustains the scopic regime of modernity (desire that is grounded in a lack or absence), but it requires a two-step reflective response on the part of the observer and provides only an inkling of the woman's state of mind.

FIGURE 4. Woman at a Window, *1822 oil painting by the German Romantic artist Caspar David Friedrich.*

By contrast, a literary text has the ability to examine the longing and desire of the individual subject through the lens of extended analytical insight into the psychological makeup of its characters. And it could do this in various different forms. With its reveling in a diverse set of literary genres—novels, lyrical and epic poetry, Gothic narratives, and Märchen, among others—Romantic literature seems to almost be flaunting its capacity to explore the inner world in ways that the visual arts could not. Novalis, perhaps the epitome of the Romantic author who reveled in the creative power of the written word, expressed this sense of the endless potential of writing in one of his most famous aphorisms: "Life should not be something that we accept as is, but rather a novel that we create ourselves" (Das Leben soll kein uns gegebener, sondern ein von uns gemachter *Roman* sein [563; translation is my own]).

With the development of more sophisticated moving-image technology throughout the nineteenth century, the visual arts would mount a challenge to writing. When film exhibition quickly became a viable cultural option to literature, the forces aligned with writing countered the threat to its hegemony in various ways, including through the remediation of literary structures and techniques in cinema. As I will examine more closely in the following sections, remediation in some ways effectively curbed cinema's potential to diminish the status of writing. At the same time, it provided the new moving-image medium with the tools that it used to establish its dominance in modernity. Friedrich Kittler draws on the gendered aspect of Romantic longing and the scopic regime of modernity to highlight how writing would have to relinquish at least some of its ground to the moving images of cinema. As opposed to a male figure that might suggest objective observation or deliberation, the choice of a female gaze for *Woman at a Window* stirs a subjective sense of longing. The gendered desire stirred by this scene had been essential to the success of prose entertainment literature that emerged in the late eighteenth century and flourished throughout the nineteenth century. Tracing the lineage of this literary tradition in Germany from Goethe to Thomas Mann, Kittler asserts that it met its Waterloo at the hands of visual technologies that could render mental processes and psychological states with more immediacy than the written word. Those young women who had sustained its success would turn to the more efficient technologies of modernity: "Entertainment writers in particular, who insist on playing Goethe even under advanced technological conditions, know fully well that Goethe's 'writing for girls' is no longer sufficient: the girls of the Magic Mountain have deserted to the village movie theater" (174). Inherent in this observation is the awareness that the moving image of cinema posed a threat not just to the mode of spectatorship that had become dominant since the Romantic period, but more crucially to the dominant cultural medium of writing.

Mechanized Culture and the Moving Image

Film's convergence with other media occurred in a modern environment where life was substantially faster and more rapidly changing than what most people had experienced during the nineteenth century. The mechanized society around 1900 challenged the sensory perception capabilities and sensibilities of a booming urban population. In the nineteenth century there were more opportunities to enjoy idyllic moments of restful retreat from the day's activities. With increasing industrialization and urbanization the senses were under more constant bombardment of forceful effects and images. In contrast to rural life, where "sensory mental imagery flows more slowly, more habitually, and more evenly," in the metropolis "the rapid crowding of changing images, the sharp discontinuity in the grasp of a single glance, and the unexpectedness of onrushing impressions" stimulate the nervous system more intensively and produce new modes of perception (Simmel, 175). The transition to an accelerated pace of living created two different needs that moving-image media could fulfill around 1900. On the one hand, moving images could offer urban residents simple, slow-paced narratives that would afford escape from a hectic, stressful lifestyle. In this case, the disembodied mode of spectatorship fostered by the scopic regime of modernity would serve the purpose well. On the other hand, visual media attuned to this new way of life could help the modern city-dweller adapt to it. The viewing experience could provide exposure to the faster pace of sensory information in a detached, protected setting and in a way that would help train the body's neural networks to process the increased load of stimuli.

Film provided a technological frame for engaging with the modern mechanized world in the second manner. The rapid and jumpy movements of early silent film corresponded to the way city inhabitants perceived the effect that the deluge of sensory information was having on the body. Modern forms of print media such as illustrated books and magazines and advertising materials contributed to the proliferation of visual images while also helping readers adjust to the constant encounter with them. The same is true of film, whose constant flow of moving images required more accommodation but also had a greater ability to promote the sensory and mental faculties needed to negotiate the metropolitan environment. Only when an aesthetic system had developed that was able to organize film images into an organic form of experience commensurate with modern life was cinema able to function as an "organ for perfecting the new reality" (Deleuze 1986b, 8). As better cameras and projectors were enabling more fluid movement of and in the image, parallel developments in aesthetics were producing a strong correlation between shot sequencing and the neurological processes that guide mental operations. Techniques such as close-ups, flashbacks, and crosscutting simulate how the mind directs attention, orders episodic events, and incorporates memory into perception. For the first time a medium was producing a real-time instantiation of how the mind processes sensory information. By structuring film images in accordance with these processes cinema could exercise these mental faculties and enhance the viewer's ability to process the more rapid flood of images encountered outside the movie theater (Münsterberg, 129).

In this regard film worked in conjunction with new means of transportation and communication that had expanded the scope of both one's real and mediated senses. The ability to capture images of distant locations and past events made film a cousin to modern technologies that had radically altered the natural limits and structures of time and space (Young, 9–10). It transported the viewing subject just as other technologies could transport the body (trains), voice (telephone), or thoughts (telegram). The travelogue lantern shows in the second half of the nineteenth century were forerunners of film in this respect but lacked the dynamic aspects that were more attuned to the increasingly mechanized mode of travel. The early film viewer experienced the stream of images on the screen like those of the countryside rapidly passing by as seen through the window of a train compartment. Film also produced some of the kinetic effects of speedy and noisy travel by train. The flicker of the film image recalled the way the telegraph poles running alongside the tracks divided the traveler's view into discrete segments, while the noise produced by the projector resembled the clickety-clack sound of the wheels on the track (Altman, 194–95). Early film producers exploited the similarity to train travel commercially. Hale's Tours, the most famous and successful of these ventures, placed viewers in a model railway car where the windows served as screens on which films that had been shot by cameras attached to a train were projected while the car was rocked to simulate the physical experience of movement (Musser 2004, 93–94; Young, 12–13).

As cinema established itself as an important art form that would reach large numbers of the population across all socioeconomic classes, cultural theorists began to assess how its direct embodied effect on the human sensorium could lead to far-reaching social and cultural change. Their ideas correspond to those espoused today by media critics who see a similar effect being exerted by digital technology. The Bauhaus artist and visionary László Moholy-Nagy saw film's ability to assimilate the populace to modern mechanized culture not merely as a potential effect of the new medium but as its essential purpose. He believed that the human sensory organs had not been able to keep up with the rapid developments in science and technology at the end of the nineteenth and beginning of the twentieth century: "With the exception of a few [sensory organs], their complex biological capacities became inert, their vision narrowed" (1947, 16). He declared that one of the most important tasks of the arts was to train and improve the sensorimotor systems on which the whole process of adaptation and progress hinged. It was not a matter of expanding and improving the function of any single organ or sensory function, rather the whole human biological organism—"the cells as well as the most complicated organs" (1922, 98)—needed to develop in coordination with changes to the social and material environment brought about by new technologies (Sahli, 21–23). As a Bauhaus principal who envisioned all forms of production contributing equally to the construction of a new society and culture as Gesamtkunstwerk, Moholy-Nagy delved into all areas of arts and design, but thought the new medium of film possessed a particularly potent capacity for adapting the sensory systems to the fast-paced demands of modernity.

Arguing in a similar vein, Walter Benjamin declared that the convergence of technologies around 1900 (film emulsion, sound recording, moving-image capture and projection) opened up the possibility of a new art for the masses with revolutionary potential. His aesthetic theory was grounded in the belief that human sense perception adapts to the technologically determined historical context it inhabits (1969b, 222). Changes made to the physical surroundings in the nineteenth century altered the mental faculties for perceiving and interacting with the world and were thus also responsible for the breakthroughs in media technology. New forms of media and communication such as photography and the telephone provided haptic and optic experiences that correspond to physical shocks and blows felt on urban streets by the modern city-dweller. Responding to "a new and urgent need for stimuli" (1969a, 175), the invention of film helped the individual and society collectively adjust to the radical changes in the cultural environment of modernity: "The film is the art form that is in keeping with the increased threat to his life which modern man has to face. Man's need to expose himself to shock effects is his adjustment to the dangers threatening him. The film corresponds to profound changes in the apperceptive apparatus—changes that are experienced on an individual scale by the man in the street in big-city traffic, on a historical scale by every present-day citizen" (1969b, 250n19). Echoing Moholy-Nagy's understanding of the role film can play with respect to the human body, Benjamin refers to it as a form of cultural adaptation: "Thus technology has subjected the human sensorium to a complex kind of training" (1969a, 175).[3] Expressed in terms of the coevolution of technology and the human, we might say that Benjamin believed that cinema offered the promise of reshaping and expanding the brain networks that produce the internal imaging of consciousness and thus also altering the processes that generate both our percepts and concepts ("apperceptive apparatus").

Hugo Münsterberg, a leading figure in experimental psychology at the time, wrote an important early treatise about how film simulates and enhances the mental operations that produce a stream of internal images in the mind. In *The Photoplay: A Psychological Study* (1916) he maintains that cinema mirrors how the brain processes perceptual and sensorimotor data to produce the mental representations that comprise consciousness (Antunes, 46–47). Explaining how certain cinematographic and editing techniques mirrored mental functions such as attention (the close-up), memory (flashback), or imagination (fantasy sequences), he proposed that film had the potential to sort, organize, and present images in a way that corresponds to these processes. Münsterberg thought that the training of these human mental functions occurs automatically, that is, without the need for conscious awareness. However, in contrast to Benjamin and Moholy-Nagy, he did not assert that they alter or augment the nonconscious processes that contribute to consciousness.

The optimism generated by the new moving-image medium's ability to engage the viewer at a physical level began to wane as the classical style of filmmaking took hold worldwide. In the 1930s both Moholy-Nagy and Benjamin believed that film had reached a stage where the financial interests of the industry had effectively negated the progressive power inherent in the medium. For Moholy-Nagy, this was due to the exclusion of experimental and independent filmmakers from mainstream filmmaking. In an open letter to the film industry published in *Sight and Sound* in 1934 he writes: "The unbiased observer cannot fail to see, to his great distress, that the film production of the world is growing more and more trivial every year" (56–57). Maintaining that the coevolution of the biological and technological is mediated through cultural practices, he declares that what characterizes humankind is that when confronted with new sensory impressions it seeks to create new forms of expression. Similarly, Benjamin portrays the plight of cinema as an inevitable fate of the revolutionary power of technologies in capitalist society. After an initial surge of innovation and creative development the forces of commodity production become the dominant influence to the detriment of the inherent progressive impulse of the new technology. Stasis sets in and blunts its revolutionary potential until the next wave of technology renders it largely obsolete. In "The Work of Art" Benjamin proclaims that new media that enable the work of art to be readily and repeatedly reproduced will destroy the concept of art as an autonomous work of creative genius. But the encouragement taken from this was tempered by his belief that commercial interests had already inserted their control between the medium of film and the public: "So long as the movie-makers' capital sets the fashion, as a rule no other revolutionary merit can be accredited to today's film than the promotion of a revolutionary criticism of traditional concepts of art" (1969b, 231). What he is lamenting here is not, as is often inferred, the decline of a cultural vehicle for conveying the message of social revolution, but rather the crippling of a technological medium with intrinsic progressive potential.

This pessimism expressed by Benjamin and Moholy-Nagy pertained to developments in film exhibition that were blunting the physical force of the image and reestablishing the mode of disembodied spectatorship that prevailed in the scopic regime prior to 1900. Cinematographic and narrative techniques that situated the viewer separate and apart from a self-contained virtual world arose in tandem with the establishment of exhibition settings that could assure sustainable profitability. Until 1905 films were mainly viewed either in "peep show" machines or in vaudeville theaters, often together with other live acts. The true commercial value of film became evident with the success of the first theaters dedicated specifically to film screenings. Nickelodeons were the main form of theater over the next ten years, until longer films became increasingly popular. During this period the burgeoning culture industry latched onto film as a means for tapping the commercial potential of the growing urban populace. Entrepreneurial producers, filmmakers, and distributors began to buy and consolidate the rights to films and to build more comfortable theaters that would justify higher ticket prices. As the trend toward integrated narrative altered the aesthetic form of films, the larger, more comfortable theaters provided the darkened, voyeuristic settings that enabled the viewers to enjoy the new feature films in anonymity. The lavish movie palaces built in the 1920s were "optical fairylands" (Kracauer 1987, 91–92) that fed cinema's meteoric rise as the medium par excellence for visual entertainment in the twentieth century. Situated facing a screen that served as a "virtual window," the body of the spectator in the darkened movie theater became cut off from the perceived external world (Friedberg 2006, 86–87). In contrast to the viewer of early cinema who was often directly shocked and physically stunned by events and attractions, classical cinema positions the spectator as an impenetrable body shielded from the experience-force of the objects, events, and characters of the diegetic film world.

The darkened theater along with the assumption of disembodied points of view within the narrative film space support this mode of spectatorship. By positing a clean separation of the observer and the object in this way, the narrative style of classical Hollywood cinema guards against the strong activation of sensorimotor responses in the viewer. This change in the viewing experience provided escape from an overload of sensory and kinetic stimuli in the modern cultural environment. Stress from life in an increasingly mechanized society took many different forms. For example, the loud noise created by trains in the nineteenth century made conversation difficult and often resulted in situations where passengers tried to avoid the gaze of those sitting across from them for the entire trip (Schivelbusch, 74–75). Journeys in horse-drawn coaches where the travelers sat facing each other were usually opportunities for interesting interaction among strangers. The high level of noise in train compartments created a new kind of social tension. Film viewing often simulated the visual and acoustic experience of train travel, while the voyeuristic setting of the darkened movie theater provided welcome relief from the awkward company of fellow travelers.

In conjunction with these shifts in the theatrical arrangement, the commercial industry developed a standard film form that served its economic, social, and institutional goals. Movies gradually became longer to meet the expectations of the viewer as customer. Essential to the success of these films and their producers was the ability to grab and hold the attention of the public throughout. At the same time, what consumers are willing to pay depends on how much they receive in return. Consequently, film companies tend to maximize their profits by making longer films, balanced off against how long a film can hold the audience's attention. Following the dictates of the profit motive, early film companies soon settled on approximately ninety minutes as the standard length for feature films. This length is a cultural adaptation that corresponds to the natural biological rhythm for activity in humans. It mirrors the average basic rest–activity cycle (BRAC). After ninety minutes of sustained action or concentration, attention begins to weaken and stray. This seems to be particularly true when the body is immobile and the mind remains active. At night, when the body-mind is in an automatic mode, the ninety-minute interval between REM sleep phases corresponds to BRAC (Kleitman). Because the darkened theater creates an environment where the viewer's mind can attend to the flow of film images much like it does to the internally generated images of dreams, one would expect BRAC to play a particularly strong role in film viewing. There is, however, one key difference between the two contexts. Because continuity editing eliminates the abrupt temporal or spatial transitions typical of dreams, this standard length serves to reinforce a disembodied mode of viewing. As movies increasingly conformed to this pattern, the more freely "sensational" mode of participation that was prevalent in early cinema waned, giving way to a more strictly optical experience of limited reach.

Nevertheless, the exploitation of cinema by the commercial film world did not extinguish the progressive impact of this modern moving-image medium. The flow of moving film images subjects the viewer to a dynamic space-time continuum that disrupts the illusion of a pre-given reality and enables a reframing of experience in unpredictable ways. Seen from this broad historical perspective, the film industry as well as the artistic activity of those involved in filmmaking are part of a singular coevolutionary process in which technological progress leads to more expansive and more plastic modes of consciousness. Technologies that are able to manifest our systems of mental processing in visual media enable us to creatively expand and refine our conceptual grasp of the effects of our actions in the world. In this big-picture view of the evolution of cinema, the commercial industry was instrumental in shaping the film image into an organic regime of sensorimotor representations, or what Deleuze calls the *movement-image*. This was the initial realization of the progressive potential inherent in the moving-image medium of film. On the one hand, it made the image more susceptible to exploitation by those who would use it to establish advantage and influence. On the other, the development of the cinematic image as a stable object (what some dismiss as a "phatic image") made it a more productive resource that expanded the extended mind's capacity for second-order theoretical processing.

As apparatus theory became the dominant influence in the 1970s, cinema scholars tended to emphasize how classical aesthetics concealed the constructed nature of the image and enveloped the viewer in a seamless film world. This produced a powerful ideological critique of the forces aligned around the film industry, but it also diverted attention almost completely away from the embodied aspects of spectatorship. Cognitivist film theory mounted a concerted opposition to the influence of psychoanalysis and apparatus theory in the 1980s, but it too ignores the medium's physical effect on the viewer. Adhering to the classic cognitivist view of the mind, it maintains that the essential structures of cognitive processing evolved through adaptation and natural selection and have remained fundamentally unchanged for many millennia (Bordwell 1989, 16). At the same time, other perspectives began to surface that resonate with Benjamin and Moholy-Nagy's ideas about film's effects on the nonconscious processes involved in the viewing experience. In his two books on cinema published in the 1980s, Deleuze stipulates that the spectator's participation in the movement of the film occurs at the neural level in the form of superceptual, physical responses to the image: "Cinema as industrial art achieves self-movement, automatic movement, it makes movement the immediate given of the image. This kind of movement no longer depends on a moving body or an object which realizes it, nor on a spirit which reconstitutes it. It is the image which itself moves in itself" (1989, 156).[4] According to this understanding of the cinematic image, engagement with the real hinges not on how the viewer reads the film as a representation of an external reality, but rather on how the viewer is moved by the film—not in the secondary sense of being emotionally moved or intellectually challenged but rather in the immediate physical sense of moving with the film images. This emphasis on movement supports Benjamin's claim that film has the potential to change the spectator in a direct physical manner. In a formulation reminiscent of Benjamin's seminal article "The Work of Art in the Age of Mechanical Reproduction," Deleuze describes the effect produced by the movement-image once it had established this connection at the sensorimotor level: "It is only when movement becomes automatic that the artistic essence of the image is realized: producing *a shock to thought, communicating vibrations to the cortex, touching the nervous and cerebral system directly*" (1989, 156).

More recently, Tom Gunning has put forward a similar argument, claiming that the ontology of the cinematic image resides in the viewer's participation in the movement of the film rather than in the indexicality of the photographic image. As he puts it, "to perceive motion, rather than represent it statically in a manner that destroys its essence, one must participate in the motion itself" (2007, 42). Gunning argues that the novelty of cinema resides not in its ability to present a compelling *illusion of reality*, but rather that the movement enables film to produce a strong *impression of reality* (2007, 40–44). Illusion of reality is linked to the past and anchored in an indexical relationship between what is presented on screen and real events that have already happened (or will happen in a future era, as in the case of science fiction). Impression of reality situates the viewer in the present, and in doing so links what appears on screen with the immediate future. The impression of reality activates sensorimotor systems and engenders "perceptual and affective *participation*" (Gunning 2007, 40) in and of itself, independent of any actual event that may be referenced indexically. This participation in the movement of the film happens in the form of subconceptual, physical responses to the cinematic image that frame the conscious cognitive reception in such a manner that one could contend: "The only truth of cinema is its movement, its ephemeral occupation of the present" (Cubitt 2004, 22). Gunning's account of how early moviegoers reacted to *Arrival of a Train at La Ciotat* and similar films supports the importance he attributes to movement. As he and others have asserted, the unconfirmed reports of frightened spectators diving behind their seats as the camera captured the train approaching them head on were most likely apocryphal.[5] Regardless of what their reactions actually were, Gunning challenges the notion that they were stimulated by an actual fear that the train might burst out of the screen and crash into the audience (1989, 35). He ascribes the spectators' astonishment at the first encounter with film not to the belief that the images provided a direct look at reality or even a representation of reality. Instead, they were astonished and thrilled by cinema's ability to produce such a powerful impression of reality, one that evoked a more powerful embodied effect on viewers than previous media.[6]

My analysis also identifies movement in and of the image as a key element determining the part cinema has played in the coevolutionary advance of the human and technology. In the remainder of this chapter I undergird this claim by situating cinema within the larger evolution of media and examining how the complex remediation between film and other major media has shaped the human as a biotechnical system. A prominent early critic who proclaimed cinema's potential as a progressive cultural force assessed its impact on the dominant medium of the day in much the same manner as I do in this study. In a 1924 essay the German writer Hugo von Hofmannsthal extols the power of film to break the chains that language and the written word have imposed on humankind. In doing so, he rejects the position of those who dismiss the value of cinema on the basis of an ideological critique. He writes that, in contrast to his view, there is another assessment of cinema that "sees nothing in all of it except a wretched confusion of industrial greediness, the omnipotence of technology, the abasement of things intellectual, and dull curiosity side-tracked in any direction" (56). In response, he asserts that this new medium that has the masses flocking into a "jam-packed, half-dark room with the pictures flickering by" has the ability to help restore what culture had diminished through the dominance of language.

Hofmannsthal reveals here a sense of a larger trajectory in the history of media that would not be formulated more fully until the second half of the twentieth century. In the following section I engage the work of media theorists from later in the twentieth century who explore the adverse effects that writing has had on human experience in more depth. At the end of the nineteenth century, technological innovation in the area of travel and communication (telegraph, telephone, railways) had already dispensed with traditional assumptions about the limits of the human body to move and communicate across space and time. This brought the hegemony of language into question. As a machinic medium closely tied to the technologies of its day, film demonstrated how the cognitive and physical responses evoked by its visual image were inseparable. This presented a further challenge to the traditional notion that language comprised an immanent and potentially universal instrument of human communication. From the present perspective of the digital age, we might say that Hofmannsthal anticipated the idea that the evolution of media over the last few centuries has followed an arc away from a human-centric form of communication based on language to a machine-centric one based on code (Hayles 2012, 113–25). In any event, the advent of film provoked an elemental clash with the most important medium for the development of human civilization over the last three millennia—alphabetic writing.

Remediation: The Convergence of Film and Writing

Whenever new forms of media appear that threaten to diminish the control the written word exerts throughout all areas of culture, a certain amount of opposition will inevitably arise. This is happening today in response to the explosive surge of new media. As the internet and mobile digital media consume a growing proportion of our attention and focus, scholars and critics warn of the detrimental effects this will have, particularly on the younger generation. At the core of the debate is the big reduction in time spent reading. Academics in the fields of education, psychology, sociology, and communication are studying how the extensive time spent on the internet and social media rather than with books is affecting critical thinking. Similar alarms were sounded when film became a popular cultural attraction. The invention of sophisticated techniques for capturing and projecting moving images in a way that engages and captivates our minds diverted significant mental resources away from the written word. Social commentators and arbiters of culture warned that the popular new form of entertainment could undermine the moral and intellectual fiber of modern society. Governments and cultural institutions took active measures to prevent film's harmful influence. However, the most productive means by which writing was able to withstand film's challenge to its status as the dominant medium were not prescriptive actions. Rather, the remediation of established literary and narrative techniques into movies served to shape cinema into a medium that supported the hegemony of the written word more effectively than any laws, regulations, or edicts.

From the broad perspective of the role media have played in human evolution, concern about the erosion of writing's place in our culture is warranted. The momentous increase in cognitive powers enabled by alphabetic writing has been the primary agent in the advance of human civilization. The offloading of linguistic thought processes into an external repository has expanded our intellectual powers at various levels of computation and analysis. Our working memory is able to entertain only a limited number of thoughts in the content workspace dedicated to online language processing (the *phonological loop*; see chapter 1). By grasping and committing these ideas to paper, we are able to refer back to them and to combine them with new thoughts as they are generated and made operational in working memory. Putting thoughts to paper, and now into digital files, has played an essential role at every stage of work on this book and every other text that requires complex analysis. The piece of writing that results then becomes available for reflective consideration and deliberation in second-order cognitive processes that can assess its merit and benefit in relation to associated texts (Clark 2003, 73–83). Over time the collection, archiving, and dissemination of written texts within and across different cultures has led to the highest levels of systematic and theoretical thinking that have produced modern technological societies. From this historical point of view, the anxiety about digital media and others before it that have reduced the investment of time and energy in the written word is understandable. One consequence of the shift away from narratively acquired and archived knowledge (written texts) toward database storage (computer and the internet) seems to be a less rigorous engagement with the network of second-order cognitive assessment of literature in any given field and thus an erosion of systematic, theoretical thinking.

At the same time, new media appear and operate as part of an overarching coevolution of the human and technology that advances with an irresistible force. As humankind develops new technologies it is perpetually driven to embrace and modify them, evolving along with them to more complex forms of existence. Thus, despite strong reservations about the effect digital media are having on the present generation, there is a concerted push to promote *media literacy* among all segments of society, including both the older generation that is less adept with the new technology and the youth who are thought to be spending too much time with it. As the term suggests, this campaign is also a means of restoring some of the dominance that print literature and the written word have yielded to digital media. Here is how the Media Literacy Project, one of the leading private organizations to partner with various state governments in the United States to promote media literacy in schools, defines its goals: "Media literacy is the ability to access, analyze, evaluate, and create media. Media literate youth and adults are better able to understand the complex messages we receive from television, radio, Internet, newspapers, magazines, books, billboards, video games, music, and all other forms of media" (Media Literacy Project). In other words, society's reaction to the fast expansion of new media is to harness their effects by subjecting them to the same kind of control mechanism provided by writing. The idea is to apply to all forms of media the sort of second-order cognitive assessment that was enabled by putting thoughts down on paper.

In the first three decades of the twentieth century there was an analogous reaction to film, one that warned about its deleterious influence while also working within the new medium to reestablish the dominance of print literature. In the course of the nineteenth century the written word, both as social or political commentary and literary fiction, had become a powerful tool for democratic reform across all social milieu. The progression of moving-image media that led up to the invention of film was itself due in large part to the democratizing influence of literature. At the same time, once the technology became efficient enough to attract a mass public, the existence of a broad literate public provided an effective base for writing's response to the challenge it faced.

The resistance to film's power to attract a broad audience and alter its relation to literary culture exerted itself in various ways. One area that has received considerable attention in film scholarship is the public discourse about the detrimental social and cultural effects of the new medium. In the initial response, up until the point where film exhibition had developed the basic structures and practices that stabilized its commercial viability, writers, journalists, and critics generally dismissed film as a cheap mode of entertainment that offered the urban masses escape from their mundane existence. Once the transition to dedicated movie theaters had occurred in the years 1905–1907 (Ben Singer), a public outcry about its potential negative influence on the urban masses arose in the United States. The fear of its effects on the moral fiber of society dovetailed with concerns about transformations caused by industrialization, organized labor, and the influx of immigrant families. An underlying anxiety about film's power to eliminate the hegemony of the written word played into this complex of concerns in a less visible manner. Analyzing the threat that electric media posed to the traditional culture based on writing later in the twentieth century, McLuhan describes the strong affective response it generated: "Our Western values, built on the written word, have already been considerably affected by the electric media of telephone, radio, and TV. Perhaps that is the reason why many highly literate people in our time find it difficult to examine this question without getting into a moral panic" (1994, 82). Certainly, the reaction to film's ascendance was fraught with a similar angst.

Responding to its own self-perceived crisis of legitimacy, the young film industry took various measures to fend off potential negative consequences for its financial interests. It established a national organization for licensing motion-picture companies and collaborated with censorship boards to avoid more restrictive intervention (Grieveson and Krämer, 135–39). Feeling the pressure of the regulatory commissions, filmmakers also began to forge narratives that framed potentially objectionable material into morally edifying contexts (Gunning 2004). This was the continuation of a comparable strategy employed in the years when the industry was first trying to find footing as a commercial enterprise (1900–1908). In response to early rumblings about the new entertainment's deleterious effects, short fiction films addressed the looming problem through metacritical allegorical scenarios. Some depict filmmakers and photographers obsessively and unwisely shooting events either to their own detriment or to that of others involved in the scene (Young, 28–32). In other films, voyeurs or photographers who direct their cameras at illicit or private scenes serve allegorically as an admonition to filmmakers that they should avoid the temptation of attracting audiences with scintillating, morally questionable content (McMahan). Not only did these films perform a self-intervention into dubious practices that could hinder the growth of this new entertainment branch, but they also enabled producers to influence the viewing practices of an unversed public.

The charge that film was having a negative effect on morals went hand in hand with the allegation that the medium was only suitable for undemanding, sensational fiction. In Europe, where literature's prominence as a key part of high culture was more widely revered, cinema had a harder time establishing its artistic validity. In Germany, for example, the first concerted opposition to film came with the establishment of dedicated film theaters in 1905–1906. The initial criticism came from the German Association of Teachers and charged that many students were spending too much time at these new theaters watching films whose content was like that of trashy dime novels. The newly formed league of theater owners responded by staging demonstrations where they refuted these claims and by issuing guidelines to its members on how to shield themselves from these attacks. It advised owners to keep their premises free of any suspect characters that might want to prey on young moviegoers. It also issued public statements declaring that film offered a new educational opportunity, particularly with respect to the dissemination of knowledge about science and the arts (Diederichs, 24–26). In the period following this first salvo directed at film (1909–1920), the German movie industry overcame the stigma of being considered an unsophisticated form of entertainment for the uneducated masses by adapting known figures, motifs, and works from the literary canon to gain legitimacy. Many of the new viewers it won by doing so came from the educated upper-middle class. Only after it had established cultural credibility in this fashion was cinema able to distinguish itself as a medium with its own unique aesthetic elements in the following decade (Kaes, 1–3). In both the United States and Europe filmmakers turned to high culture and literature in particular to counter the charge that the new medium was detracting from the reading of more demanding texts and thus diminishing the stature of knowledge and critical thinking. Here too, the written word was reasserting its hegemony by making the legitimacy of film dependent on critical literature that assesses its aesthetic, social, and moral value.

The most critical factor in the remediation process was not the incorporation and repurposing of content from literature, but rather the appropriation of formal techniques and structural features. In search of a viable film form, filmmakers turned to the proven practices of existing media, first to those employed in theater and then increasingly to literary fiction. In documenting the shift from monstration in early film to cinematic narrative, André Gaudreault argues that the new cultural institution discarded its reliance on techniques it had adopted from theater in favor of "textual literariness" (159). Rejecting the traditional distinction between narrativity and theatricality established by Jean Mitry, he asserts that in their convergence with film both theater and literary fiction contributed to the formation of the cinema of narrative integration. Still, for Gaudreault, literature became the dominant intermedial force when filmmakers embraced "cinema's language-like ability to produce different *énoncés* at a higher level of abstraction than the mere monstration" (161). As the term "literariness" indicates, the mode of enunciation adopted as cinema became established as a major cultural institution was not the spoken word, but rather the written text. As the ability to attract audiences with displays of film's novel technological features waned, producers and exhibitors turned to narratives that depended on psychological character development, intriguing plot lines, and dramatic action. In the process of their remediation into film the aesthetic strategies of literary fiction were adapted to the new medium. Certain style elements of nineteenth-century prose proved particularly compatible, and their remediation into works for the big screen was instrumental in shaping the standard narrative feature film. In particular the advent of descriptive prose that enabled the reader to conjure up in the imagination a more detailed diegetic world was adaptable to film. Description of what one would see, hear, touch, smell, or taste in a fictional setting provided a sensory dimension to literary texts that had previously relied more heavily on story to sustain the reader's absorption in the text.

The development of literary mise-en-scènes in the nineteenth century constituted a relative shift in emphasis from the temporal dimension of narrative to a spatial orientation that corresponds to film's enhanced ability to create a diegetic effect based on sensory data. The steady stream of projected images could produce a coherent diegetic space independent of either an overarching narrative or the aggregate space generated to accommodate the narrative. However, as aesthetic strategies for structuring film space evolved, the remediation of literary elements curbed the potential for sensory engagement by the spectator. Editing techniques were developed that privileged spatial unity over strict temporal continuity and produced a film syntax that relied on the virtual mobility of the camera-eye to piece together a unified diegetic space within which the film scene unfolds (Gunning 1991, 290–91). At the level of the film as a whole, there was a composite space of diegesis that encompasses all the places and events included in the story, whether they appear on screen or not. This virtual film world conforms to our conception of global space as an aggregate of separate locations where significant instances of production, consumption, convergence, or contestation are occurring. In this way, film combined the diegetic techniques of its literary predecessor with the medium-specific attributes of the photographic image to create a continuous and seamless world onscreen. In conjunction with this spatial construct, the movement in and of the film image empowers "unfamiliar explorations of flexible coordinates of space and time" (Gunning 2007, 40). But this in itself does not necessarily promote either embodied spectatorship or adaptation to changing environments. It can also serve diegetic absorption in story and plot, and this became the main emphasis along the path to classical cinema. As a result, the assimilation of narrative techniques from nineteenth-century literary prose assured that film viewing remained more closely aligned with the slower process of visualization that occurs during reading.

As the cinema of narrative integration became the standard film form, the autonomous force of the moving image gave way to a more abstract spatial orientation. The style of dominant cinema that emerged was designed in part to stifle film's ability to stir affective participation in the moving image and to situate the viewer as a passive spectator who takes in the film with detached, disembodied vision. This development occurred as part of a larger complex of mediation that has determined how film and subsequent innovations in moving-image technology have been integrated into and altered the visual arts and entertainment culture throughout the twentieth century. The role played by alphabetic writing and literary culture in this process cannot be divorced from a variety of other material forces. This includes factors such as production companies and the institutional structures that govern filmmaking, movie theaters and other exhibition sites, the aesthetic paradigms for products such as a feature film, and the technological innovations that change the material conditions of the medium over time. At times, these various elements work in unison to promote a certain mode of spectatorship. At other times, they may operate at cross-purposes, particularly when new technologies disrupt the status quo and enable new patterns of mediation to form. In the first two decades of the century, when the consolidation of a commercial film industry was the dominant factor, they were strongly aligned in shaping a film experience that engaged the senses in much the same way as writing. Film viewing became a largely disembodied act of vision that worked in isolation from the other senses and minimalized the reorganization of the human sensorium enabled by the new moving-image technology.

Even as the film industry was working toward a standard form that could sustain the interest of the viewing public and creating the appropriate exhibition setting for it, filmmakers were training viewers how to position themselves with respect to the narrative feature film. The basic orientation of the spectator to the image was the same as that of the observer of Renaissance perspective painting. The viewer is immobilized and the gaze is directed onto the framed image as if looking through an open window. In the continuity system of classical Hollywood cinema, space and narration function to maintain a consistent viewing perspective "outward from the spectator's eye" (Thompson, 215) in every shot and collectively for the film world as a whole (Bordwell 1985, 55–56). However, the perspective within the diegetic space of a film scene shifts constantly across cuts such that the unified vision of the film as a whole must be sutured together from different points of view. When the emphasis shifted from temporal to spatial continuity starting around 1906, the viewer needed to be drawn into the spatial construct of the film world (Gunning 1990, 91–93). As the cinema of narrative integration was taking shape, characters in hidden viewing positions within a scene would mark the internal perspectives the spectator was to inhabit. By identifying with the point of view of characters who were seen secretly watching or recording a scene in the movie (a voyeur, photographer, or spying lover), the movie-goer was first drawn closer to the edges of the onscreen space and then eventually into the narrative space of the film itself (McMahan). As these embedded subjective points of view gave way to the invisible eye of the camera, the viewing subject would assume the constantly changing point of view and become the locus of a unified viewing perspective. This development in early cinema parallels the transition in the Romantic period from the classical Renaissance view onto the external world to one endowed with a more subjective orientation. The embedded observers in the early transitional films influenced cinematic spectatorship in much the same way that the woman standing at the window in Friedrich's seminal work had shaped the viewing experience for painting. They keep the disembodied perspective of a disengaged observer intact, while also promoting subjective involvement in the film world. As the cinema of narrative integration matured, this effect was reinforced by stronger character development. Moreover, when the camera became attached to a protagonist, identification with the character enabled the spectator to better negotiate the many shifts in location and perspective across cuts and provided spatial orientation for the audience and coherence to the film.

At the same time as the remediation of literary elements into film was dampening the affective force of the film image, a virulent criticism was emerging, particularly in Europe, of what some intellectuals deemed the tyranny inflicted on humankind by the all-powerful medium of writing. Drawing on Rousseau and other Romantic writers, its proponents charged that the establishment of a modern society grounded in the accumulation of knowledge and intellectual thought had eroded human emotional life and powers of imagination. Harboring reservations that ran deeper than those expressed by Romantics a century earlier, they articulated a deep-seated skepticism of both the written and spoken word that in the German context became known as the *Sprachkrise*. Hofmannsthal, whose fictional prose work "The Letter of Lord Chandos" (1902) gave rise to this term, wrote that the "language of the educated and semi-educated, whether written or spoken," loosens perhaps "the shackles that they [the inhabitants of the modern city] feel wrapped around their hands . . . for the moment—in pretense—in order then to perhaps draw them together even more tightly" (2004, 54). Marxist writer and film critic Béla Balázs expressed similar concerns about the oppressive power exerted by language: "The word seems to have taken men by brute force; over-rigid concepts have obliterated much, created an absence which we now feel keenly, and which music alone does not suffice to fill. The culture of words is dematerialized, abstract and over-intellectualized; it degrades the human body" (11).

In the second half of the century media theorists and culture critics offered a more differentiated analysis of the detrimental effects of language, focusing in particular on alphabetic writing. In *Gesture and Speech* André Leroi-Gourhan presents an anthropological theory of how the communication of human thought in external media evolved from Paleolithic cave painting to written language. Focusing on the role that visual media have played in human evolution, he assigns a generative function to pictorial representation and maintains that it complements symbolic thinking in important ways. Paleolithic cave paintings, he argues, present a "symbolic assemblage of figures" (196) whose form of expression differs fundamentally from our conceptual scheme that is shaped and dominated by written language. He asserts that these paintings manifest a figurative attitude that modern humans, who have been conditioned by four thousand years of linear writing, can only recapture through concerted efforts of abstract reasoning (192). To explain the chasm that separates us from our Paleolithic ancestors, Leroi-Gourhan offers a detailed account of the process that leads from the multidimensional assemblage of graphic symbols to alphabetized writing. Tracing the use of pictograms as graphic symbols for bookkeeping in early agricultural societies and then as symbols in the ideographic alphabets of Egypt and China, he establishes how *linearization* was the key to the development of alphabetic writing. He describes how writing, in the process of its gradual evolution, tended toward stricter linearization and the constriction of pictorial elements. This development was driven in large part by the need for greater utilitarian efficiency in the use of symbols to record and communicate the affairs and business of increasingly technological societies. Efficiency is gained by the reduction in the gaps between the linearly aligned symbols: "Material civilization rests upon symbols in which the gap between the sequence of emitted concepts and their reproduction has become ever more narrow" (213). The functional efficiency dictating these changes to alphabetic writing mirrors the advances in socioeconomic organization that were driving the expansion of the new agri-cultures. Put differently, in the development of alphabetic writing the emerging agricultural societies were adhering to the same economization of resources that was responsible for their affluence.

Along with the advance in efficiency, and this is the key point for Leroi-Gourhan's account of what was lost with the ascendance of writing, the figurative force of the graphic image declines proportionately with the diminishing of the gaps. In a reversal of the accepted view of the origins of writing, he asserts that this loss was not a result of a paradigmatic shift from oral to written language. Rather, taking a radically different view (one that influenced Jacques Derrida's view of the structural relation between oral and written language in *Of Grammatology*), he argues that linearization represented a return from the more freely organized spatial and temporal settings of what he terms *picto-graphy* to a form of writing that conforms to the temporality of speech: "Written language, phoneticized and linear in space, becomes completely subordinated to spoken language, which is phonetic and linear in time. The dualism between graphic and verbal disappears, and the whole of human linguistic apparatus becomes a single instrument for expressing and preserving thought—which is channeled increasingly toward reasoning" (210). In his critique of language Hofmannsthal had expressed a similar idea in a more figurative manner: "[Language] ruffles the surface, but it does not awaken what slumbers in the depths. There is too much algebra in this language; another numeral covers every letter, the numeral is an abbreviation of reality" (54). The vital question here is what was sacrificed in terms of our ability to entertain and manipulate visual images. Leroi-Gourhan's answer to this question provides a theoretical base for the defense of silent film offered by the *Sprachkrise* critics:

> Writing is unquestionably a most efficient adaptation of audiovisual behavior, which is our fundamental mode of perception, yet it is also a very roundabout way of achieving the desired effect. The situation now apparently becoming generalized may therefore be said to represent an improvement in that it eliminates the effort of "imagining" (in the etymological sense). But imagination is the fundamental property of intelligence, and a society with a weakened property of symbol making would suffer a concomitant loss of the property of action. In the modern world the result is a certain imbalance . . . the phenomenon of loss of the exercise of the imagination in vital operating sequences. (213–14)

For Leroi-Gourhan, the development of writing subordinates "the whole of human linguistic apparatus" (210) to a technical utilitarianism that serves the preservation and dissemination of thought, but at the cost of a weakened ability to arrest, entertain, and manipulate vibrant new mental images.[7] However, the mode of internal image generation that produced the earliest cave paintings has persisted during the long evolution of *Homo sapiens* and continues to underlie a significant part of human behavior (Leroi-Gourhan, 196).

McLuhan evaluated the influence of alphabetic writing in a similar fashion, up to a point. He sees the invention of the phonetic alphabet as the first of three major technological innovations—the printing press and the telegraph being the other two—that have shaped the cultural evolution of humankind most dramatically.

He, like Leroi-Gourhan, emphasizes the shift from pictographic to symbolic writing as a crucial step, but assesses its effect mainly in terms of a reorganization of the senses in a given culture. According to his general theory of media convergence, when a powerful new medium challenges the dominance of the currently prevailing ones, the bodily senses get drawn into the fray and the result is a re-alignment that correlates to the shift in the media landscape. In the case of writing, he argues that the phonetic alphabet divorces the semantic properties of language from both the visual signs of writing and the sounds of the spoken language. As a result, a detached, disembodied mode of vision gained dominance over the other senses. As vision became increasingly extended into this powerful new medium, hearing, touch, taste, and smell remain more closely linked to each other, united in a more general, primary mode of sensation that in his later work Maurice Merleau-Ponty calls *primordial tactility* (2004). The result was an imbalance among the senses that is reflected culturally in the idea that touch, taste, and smell are lower, more carnal senses that have not been subjected to the same degree of sublimation as sight, and to a lesser degree also sound. Similar to Merleau-Ponty, McLuhan defines tactility as the "interplay of the senses" and sees a shift away from the vision-dominated influence of writing as the way to restore "a unified ratio among the senses" ([1964] 1994, 60).[8] On the threshold to a new age of computers, he saw the rise of digital technology as the path back from the dominance of writing, which he declares "was long held to be the mark of our *ratio*nality" ([1964] 1994, 60).

For both McLuhan and Leroi-Gourhan, the invention of alphabetic writing was the pivotal event in the long cultural evolution that established disembodied vision as a key component of human culture. However, the written word no longer provided a sufficient frame for harnessing lived experience in modern technological society. Hofmannsthal and Balázs both saw the surge in performance arts that did not entail language, such as dance and pantomime, as a reaction to the oppression that people felt from the overwhelming profusion of words, concepts, and knowledge. For both, silent film attended to the "painful yearning to be human beings with our entire bodies, from top to toe and not merely in our speech" (Balázs, 11). Situating the human ability to produce symbols in precognitive processes, Balázs calls for a return to nonlinguistic modes of visual imaging: "We evidently have many things to say that cannot be expressed in words. Now that the secondary and derivative modes of our culture appear to have ended up in blind alleys of different sorts, we are reverting to primordial forms of expression" (11). Hofmannsthal surmises that although our society proclaims that "knowledge is power," for the modern masses "the cinema calls more strongly: it calls with images," because they "fear language; they fear in language the tool of society" (54). Hofmannsthal attributes to "the pictures flickering by" in the movie theater a similar power: "the symbol arises from the being's depth like lightning: the physical image for intellectual truth that is unattainable by reason" (56).

The emergence of film as a powerful new visual medium was part of a larger shift in the relative influence of existing media and corresponding changes in the human sensorium. To attribute film's influence more strictly to the distinction between the visual and the verbal would fail to give full due to the role played by mechanization and automation. It would not explain, for example, why film challenged the hegemony of writing, which according to McLuhan had established vision as the predominant sense in human culture. In the case of both alphabetic writing and visual media, mechanical means of reproduction were the essential element that altered the process of production and reading/ spectatorship and caused a substantial reorganization of the senses. For example, Kittler asserts that the invention of the typewriter at the end of the nineteenth century eliminated the need for a guiding eye to be trained on the line of written text to control every move of the hand as it moves the pen. Liquidating "the media-technological basis of classical authorship" (203), this new writing machine dismantled as well, according to Kittler, a whole range of classical humanist assumptions linked to authorial subjectivity. Similarly, film dispensed with vision's role in directing the hand of the classical pictorial artist, the painter. In doing so, however, it undercut vision not only by automating the production process, but more importantly by simulating the entire mental apparatus that produces visual consciousness. Thus, the projected film image shocked and fascinated early spectators primarily not because of its ability to capture and present reality, as is often claimed, but because of the power of its moving images to activate sensorimotor and affective systems that had long lain relatively untouched by both external images and the physical act of writing/reading.

Media technologies make us more efficient by pushing body technics to new frontiers, but they can also stall and support habituated modes of experiencing the world. Aesthetic strategies harking back to the Romantic period and beyond were crucial in determining to what extent the viewer would be able to establish a more expansive physical engagement with the cinematic image. In terms of McLuhan's account of the interplay between media and the senses, the remediation of literary elements into cinema was a reaction to the reorganization of the sensorium caused by film. At stake was whether film would be allowed to develop its potential to expand the human sensorium or succumb to cultural practices that reinforced existing patterns of perception and sensorimotor reaction. This disruption of the existing allocation of energies across various media networks stirred resistance and reaction in the sensory processing networks of the individual organism and reverberated all the way up to the most eminent cultural pursuits. The tension between moving visual images and alphabetic writing played itself out at basic levels of mental processing in ways that then manifested themselves in the cultural wars fought over film and literature. In the first two decades of the century the film industry called on literary forms and techniques to create a standard film form that was familiar to the movie-goer and could be more readily consumed within her existing comfort zone. In effect, literature inserted its form of interface between the spectator and film, adapting the new medium to cultural and social practices that corresponded to the traditional technologies of writing. The style of cinema that emerged was designed to make film more accessible and profitable, but it also served to constrain its power to activate and change the viewer. What was diminished was the moving image's ability to form a progressive alliance with other visual and communication technologies as they worked to reenergize the original tactility of the body, its ability to engage the world with all of its senses at once (McLuhan and Powers, 95). These forces of mediation diminished the affective and participatory power of film, but they could only partially sublimate it, not eliminate it. The developments in moving-image technology that began with film have continued to have an effect on the human sensorium that could only be partly contained.

Film and the Tyranny of Writing: Franz Kafka

Until now, my discussion of the remediation process involving film and literature has concentrated on how the latter exerted influence over the new medium. Remediation also works in the reverse direction. As the medium of writing and literature in particular shaped film in ways that mitigated its challenge to their dominant position in society, cinema had a reciprocal effect on a broad array of established practices involving the written word. Given writing's ubiquitous and indispensable role in almost all spheres of modern society, the changes introduced by the new moving-image technology were diluted and for the most part not readily detectable. Even in the case of creative writing, where intersection of the two media was the strongest, the impact of film seems marginal. However, it created disruptions in the literary culture of modernity beyond just the assimilation of film aesthetics or style into literary fiction.

To explore what the effects of film on literary culture might reveal about its larger role in the coevolution of the human and technology/media, I turn to Franz Kafka, whose literary career began just as cinema was developing its standard narrative form and ran parallel to the evolution of classical cinema (1906–1924). Several aspects of his personal and professional life make him a prime candidate for this analysis. He considered himself an intensely visual person and believed that his keen observation of everyday activities and social interactions among his fellow human beings informed his work as a writer. It is then not surprising that he was attracted to the cinema, which became popular in Prague during his formative years as a creative writer. As he began to visit the movies with increasing frequency, cinema did not however become a source of inspiration for his literary work. Rather, he saw the simulated visual consciousness projected onto the film screen as an alternative mode of seeing that threatened his own creative vision. This precipitated a writer's crisis that caused him to stop going to the cinema and reverberated in his writing throughout the rest of his life.

The first part of this section chronicles Kafka's firsthand experience with film and examines what part it played in his literary crisis, particularly in its most intense period in the years 1912–1914. My analysis traces correspondences between cinematographic techniques and Kafka's style of descriptive prose that lead up to two indirectly autobiographical stories in the year 1914. In a key passage at the end of each text, Kafka employs a decidedly camera-eye perspective to "write himself free" from the personal and professional crisis that had beset him. These prose works, and the two final scenes in particular, also serve as a cathartic purging of cinema's influence over his literary vision. However, the clash between film and writing that Kafka experienced in his life as a literary author continued to manifest itself in his writing in a different fashion after 1914. The second part of this section considers how the encounter with cinema contributed to Kafka's broader exploration of the effects writing exerts over the individual and society at large. In his later writings, and in particular in his two major unfinished novels, he grapples with the effects of the other kind of professional writing he produced as a bureaucratic official in the Workmen's Accident Insurance Institute for the Czech Lands. Although these works contain few passages that describe the action through a cinematographic lens, those that do suggest how the medium of film threatened to expose and undermine the repressive reach of writing in modern bureaucratic society. Kafka's work both manifests the complex process of remediation between film and literature and illuminates one dimension of the emancipatory potential that the new moving-image medium possessed.

Writerly Vision and the Camera-Eye

We know from letters and diary entries as well as the biography written by his friend and confidant Max Brod that Kafka was attracted to and fascinated by film. Starting most likely in 1907 when the first two large movie theaters opened in Prague, he made occasional and at times even frequent visits to the movies. We also know that these ended almost altogether in 1913 when his work as writer assumed an existential urgency and began to take precedence over other interests and pursuits. In the transition years of 1912–1913 he was first drawn more closely to cinema and then disengaged from it with a certain degree of agitation. Given the close, complex relation Kafka had to film, it is not surprising that his literary texts exhibit a diverse set of style elements and aesthetic techniques associated with it. And yet, even though Kafka is one of the most prolifically studied modern authors, the influence film had on his writing and his identity as writer remained largely unexplored until Hanns Zischler's 1996 book *Kafka geht ins Kino* (*Kafka Goes to the Movies*, 2003) triggered a flurry of critical work on the topic that still continues today.[9] In the wake of Zischler's work subsequent studies have focused mainly on the affinity between Kafka's "visual method" of writing and cinematic forms of representation and narration (Beicken, 2011). What remains for the most part unexplored, and will be the key question driving my analysis, is how the incorporation of filmic elements into his literary works reveals major fault lines created by the convergence of moving-image technology not just with literature but with the medium of writing per se.

One constant among all those who have addressed the topic of Kafka and film is the importance of visual observation in his writings. However, this in itself is not evidence of the influence of film. In the nineteenth century there had already been a shift toward visual description in literary prose. This trend became more extensive and diverse as the flaneur became an important literary vehicle for exploring the modern urban environment. Some have argued that Kafka's protagonists often seem to be flaneur who have lost their calm, leisurely stance in the increasingly fast-paced city. Peter Beicken and Rolf Goebel each argue that a protagonist in one of his key early works that features aspects of cinematic vision reacts like a flaneur who "is threatened with the loss of independence," ready "to succumb to the rush of the world" (Beicken 2000, 4) or who "is unable to experience any redemptive qualities in the street's physical reality, as a cinematic *flâneur*" (Goebel 2000, 14). As they and others since them have rightly noted, Kafka describes the world seen through the eyes of his early protagonists from a narrative point of view that is "grounded in cinematic perception and motion" (Beicken 2000, 6). The street scenes in his early short prose pieces are described in distinct sections that are structured like a sequence of camera shots. When the people and objects within the scenes are in motion, the descriptions correspond to the varying distance of the narrator from them. This produces the literary equivalent of long and medium shots as well as close-ups. In "Wedding Preparations in the Country" (written in 1908[10]) he employs the literary equivalent of filmic techniques, such as establishing shots, varying shot distances, zoom shots, and in one case, a masking shot like those used frequently in early cinema, to present the observations of the protagonist Eduard Raban (Beicken 2011, 168). Similarly, the literary style used to describe what the unnamed narrator of "Description of a Struggle" (1909) sees as he walks at night through the streets of Prague replicates filmic techniques such as rapid changes of scenes, camera movement, point-of-view shots, establishing and panorama shots, close-ups, and shot/reverse shot sequences (Goebel 2000, 14).

The correspondences that Beicken and Goebel establish between these two texts and film techniques are valid, but they do not appear to stem from film viewings. One of them ("Wedding Preparations in the Country") and possibly both were first drafted before Kafka had actually watched a movie. Also, most of the film techniques, especially those noted by Goebel, were not developed until a few years later. Neither he nor Beicken claims that Kafka picked up the visual style of these early works from movies. Rather, each suggests in his own way that through careful observation of life on the streets in the modern urban environment Kafka had developed a filmic mode of seeing that he would find mirrored in the camera-eye of cinema. They both see it as a prefiguration of cinematic vision that arose during the transition from the flaneur phase of modernity, where the individual could still gather in the fleeting images of urban life with reflective calm, to a more mechanized culture that overwhelms the observer.

With respect to a direct effect of film aesthetics on Kafka's literary techniques scholars have concentrated primarily on the period from 1908, after the first documented visit to the movies, through 1914. They cite mainly the later stories in the *Contempla-tion* collection (1912), the unfinished novel, *The Man Who Disap-peared* (1914), and the pivotal 1912 story "The Judgment" as texts displaying style elements drawn from early film. Zischler's book, in which Kafka's withdrawal from cinema in 1913 plays a prominent role, seems to have directed the attention of subsequent scholarly work away from his later writings. This changed when in his 2009 monograph *Kafka und der Film* Peter-André Alt claimed that the adaptation of cinematic strategies factored into his literary work more than had been previously noted. He focused in particular on the last two unfinished novels (*The Trial* and *The Castle*) as well as some of the later stories (including, "A Fratricide" and "The Hunter Gracchus") to trace a continual, even if changing, pattern of "cine-matic narration" throughout all periods of his writing. Drawing on diary entries from the years 1911–1914, Alt argues that cinema was for Kafka a form of escape that left him in a depleted mental state where his imagination could generate new images and views of life that spurred creativity (36). Film plays this role for Kafka, according to Alt, because it supports a way of seeing the world without either getting caught up in it or trying to grasp and master it. Goebel assesses Kafka's relation to cinema similarly, but draws a very different conclusion about its effects on his writing. He con-tends that for Kafka film offers sensuously appealing images that the spectator can observe in a position of safe remove from real life, but it does so in a manner that "turns authentic fullness of life into an artificial spectacle, a performance, a phantasmagoria" (2000, 16). Pushing this argument further in a later article, Goebel identifies a strategy in Kafka's literary works for resisting threats posed by film as well as other modern media (telegraph, telephone, gramophone) that were challenging the hegemony of writing. More specifically, he contends that Kafka's texts reveal how modern me-chanical media exert an overbearing physical force on the user that overrides their content and results in "the loss of the individual's capability for seeing material reality directly and authentically" (2011, 160; also 152).

In the critical literature exploring Kafka and film Goebel stands out as, to my knowledge, the sole scholar who addresses the issue in the context of the clash between new technological media and the medium of writing. In examining how film is remediated back into his literary works, he asserts that Kafka employs a "totalizing strategy" to reinforce "the classical position of privilege held by writing as the primary repository of truth, beauty, and moral authority" (2011, 161). Like other scholars who have focused on the crisis period 1912–1914, Goebel stakes out his position on the basis of passages in the diaries and letters that address the role film played as Kafka began to assert his identity as writer more emphatically. In the following analysis, I also take this pivotal point in his self-understanding as a writer as the starting point for constructing an alternative view of Kafka's ideas about writing, one that sees a deep-seated ambivalence about both film and writing.

Kafka's decision to stop going to the movies came at a time when he was feeling anxious about his ability to pursue his calling as a writer while holding down his job at Workmen's Accident Insurance Institute for the Czech Lands in Prague and entering into marriage with his fiancée Felice Bauer. Even before his proposal in a letter at the end of July 1913, he was expressing deep concerns in his diaries and letters about how marriage would affect his writing. In April, he reveals them rather directly to Felice in a manner that offers a hint of the two failed engagements that would follow. He writes, "If I could write, Felice! I am consumed with the desire to do so. Above all, if I were only free enough, and fit enough! I don't think you have properly taken in that writing is the only thing that makes my inner existence possible" (1973, 245). In the previous November, just three months after they had first met, he had already confided to her that his "mode of life is devised solely for writing, and if there are any changes, then only for the sake of perhaps fitting in better with my writing" (1973, 21). These declarations become even more pronounced once they are formally engaged. On August 14, his letter to Felice contains what has become an oft-cited formulation of how he had become completely consumed by the drive to be a writer: "I have no literary interests; but am made of literature, I am nothing else, and cannot be anything else" (1973, 304). As writing takes on this existential meaning for Kafka, he becomes increasingly frustrated that he is not able to produce texts that satisfy him and could justify his life as writer. He writes to Felice in March 1913 that he has destroyed two hundred pages that comprised the first version of his novel *The Man Who Disappeared* (1914), describing it as "completely unusable" (1973, 218).

During this period as he tries to juggle the demands of his job with his literary ambitions and complains of the stress it is causing him ("what I overcame [suffered] while writing this afternoon" [1965a, 264; June 6, 1912]), cinema serves as an outlet that helps him sustain the energy he needs to write. Shortly after writing "The Judgment" in a single sitting on September 22, 1912, he notes in his diary, "tore myself away from writing" (1965a, 278) to go to the Landestheater cinema in Prague to see a set of short films that included *Lützow's Wild Chase*, an action-filled historical piece about the Romantic author and fallen war hero Theodor Körner (d. 1812). Despite the correspondences between visual description in his writing and film aesthetics, it seems that for Kafka cinema served mainly as escape from the tensions and pressures that burdened him as he tried to carve out an identity for himself as a writer. However, in 1913, with his engagement to Felice, as he becomes increasingly worried that marriage would undermine his devotion to writing, he begins to consider everything else a distraction. Viewing both cinema and his fiancée as a threat to the core of his self-identity, he draws this connection between them vividly in March 1913 in a metaphorical fantasy that has him storming "the film palace 'Felice'" [*Kinopalast 'Felice'*] with his writing (Zischler, 227). Then, shortly after his marriage proposal and before the formal engagement occurs in May 1914, it seems that Kafka stops going to movies almost entirely. In his diary and letters the frequent mention of cinema or of particular films is concentrated mainly in the years 1910–1913. These instances spike in the second half of 1913, with a series of references that extend from a summer trip to Verona through his return to Prague, before ending in November (Zischler, 89–107).

Although Kafka considered himself a "person who takes in the world with his eyes" (*ein Augenmensch*; Janouch, 93) and had an intense interest in film during the first half of his career as writer, there is no evidence that he drew on film for material or inspiration for his writing. The allusions to cinema in his private writings often contain cinematographic descriptions of individual scenes and images that stuck with him from his film viewings. However, no trace of these can be found in his literary texts, nor does Kafka ever mention that he incorporates visual memories from cinema into his writing (Zischler, 57–58). He also never expressed concern that what he took away from his film viewings might interfere with his ability to come up with original content for his stories. Nonetheless, the question remains whether Kafka came to believe, as Goebel argues, that there was an irreconcilable conflict between the form of literary production that he was pursuing and the medium of film. The prevailing view, to which Alt represents an exception, is that Kafka resisted the way the viewer is pulled along with the constant movement of film images and not able to stop and observe a scene reflectively. The claim is that this disrupts the form of visual perception that fueled Kafka's literary imagination (Jahraus, 227–28). In a formulation that has influenced subsequent scholars, Zischler asserts that for Kafka the "almost demonic technological element challenges the way we have learned to see, confronts the author's powers of sight and writing with very great, agonizing demands" (16). Or put differently, the simulated visual consciousness projected onto the film screen trains the individual to organize perceived objects and events in a mechanical fashion that interferes with the visual acumen and creative writing talents of Kafka the literary author.

There is considerable evidence to support this idea. In 1911 while on an extended business trip through the industrial area of Bohemia, Kafka complains of the limited cultural opportunities. In a diary entry, he writes that the only entertainment option in the town of Friedland was a Kaiserpanorama, an installation where up to twenty-five visitors could view a series of rotating stereoscopic slides that produced a 3-D effect. After noting that he was surprised by the elegance of the establishment and the apparatus, Kafka describes in short, precise sentences first what he observed as he entered the establishment and looked at the installation and then the scenes he sees when looking through the eyepiece. He then notes this impression: "The pictures more alive than in the cinema because they offer the eye all the repose of reality. The cinema communicates the restlessness of its motion to the things pictured in it; the eye's repose seems to be more important" (1965b, 241). As opposed to most early viewers of film, who were generally struck by the close affinity between film images and reality, Kafka equates reality with a lack of movement. We get here important insight into the difference between his mode of visual description in his literary texts and cinematic perception. In this journal entry, he goes on to make another comparison between different ways of depicting reality: "The gap between simply hearing about a thing and seeing lantern slides of it is greater than the gap between the latter and actually seeing the thing itself" (1965b, 241). In his view, the writer as well as any mechanical visual medium can do no better than provide a still image or a descriptive passage that enables the viewer/reader to take in a scene leisurely, with time allowed for reflective observation. This preference is evident in the evolution of his writing from the early prose texts where scholars have detected a closer resemblance to cinematic vision to the later writings where what we see through the protagonist's eyes is described more like a panorama scene or a stereoscopic slide. The latter not only entails more descriptive detail, but it also enables the insertion of the narrator's mental reactions to what he observes. For example, in his post-1912 works, the assumptions his protagonists make about the thoughts of the people they encounter are an essential component of his singular literary style. This method of exteriorizing psychological experience and conveying it via visual observation is one of his writing's most distinctive features.

This predilection for the quiet gaze also reveals itself in later diary entries and letters where Kafka develops an interest in film posters that seem to serve as an adequate substitute for the actual screenings that he no longer attends (Zischler, 77–78). A letter to Felice, written March 13–14, 1913, offers insight into his preference for the still image and expresses an ambivalence that seems to have influenced his decision to abandon cinema. He writes that his sister dropped by his apartment on the evening of the 13th after having been to the cinema:

> My sister talked about the performance, or rather I questioned her about it, for although I myself rarely go to the cinematographic theater, I usually know by heart almost all the weekly programs in every one of them. My need for pleasure and distraction feeds on posters; when looking at

FIGURE 5. *A drawing of the Berlin Kaiserpanorama from Walter Benjamin's autobiographical recollections* Berliner Kindheit um Neunzehnhundert *(Berlin childhood around 1900). 1987, Frankfurt: Suhrkamp, 15.*

posters I derive some relief from my habitual inner uneasiness, that everlasting feeling of impermanence; whenever I returned to the city after the summer vacation, which invariably turned out to have been unsatisfactory, I felt a great thirst for posters, and, from the tram on my way home, swiftly and with some effort I used to read fragmentary snatches of the posters we were passing. (1973, 221)

Kafka's ideas about how visual media benefit him appear fraught with contradiction. When away from the bustling city streets of Prague he lauds the restfulness provided by the still images of the Kaiserpanorama, but when he returns, whether from summer vacation or business travel through smaller, quieter towns, he feels unsatisfied and seems to crave the fleeting, quick view of images flowing past the moving window of the tram. He confides that the posters provide him some relief from his "habitual inner uneasiness," but they seem to do this best when he views them from the moving streetcar that effectively turns the still posters into moving film images. It is not the restfulness of the still image that eases his inner restlessness, but rather the film-like stream of images that are attuned to life in the mechanized urban environment.

With the tension inside him building as he contemplates proposing to Felice, his desire to lose himself in moving images apparently becomes stronger as well. He begins to go to the cinema more frequently and continues to do so until he stops altogether at the end of November 1913. In March of that year, the same month when he described the experience of viewing posters from the tram, he had stated that he rarely goes to the movies. But he then begins to visit the cinema more frequently throughout the summer and fall, almost as if driven by an addiction. In the final diary entry about film before they cease in November, he describes himself after a night at the movies much like a junkie who has come down from a high and realizes the futility of taking the drug: "Am entirely empty and insensible, the passing trolley has more living feeling" (1965a, 310; November 20). In contrast to what film can offer him, writing offers the hope of something more solid, more permanent. One week after the unsatisfactory visit to the cinema, in an entry that stands in stark juxtaposition to the earlier one, he describes the recuperation writing brings him: "The firmness, however, which the most insignificant writing brings about in me is beyond doubt and wonderful. The comprehensive view I had of everything on my walk yesterday" (1965a, 310; November 27). In place of the fragmentary glimpses of posters he snatches while on the tram, the stable view he gains on foot quiets his unease, as the literary gaze of the flaneur returns to banish the feverish observation of the film viewer. Losing control and being swept away by the film image provides temporary relief, but in doing so it diverts his focus away from what he sees as "the only thing that makes [his] inner existence possible" (1973, 245), his writing.

A short early piece that scholars have cited as an example of Kafka's filmic mode of description (Beicken 2000, 4–5, Alt, 39–40) prefigures the tension between literary flaneur and film viewer that comes to a head in 1913. In "On the Tram" (1908) the narrator's close observation of a girl who is preparing to step off the tram as it approaches a stop may well have been influenced by Kafka's visits to the cinema. Regardless of whether there is a direct connection or not, the paragraph describing what he sees is structured in much the same way a camera might study its object. First a medium shot catches her as she moves toward the steps, preparing to get off. Then the look moves in closer, noting details such as the folds of her skirt, the collar on her blouse, and her hand holding onto the car as the tip of her umbrella is planted on the second step from the top. Finally, a close-up zooms in on her face, her nose, her hair, strands of it falling down on her temple, and the back of an ear. In the opening paragraph, before assuming the camera perspective, the passenger/narrator reveals that as he stands on the platform of the streetcar he is "completely insecure about his standing in the world, in this city, and in his family" (1994, 27; translation my own). Alluding to what Kafka would later call his "habitual inner uneasiness," the narrator links his insecurity to his status as a passenger, in contrast to those pedestrians who "move out of the path of the streetcar or walk calmly or stop in front of the shop windows" (1994, 27; translation my own). Here, as in the later diary entry about viewing posters from the streetcar, Kafka distinguishes the mode of seeing of a rider on the tram from that of the flaneur. He also expresses an obscure need to defend taking the streetcar while others walk calmly through the streets. The external constellation that evokes the narrator's guilt in "On the Tram" recalls the way Kafka described his emptiness after he had taken refuge in the cinema in November 1913: "the passing trolley has more living feeling."

In the crisis period of 1912–1914 Kafka liberates himself from the "demonic" filmic way of seeing not only by stopping his visits to the cinema. He also writes his way free of its influence in his literary works. The passages at the end of the two major stories written during this phase depict a scene much like those found in early cinema. In both cases they complete the demise of a protagonist whose seemingly secure employment and relation to his father, with whom he still lives, have crumbled in the course of the story. In "The Judgment" Georg Bendemann learns that his father has been secretly corresponding with an old friend of Georg's who had emigrated to St. Petersburg, conspiring to expose at the most opportune moment his son's self-centered abandonment and betrayal of his best friend and his father. As he does so dramatically, throwing off the covers and standing up in bed in a theatrical show of unsuspected strength that borders on slapstick comedy, the father abruptly and unexpectedly condemns Georg to death by drowning. Bewildered by this bizarre occurrence, Georg rushes out of the room and heads toward the nearby bridge over the river. The description of his mad rush to the bridge and plunge into the water below resembles the depiction of action in silent film (Alt, 74–75). The "shot" of his dash down the stairs where he nearly knocked the maid down is followed by a "cut" to a "camera" stationed outside the building that captures him coming out the door and crossing the street heading toward the river: "On the staircase, down whose steps he raced as if down a ramp, he nearly bowled over his cleaning woman, who was just coming upstairs to tidy the apartment after the night. 'Jesus!' she shouted, covering her face with her apron, but he was already gone. He leaped out of the gate, across the avenue, driven on toward the water" (2007, 12). There is then a second cut to him already on the bridge holding onto the railing: "He was already clutching the railing the way a starving man clutches food" (2007, 12). The final scene plays out as a single shot showing him slowly loosening his grip on the railing, until a bus passes by in the background, creating enough noise to drown out his cry as he lets go and falls into the river. As in silent film, we would see his lips moving but not hear what he is saying, having rather to rely on an intertitle to disclose his final words: "He swung himself over, like the excellent gymnast he had been in his youth, the pride of his parents. Even as his grip weakened, he continued holding on, between the bars of the railing he caught sight of a bus that would easily muffle the sound of his fall, and crying out softly, 'Dear parents, I really always loved you,' he let himself drop" (2007, 12). The final sentence of the story ends this scene in much the same way a film would cut back after he has fallen to the same shot of the bridge above, showing the traffic streaming across it behind where he had been holding onto the railing. "At that moment, the traffic going over the bridge was nothing short of infinite" (2007, 12). In its structure and pacing this final sequence not only resembles something Kafka would have seen in his visits to the cinema, it also anticipates filmic techniques of classical cinema and supports Beicken's claim that Kafka learned from going to the movies "how to incorporate additional film elements and structures into his narratives beyond the cinematic culture of the gaze in his early works" (173).

Kafka resorts to this filmic visual style to describe the dynamic action that occurs after the father's outburst disrupts the years of stasis and inaction that had developed in their relationship. Until the father suddenly resists Georg tucking him into bed, the narrative had consisted almost entirely of direct and indirect discourse between Georg, his fiancée, and his father, Georg's inner monologue about his reasons for not maintaining contact with his friend, and the text of the letter he had just written to him telling about his engagement. Once this tortured constellation of thoughts, speech, rationalizations, and guilt ruptures, the story breaks into dynamic action described in the visual style of silent film that leads to Georg's suicide. Kafka follows the same basic pattern in "Metamorphosis." In the course of this considerably longer story there are occasional interludes of frantic action that are described visually in a manner that evokes film scenes. These occur when Gregor comes out of his room to speak with the bank manager or to listen to his sister play the violin for the boarders the family had taken in and is driven back into his room by his father's threats of violence. The last of these episodes takes place when his sister and mother venture into his room to remove some of the furniture. Similar to the scene in his father's room in "The Judgment," these are bizarrely dark, comical moments that lead up to Gregor's elimination from the family. In this final encounter his father bombards him with apples and in doing so inflicts a mortal wound. The description of the movements and gestures involved in these frantic skirmishes also corresponds to the way action is staged in early film.

In another parallel to "The Judgment," the final shot in "Metamorphosis" also marks a transitional juncture between Kafka's earlier stories that rely more on observations described as if seen through the eye of the camera, and his two late novels that reflect inner psychological processes via narrative structure and dialogue. Similar to the ending of "The Judgment," this pivotal moment occurs after the protagonist's death:

> Then all three of them left the apartment together, something they had not done for months, and took the electric tram all the way to the open countryside at the edge of town. The car in which they sat all alone was entirely

suffused with warm sunlight. . . . As they were conversing
in this way, Herr and Frau Samsa were struck almost as one
while observing their daughter, who was growing ever more
vivacious, by the thought that despite all the torments that
had made her cheeks grow pale, she had recently blossomed
into a beautiful, voluptuous girl. Growing quieter now and
communicating with one another almost unconsciously by
an exchange of glances, they thought about how it would
soon be time to find her a good husband. And when they
arrived at their destination, it seemed to them almost
a confirmation of their new dreams and good intentions when their daughter swiftly sprang to her feet
and stretched her young body. (2016, 46–47)

Gregor's death liberates the family from the burden that he had
been for them, which is signified by his transformation into a
vermin [*Ungeziefer*]. His death also enables the shift in narrative
perspective from Gregor's, which was confined to the interior of
his room, to that of his parents, who leave the apartment and feel
their relief reflected in their ability to now move freely through the
streets of the city.

We have here the high point of Kafka's remediation of the
camera-eye back into literary prose. The daughter stretching her
nubile body as she experiences her sexuality, although not yet consciously, evokes an embodied response typical of film. The indirect
point of view through the eyes of the parents correlates to the use
of indirect subjective looks in early film that predated direct point-
of-view shots. As discussed in the last section, these instances of
embedded looks from the point of view of a character included
those of a hidden photographer or voyeur secretly watching or
recording a sexual encounter or erotic scene. With Gregor now
removed from the picture, the indirect look at the sister in the
streetcar provides insights into the thought processes of the parents. Describing the daughter's movement as it might be captured
by a film camera, Kafka evokes a sensual response to convey the
liberation the family experiences once Gregor has been eliminated.
In "The Judgment" and "Metamorphosis" he employs these moments of filmic literary description to literally write himself out

of the tortured family relations and professional life in which he felt entrapped. In doing so, he realizes that whatever liberation he might gain does not come from the representation of a way out, but rather the process of writing itself would offer him whatever salvation he might hope to find in literature. He articulates this in his increasingly emphatic declarations that writing is his only hope for an "inner existence" and that he is "made of literature," and is indeed "nothing else, and cannot be anything else." And he affirms this after he came away from the cinema feeling empty in November 1913, when he proclaims the "firmness" he gained by even the most insignificant writing, explaining that it empowered him to see everything more clearly and comprehensively.

Writing and the Restraint of Vision

When Kafka emerges from the crisis period during which these two transitional stories were written, he no longer produces autobiographically inflected texts that enact his extrication out of a torturous private and professional life. As Alt has shown, he continues to employ his literary version of the camera-eye in his two unfinished novels written after 1913, *The Trial* and *The Castle*. However, the later works lack the kind of "redemptive" moments found at the end of "The Judgment" and "Metamorphosis." He had gained from this crisis phase the insight that the failures he experiences with respect to familial, social, and professional expectations are not primarily a matter of individual guilt or psychic frailty, but rather are built into the systematic structures that define interaction with others in these spheres (Abraham, 431). The complex psychological makeup of the two protagonists of his late novels reflect, among other things, how control in a bureaucratic society is structured through and sustained by written texts. Josef K.'s exposure to an inscrutable, byzantine justice system in *The Trial* and K.'s enmeshment in a comparable network of institutional authorities in *The Castle* expose uncentered agencies through which the power of language is exerted almost imperceptibly. In this context, the "camera-eye" style of description found in his earlier stories gives way to more strictly literary techniques, such as free indirect speech, that depict the linguistically formulated thought processes of the anxious protagonists of his later novels. When Kafka includes moments of filmic visuality in his final two novels, he does so to reinforce the protagonist's entrapment in a network of indecipherable rules and laws.

As the frame of reference for the intricate mental worlds of Kafka's protagonists undergoes this shift, the scenes described in a cinematic visual style take on a different form and purpose. One such passage is found in the opening chapter of *The Trial* where K. discusses his situation with the inspector after they have moved from his room into the one rented by the typist Frau Bürstner. K. looks out the window to the building across the street where an elderly couple has been watching the proceedings in his building in the company of an officer of the court. Spying them again, he reacts:

> Across the way the group was still at the window, their peaceful observation now slightly disturbed as K. stepped to the window. The old couple started to rise, but the man behind them calmed them down. "There's more of the audience over there," K. cried out to the inspector and pointed outside. "Get away from there," he yelled at them. The three immediately retreated a few steps, the old couple even withdrawing behind the man, who shielded them with his broad body and, judging by the movement of his lips, apparently said something that couldn't be understood at that distance. They didn't disappear entirely, however, but instead seemed to wait for the moment when they could approach the window again unnoticed. (1998b, 15–16)

Several aspects mark this scene as decidedly filmic. First, the characters' movements, gestures, and postures recall those commonly seen in early movies, and K. reads them much like a film viewer to gauge their emotional reactions and intentions. Also, K. watching the neighbors talking without being able to hear them mirrors the visual scenes of silent film. And finally, the internal framing of these "shots"—his point of view is framed by the window of Fraulein Bürstner's apartment and what he is observing is framed by the window on the other side of the street—reinforce this effect.

The occasional filmic moments in *The Trial* differ in important ways from Kafka's early writings that display aspects of a cinematic literary style. The entire text is not structured around the visual observations of the protagonist, focused like a camera on "the cityscape from his vantage point vis-à-vis the bustling life rushing by in front of him," as in his early novel fragment "Wedding Preparations in the Country" or "Descriptions of a Struggle" (Beicken 2000, 6). Rather these isolated instances of the camera look remain consistent with the unique combination of authorial and figural narration he employs in his final two novels (Stanzel 1984). In terms of the overall narrative perspective, the later style corresponds more closely to cinematic narration. Blending free indirect discourse with figural narration, Kafka is able to structure "the entire fictional world as an uninterrupted *vision avec*" (Cohn, 111–12). Passages like the visual description of what is happening in the apartment across the street offer a filmic version of this literary technique. The conclusions drawn about the intentions of the elderly couple correspond to Kafka's frequent use of free indirect discourse to express his protagonist's assumptions about how the people he encounters judge his actions. The relatively small, seemingly insignificant instances of camera-like visual perception in *The Trial* and *The Castle* are similar to close-ups in a film that focus in on individual objects or parts of the body within a larger diffuse background. In this case, that diffuse world in which these momentary visual episodes appear is not the larger street scene as described by an observing narrator. Rather, it is the novel's long, intricate account of K.'s attempts to come to terms with the impenetrable set of precepts and provisions that have taken control of his life. Just as Kafka's free indirect style echoes the many assumptions, reflections, and imaginings coursing through K.'s thoughts, these visual observations offer insight into his frame of mind as he attempts to construct a defense.

There is another such scene early in chapter two of *The Trial* as K. makes his way to the court for the first time. As is typical of passages associated with film in both his private writings and his literary texts, a streetcar figures prominently here. It also features the same constellation of the three elements found in "On the Tram"—a streetcar, a filmic point of view, and the compulsion to mount a defense against an undefined charge. On the way to the court he sees the three clerks from the bank, whom the officer of the court had summoned to his apartment, supposedly to make his late arrival at the bank less conspicuous.

> Strangely enough, although he had little time to look about, he ran across the three clerks who were involved in his affair: Rabensteiner, Kullych, and Kaminer. The first two were riding in a tram that crossed K.'s path, but Kaminer was sitting on the terrace of a coffeehouse and, just as K. was walking by, leaned inquisitively over the railing. They probably all gazed after him, wondering why their supervisor was in such a rush; some sort of stubbornness had prevented K. from taking a cab; he had an aversion to even the slightest outside help in this affair of his. (1998b, 37–38)

This brief interlude also has the earmarks of a film scene. Between his apartment and the court we have only this one scene inserted much in the way films often include transitional markers when there is a move to a new location. The parenthetical remark "although he had little time to look about" situates the two images of his coworkers not as subjective camera shots from his point of view, but rather as visual observations from the perspective of an accompanying camera (*vision avec*). The sighting of the first two colleagues through the window of the streetcar again reinforces this effect by suggesting a framed film image. And the description of Kaminer leaning over the balustrade to peer at K. brings to mind the gestures, actions, and facial expressions that played a prominent role in silent film.

Here as well the sighting of the three bank employees serves the same purpose as Kafka's use of free indirect discourse. The glimpse of Kaminer watching K. pass by prompts assumptions— that they were observing him and were surprised how he was walking hurriedly—that are not explicitly designated as K.'s. However, the subsequent, convoluted account of why he chose to walk marks them clearly, even if indirectly, as part of his mental response to what he sees. The inclusion of this kind of filmic scene does not merely support the literary construction of a mental world wracked by ambiguity and paranoia. K.'s inability to abide by visual observation without resorting to perspective-taking and linguistic, cognitive interpretation of what he sees is a constituent element in the sociocultural dynamic Kafka is exploring. Even when the text provides detailed description that functions much like mise-en-scène in cinema, the protagonist and the reader become caught up in a process of dissecting the presumed thoughts, assumptions, assessments, and judgments of the other characters that eclipses visual observation. At the level of K.'s interaction with everyone he encounters, language dominates not only when there is direct speech, but even more perniciously when free indirect speech represents their thoughts about him and his situation. As the protagonist becomes locked into a reciprocal relation with the external world that is dominated by the dictates of language, he loses the capacity to see. With respect to the most basic interaction with others, the preponderance of language eclipses the power of vision to establish *embodied social cognition* prior to the cognitive processes of situation modeling and perspective-taking that rely on linguistic analysis (Cook 2015). What K. needs and cannot establish is "intersubjective acknowledgment" and "reciprocal recognition" (Corngold and Wagner, 122). The text offers the possibility for the kind of visual observation that Kafka prized as an *Augenmensch,* only to counter it by engaging the reader in the protagonist's contorted inferences about what is expected of him. This clash between seeing and saying mirrors Kafka's ambivalent relation to cinema and reflects the underlying tension between writing and film. On the one hand, visual description in his literary works creates a perspective closely related to the "eye" of the film camera. On the other hand, he became disenchanted with the movies because the rapidly changing and moving images disrupted the mode of detached viewing and contemplation that sustained him as writer.

In *The Trial* the subjugation of vision to discourse is part of a larger thematic that implicates the written word. The mere presumption of a written law renders K. unable to disengage from the ungrounded dictates of the court and its peculiar officers and minions. He never gains access to the actual documents that govern his fate, but just the assumption that they exist prevents him from seeing things freely and clearly. Kafka provides K. and the reader a parable that addresses the pervasive but also elusive control exerted by writing. The insights it offers are presented in an enigmatic fashion that exceeds the powers of K.'s determined hermeneutic efforts and has spawned a multitude of diverse interpretations in the critical literature.[11] The priest K. encounters when he visits the cathedral tells K. that he is deceiving himself in his view of the court that has summoned him. He then recites a story from the introductory writings to the Law that, according to the priest, explains how K. is deceiving himself. The parable, published by Kafka separately in 1915 as "Before the Law," tells of a man from the country who approaches the Law and seeks entry into it from a doorkeeper who controls the entrance. But when the doorkeeper says he cannot allow him to enter now, but possibly at a later time, the man decides to wait. The doorkeeper suggests that he could try to pass through despite his interdiction, but warns that inside, from room to room, there are other doorkeepers each more powerful than the previous ones. After years of waiting, during which he beseeched, cajoled, and attempted to bribe the doorkeeper, his powers, and his vision in particular, grow weaker, until the doorkeeper realizes that he is at the end of his strength. As he gets up and closes the door, the man asks why during all these years no one else has come seeking entry. The doorkeeper replies that no one else could have entered here because this door was intended only for him, and goes to close the door.

The interpretation that is important for my purposes concerns what the parable has to say about the written word. As the priest suggests when he introduces the story, the presence and authority of the Law depends on its documentation in writing. And yet the exercise of this authority does not depend on what the texts actually say. In fact, merely the word of the doorkeeper, who, as K. points out, contradicts himself, suffices to uphold its dominion. But of course, the doorkeeper's statements have been committed to writing as part of the story as it appears in the introduction to the Law, and the priest emphasizes that he has recited the story word for word (*im Wortlaut der Schrift*, literally, "in the wording of the text"). Also, in the ensuing discussion of the story the priest provides an exhaustive exegesis that parses every possible way of interpreting what the doorkeeper says. He does so in response to K.'s curt analysis as soon as the priest finishes the story: "'So the doorkeeper deceived the man'" (1998b, 217). The priest's counter-arguments, which are as exhausting as the doorkeeper's stance toward the man had been over his many years of waiting, repeatedly stress unerring commitment to the written word of the Law: "'But there is no contradiction'"; "'He [the doorkeeper] appears to love precision'" (1998b, 218); and to K., "'You don't have sufficient respect for the text'" (1998b, 217). In the end, the priest's analysis wears down K., who has no other retort than to ask, "'Do you want anything else from me?'" (1998b, 224). Confirming that he belongs to the court, the priest deflects this charge with a response that *mutatis mutandis* mirrors the doorkeeper's stance toward the man from the country: "'Why should I want something from you? The court wants nothing from you. It receives you when you come and dismisses when you go'" (1998b, 224).

The source of the power that the court exerts over K. and the Law exerts over the man from the country does not reside in the wording of authorized texts, but rather in language itself, and more specifically in the medium of writing. "Before the Law" suggests that the maintenance of this form of control depends on the suppression of precognitive forms of apprehension, and of vision in particular. As the man yields to the power of the Law without reason, he loses his ability to *see* for himself. When the doorkeeper tells him that it is possible for him to enter through the door, but not yet, he leans forward peering through the door to see what lies inside. This draws a laugh from the doorkeeper, who invites him to try and enter in defiance of his prohibition. But his warning of the other, more powerful doorkeepers that await him inside, the third of which this doorkeeper cannot even bear to look at, convinces the man that it is better to wait here until a more opportune time. From this point on his look is restricted to the doorkeeper, whom he observes relentlessly for many years. The absurdity of this decision (and Kafka's unique sense of humor) is demonstrated when he notices the fleas in the doorkeeper's fur collar and asks them to help him persuade the doorkeeper to grant him entry. At the end, his eyesight weakens, and it at least seems to be getting darker, until an inextinguishable glow emanates from inside the door. Now that the man no longer has the capacity to see clearly or freely, the Law that has eclipsed his vision and held him in abeyance over many years sends out a final beam of light confirming that the source of its power is not the legal text, but rather the underlying cultural mechanism that gives it authority, the medium of writing. The man's failure to *see past* this inscrutable force corresponds to K.'s inability to view the world he lives in without becoming entangled in the presumed words of others that condemn his failure to meet the expectations placed on him by the world at large. Indeed, the reciprocal relation that holds K. and all those he encounters in check suggests that their lives are grounded not in particular texts, but in the power of writing per se to organize the senses and structure all experience accordingly.

In *The Castle* Kafka uses a narrative construct similar to that in *The Trial* to further explore how writing exerts a pervasive but intangible form of control across all different spheres of modern social life. As K. struggles to determine why he has been summoned and to prove his relevance, he encounters at every turn officials who present or refer to written documents that determine all manner of procedures and power relations in the world of the castle. Neither the inhabitants nor the castle officials know by what authority these texts have legitimacy, but they all proclaim their infallibility and circulate them dutifully. This results in nonsensical attention to the letter of the law that, when warped by carnal impulses and molded by Kafka's literary imagination, results in comic-grotesque behavior. In this regard, the castle is an allegorical figuration that enabled him to express his intense dislike of the professional world that shaped his experience and identity as much as his literary work. In the bureaucratic sphere of his life as a writerly being he composed legal interpretations for the Workmen's Accident Insurance Institute. In this capacity, he became an agent for a bureaucratic system whose comprehensive social organization reaches into all corners of modern life. As the etymological origins for this form of institutional power suggest (*bureau*, as a desk that has drawers for holding documents), its authority resides in the production and accumulation of written texts that fix laws, prescribe rules and regulations, and archive examples and precedents that undergird hypothetical situations with actual lived experience.

Because of *The Castle*'s thematic focus on the control exerted by written documents, scenes described in the visual style of film are less frequent in the novel. There are such passages, but they are concentrated at the beginning of the text and play a smaller role after K. is drawn into the intricacies of the castle world.[12] Perhaps the most dramatic of these is the famous opening scene of the novel that functions like an establishing shot, or more precisely, a blank establishing shot, where the obscured view of the castle foreshadows K.'s interaction with the village and castle that is to come:

> It was late evening when K. arrived. The village lay under deep snow. There was no sign of the Castle hill, fog and darkness surrounded it, not even the faintest gleam of light suggested the large Castle. K. stood a long time on the wooden bridge that leads from the main road to the village, gazing upward into the seeming emptiness. (1998a, 1)

What K. sees as he looks up from the wooden bridge into the fog toward where the castle should appear prefigures the chameleon-like character of the castle. When K. is able to catch sight of it the following morning, Kafka provides a detailed description of the imposing structure, which is more like a village than just a single structure.[13] However, the exactness with which K. describes the layout does not help him understand its methods and practices. As he tries to work his way into its circle, the castle society continues to change its demands, constantly morphing in ways that require K. to adjust accordingly as he doggedly pursues his goal. In the end, the filmic form of visual description that Kafka uses when K. first lays eyes on the castle proves inconsequential, because the bureaucratic network it embodies turns out to be an amorphous system of writing that cannot be firmly apprehended.

In this final attempt at a novel Kafka reveals what unites the two seemingly opposed spheres of his life as writer—his work as a literary author and the institutional world of the government bureaucrat. In both cases his identity is constructed in relation to an unanchored network of rules and principles that is always subject to change by the next act of writing. The rules and practices that govern the castle, like those that govern modern bureaucratic society, cannot be grasped and understood, because they are constantly writing themselves anew: "The castle and its environs are a single bureaucratic institution, marked by the ubiquity of its written signs and the untraceableness of their circulation: it is chiefly in this sense that the castle is a figure for the 'house' of writerly being, *Schriftstellersein*" (Corngold and Wagner, 123–24). In this respect, K.'s attempts to discover his place and establish his identity in the castle society is a figuration of Kafka's resolve to write *The Castle* (Corngold and Wagner, 121). The castle does not merely embody what Kafka was up against in his struggles to establish himself as a literary writer. It also reflects the dichotomy in his writing between personal failings that are reflected in his protagonists and his exploration of the social and cultural forces that bear responsibility for those failings.

When Kafka employs a camera-eye perspective at the end of "The Judgment" and "Metamorphosis" to purge himself of the tendency to write in a filmic style of visual description, he is also abandoning his literary focus on his anguished family and work situation. In getting rid of Georg and Gregor he is literally writing himself free of his fixation on personal deficiencies and guilt. In his subsequent texts vestiges of such topics as his bachelorhood and his intense dislike of his job remain, but they are integrated into the thematic analysis of more universal social dysfunction. In a 1920 diary entry, he describes the power of the family over the individual in a third-person account of his own situation:

> He does not live for his personal life; he does not think
> for his personal thought. It seems to him that he lives and
> thinks under the compulsion of a family, which is surely
> itself overabundant in the power of life and thought but for
> which he signifies, in accordance with some law unknown to
> him, a formal necessity. For this unknown family and these
> unknown laws he cannot be released. (2007, 207)

The practices and routines that structure family life in modernity mirror those at work in the office and those that incapacitate the Josef K./K. dyad of his late novels. The impenetrable network of officials and writings that impose an unfounded yet sovereign set of expectations and define individual identity in *The Castle* is the same agency that "wrote" Kafka into a reified family organism.

Kafka's frequent statements in his diaries and letters about the importance literature held for him provide insight into how both the personal and professional spheres are subject to the dictates of writing. From the beginning of his relationship with Felice (1912) he repeatedly professed that his well-being was dependent on his ability to establish himself as a literary writer (*Schriftsteller*). The urgency to realize this goal gradually increased as his health worsened and he remained unfulfilled by what he had produced with his writing—for which he declares he was sacrificing everything. Near the end of his life, at the time he was working on *The Castle* (1922), he describes his life as an abject failure in every important regard. In a letter to Max Brod he depicts himself as "a son incapable of marriage, who produces no carriers of the name; pensioned at 39; occupied only with an eccentric writing that aims at nothing else than the salvation or damnation of his own soul" (2007, 212). What he means here with "an eccentric writing" is not that his literary work is driven by personal ambition or the individual pursuit of meaning. Rather, the dissatisfaction he expresses suggests that he was never able to sufficiently extract his sense of psychic frailty and feelings of personal guilt from the complex of pervasive social forces he was addressing in his literary texts. The personal was always surfacing in ways that interfered with his attempt to expose how a pernicious "formal necessity" was inflicting harm on the lives of everyone in modern bureaucratic society. As he examines how the archiving and circulation of written documents exerts an arbitrary, harmful form of control, his own sense of personal weakness continues to haunt his late writings. Even as he strove to write himself free of the shackles of the written word that afflicted him in both his personal and his professional life, he only reaffirmed the tyrannical hold it had on his existence.

3

2000

Cinema and the Digital Image

Intermedial Constructions of Cinema's Virtual Reality

Cinema's role in shaping how we engage with new media has been variously interpreted. Manovich argued that the film image would be the predominant influence determining our aesthetic interface with computer technology: "Cinema, the cultural form of the twentieth century, has found a new life in the toolbox of the computer user. . . . Cinema's aesthetic strategies have become basic organizational principles of computer software. The window into a fictional world of a cinematic narrative has become a window into a datascape. In short, what was cinema is now the human-computer interface" (2001, 86). He has since retreated somewhat from this claim and subscribed to the more prevalent view that digital technology is spawning a qualitatively new image. However, his overstating of cinema's influence should not obscure the fact that in the early stages of the digital age a vibrant mutual exchange of aesthetic features and structural conventions occurred between film and new media. As moving images appear more frequently on new devices at a dizzying clip, speculation about the demise of cinema surfaces regularly. But the transition from one medium to the next is never a clean break, with one disappearing and a new one replacing it. Instead it involves a complex convergence of an increasingly broad array of diverse media. At the time he was writing, McLuhan considered television as the new medium that was influencing the cultural landscape and the human nervous system most dramatically, even as he pointed ahead to computers as the next technological innovation that would soon produce momentous changes. Nonetheless, he maintained that other contemporary media, such as radio, photography, movies, the press, and the telephone, among others, were continuing to have substantial effects on the human organism.

At the present we are in a period of an even more complex confluence of mediation among electronic and now digital media that is radically transforming cinema: "As a result of the developments in information-communication technologies and the emergence of electronic media and multimedia, the situation of cinema/film—the first form of moving image media art—is changing to an extent that far outweighs the intensity of all its previous transformations" (Kluszczynski, 209). The current process of convergence has many of the earmarks of what happened a hundred years earlier when film was the new medium producing ripples throughout the information and entertainment industries. At that time, formal and narrative strategies from literature and theater were instrumental in shaping motion-picture storytelling. Conversely, as fiction film quickly became a widely disseminated form of popular culture, its medium-specific faculties for conveying our mental life were remediated back into those forms of expression and expanded the reach of the written word and stage production.

Today, a similar dynamic is at work between cinema and digital media. Moving images themselves have moved, migrating from the fixed movie or television screen to all manner of handheld devices and screens affixed to moving vehicles (planes, trains, and automobiles) or to the exteriors of public buildings. The user views these new screens with a look that has been shaped by mainstream film viewing and its dissemination through other twentieth-century visual media (including television, video games, and DVD players). There is an ongoing mutual exchange among them of techniques and structural conventions stemming from early cinema, such as narrative patterns, spatial construction, editing, framing, and viewer orientation. Just as the remediation of narrative and visual elements from previous media was an integral part of cinema's path to a standard form, new digital media have incorporated the aesthetic techniques and structures of cinema into their forms. Furthermore, the number and kind of formats for assembling and recording moving images have expanded along with an extensive set of digital systems that can be used in various contexts. As moving-image media have become a major platform for providing basic services throughout all sectors of the economy, ranging from entertainment to education, research, job training, military operations, and more, the basic filmic techniques developed for cinema become disseminated ever more widely and diversely.

At the same time, cinema has increasingly and to great effect incorporated digital technology into all phases of its production and exhibition over the last two decades. The growing use of digital imaging and CGI-generated special effects has also changed cinema in fundamental ways, such that the film image that is being remediated into the whole range of digital devices has itself been altered by the new media. What is often obscured as divergent interests and competing forces drive the convergence of existing and emerging media are the multiple recursive forces at work between the two and the dynamic state of hybridity they produce. When digital imaging became commonplace in cinema, practices and techniques developed in new media began to fuse with standard film elements to produce new hybrid forms (Kluszczynski, 211–12). What works its way back into film are new media practices that have already been substantially shaped by their fusion with cinema. As new media follow conventional film principles in dramatically altered environments, the cinematographic techniques are transformed in the process and these changes are remediated back into cinema. This is of course not a pattern unique to the digital age. Television expanded the exhibition setting to include individuals, families, or small groups of friends viewing together either at home or in public places such as bars, the workplace, airports, and schools. As has been widely documented, the aesthetic practices developed for television then had a wide-ranging influence on cinema.[1] However, the current process of reverse remediation is producing more dramatic changes in one important regard. The interactive nature of new media has led to embodied modes of engagement with the moving image that are now radically altering the act of film viewing across all devices and venues.

The basic principles of cinematography are undergoing extensive transformation as they are applied in ever more contexts and to various kinds of screens that serve many different purposes. The film image has been set loose from its confinement in a screening environment that promotes focused attention, with the result that increased mobility and distraction are becoming crucial aspects of the viewing experience. Computers, tablets, cell phones, and other mobile devices have brought moving images to an ever-expanding set of new environments and media (games, surveillance cameras, training devices, scientific and medical equipment, and amusement parks, among others). Our experience of the visual image in these contexts is increasingly mediated through kinesthetic and tactile engagement with the technology in various ways. The touchscreen enables the user to control or alter images by direct touch. Various new media devices enhance the visual image with haptic effects, such as reverberating sound, vibrations and tactile signals delivered to joysticks and other control units, or feedback from remote tactile sensors. The user's sensorimotor systems that provide spatial orientation also play a greater role in virtual reality and web environments where there is an enhanced sense of virtual body movement within moving-image representations. What is now being remediated back into cinema is then not merely the specific technology of digital imaging, but rather the whole complex of altered bodily functions in the new media environment. When digital imaging is used to stir kinesthetic and tactile responses in the film viewer all these modes of physical engagement with the transformed cinematographic image are called into play in the movie theater as well.

The incorporation of aesthetic techniques from new media into cinema has resulted in a shift away from classical narrative. Digital technology's ability to generate a more participatory user experience threatens to dislodge the mode of spectatorship that has dominated cinema since narrative integration became the operative paradigm for classical cinema. Still, Hollywood tends to fold the disruptive force of the digitally altered film image back into mainstream cinema in ways that reinforce the traditional mode of spectatorship (Young, xxi). Digital imaging can also be employed to produce a more consummate version of the diegetic film world, thus cementing the conventional relation to the cinematic image. Just as sound, more sophisticated cameras, and more sensitive film stock were appropriated by the film industry to strengthen classical continuity, digital imaging may also be used to solidify the diegetic unity of the film world. Arguing that classical continuity has emerged unscathed by the remediation of digital technology, Bordwell contends that even in the accelerated dynamics of contemporary cinema "narrative functions tend to tame visual effects" (2006, 14). In adapting CGI to its traditional standards, Hollywood has, he claims, neutralized the disruptive potential of digital imaging to actually strengthen continuity.

Those who, like Bordwell, emphasize the endurance of narrative continuity tend to overlook the erosive effects of a new aesthetics of spectacle that foregrounds the wondrous capabilities of digital imaging technology. Cinema is but one of a whole array of entertainment media that brandish and exploit an enhanced ability to produce illusions that can stand in almost seamlessly for our perceptions of reality. Digital technology is employed across a constantly expanding set of media to make virtual images seem increasingly real. IMAX theaters, virtual reality and other immersive multimedia environments, online role-playing games, and even amusement park rides, theme park attractions, and movie studio tours all exploit the ability to simulate reality in ever more convincing ways. Video games, in particular, "flaunt their capacity for making a reality out of an illusion" (Ndalianis, 207). In all these areas of the entertainment industry, the dual nature of "the fantastic illusion both as a technological achievement and as an alternative reality" (Ndalianis, 213–14) generates ambiguity. The wonder evoked by new modes of visual representation is mixed with a loss of belief in a stable world and the traditional view of the human's place in it. The incorporation of digital imaging into mainstream cinema erodes the faith in the power of the cinematic image to represent reality. With its ability to alter the profilmic event and still generate a sense of even more complete realism, digital technology is seen to be dangerously deceptive. As this deployment of digital imaging upends existing conceptions of reality, it also opens up fissures in spectatorship as it has been fashioned by classical cinema.

As Hollywood began to fully exploit digital technology in this manner, a series of sci-fi films at the end of the millennium began to explore how mainstream cinema has purported to represent reality in its diegetic fiction. One way they do this is by creating multiple simulated realities that are at times indistinguishable from the base diegetic reality in their stories. Films such as *eXistenZ*, *Open Your Eyes*, *The Thirteenth Floor*, *Dark City*, and *The Matrix* invoke the contemporary viewer's familiarity with immersive digital environments to facilitate fluid movement between different diegetic worlds. As key plot elements in these science-fiction films, the simulations are fashioned according to the basic constructs of film narrative and thus are on the most fundamental level unmediated manifestations of cinematic representation. These films are then also rife with metacinematic figures and allusions that link the simulated worlds in their stories to the diegetic reality produced in narrative cinema. However, they do more than merely provide a critical lens for assessing the effect produced by the dominance of a narrative cinema keyed to diegetic reality. They wield the power of digital imaging to disrupt habituated modes of spectatorship, altering the interface not only between the viewer/user and the image, but also between the human nervous system and the cultural environment created by the new technology.

All the films discussed in this chapter allude in some way to the conventional mode of representation in narrative film. *eXistenZ* draws perhaps the most explicit comparisons between digitally created virtual worlds and cinema. In the opening scene, a focus group is getting ready to test the new virtual reality game (*eXistenZ*) of a leading game designer, Allegra Geller (Jennifer Jason Leigh). As the participants start porting into the game, an assassin pulls out a crude pistol made of bones and fires it at Allegra, hitting her in the shoulder. Ted Pikul (Jude Law), a security officer who has been screening people coming into the room, grabs the gun and whisks Allegra out of the building. Fearing that the sole gaming device containing *eXistenZ* has been damaged, she convinces Ted to have a game port (a bio-port) installed in his body so that he can accompany her into the game to test it. With this begins the pair's adventure, as they encounter strange allies and foes while traversing various stages of what turns out to be a game-within-a-game scenario. Director David Cronenberg overlays the game experience directly onto film spectatorship by creating a diegetic reality that is itself a game environment, one that turns out to actually be multiple levels of interlocking game realities. Throughout the film, allusions to cinema, sometimes direct and at other times more implicit, repeatedly focus attention on the question of spectatorship. In the game world of *eXistenZ* Ted (Jude Law) assumes a role that is typical of the protagonist in a certain type of Hollywood genre. He is the naïve and cautious male lead who only becomes more adventuresome after he has been seduced by a strong woman. The film is replete with other stock Hollywood characters as well, such as the fatherly scientist Kiri Vinokur (Ian Holm) who turns out to be evil. The style of acting within the game is excessively histrionic in a notably Hollywood manner. When the characters return from the game to the supposed base diegetic level of film reality they assume a more naturalistic mode of acting: not exaggeratedly coded as cinematic, but still common to narrative film. Similarly, the film is full of one-liners that mark classical Hollywood dialogue. When Ted says to Allegra, "That's two people in one day who wanted to actually kill you," she retorts, "I've never been more popular." When Ted and Allegra begin to get sexually aroused and start passionately caressing each other, the scene unfolds playfully as a mock-up of how Hollywood deals with sex. After licking Allegra's bio-port as if it were another female orifice and then kissing her hard on the mouth, Ted demurs that it was not him, but rather his game character who was acting this way. Allegra's response indicates that it is all indeed scripted like a movie: "You're right. Our characters are obviously supposed to jump on each other. Probably to create emotional tension when danger happens. No use fighting it." As their foreplay begins to heat up toward what is clearly going to be passionate sex, the film cuts suddenly away to Ted standing at an assembly line at the mutant trout farm. This abrupt change mirrors the common Hollywood tactic of cutting away from lovemaking scenes before actual intercourse, while the starkly nonromantic ambience of the fish farm provides humorous self-reflection on the cinematic nature of the cut. At times, there are metacinematic elements that allude specifically to how the game design remediates the basic structures of mainstream cinema. Trying to convince Gas (Willem Dafoe) that his scheme to kill her and get the reward won't work, Allegra wisecracks: "Don't you ever go to the fuckin' movies?" To which he responds, "I like your script. I want to be in it."

The film taps into viewers' familiarity with interactive game

FIGURE 6. *Ted at the mutant trout farm after the cutaway from a passionate caress in* eXistenZ.

environments both to engage and to establish a certain degree of stable orientation within the strange film world. But the mode of representation remains moored to cinema, and this generates an alienating disorientation. The editing required to transition between the different game environments disrupts classical continuity even as it signals a shift in the diegetic setting. When Allegra and Ted plug into *eXistenZ* for the first time, the scene shifts from the base diegetic reality (which we later find out is also a game reality) to a media store that exists in the game. This occurs via a cut from an astonished look on Ted's face to a subjective shot of the new environment that surrounds him. When the film cuts to what he sees, the viewer too is suddenly transported from the diegetic real world of the film to the simulated game environment. Ted's first words once he has collected himself, "That was beautiful," expresses the wonder that the viewer is supposed to feel when experiencing the ambient image of the new cinema. As he continues to express his amazement, his reaction suggests that this kind of novel shift between scenes frees up the viewer/participant from the more artificial constructions of reality typical of classical cinema: "I feel . . . just like me. Is that kind of transition normal, a kind of smooth dissolve from place to place?" Allegra's description of the techniques she employs in *eXistenZ* alludes to the expanded repertoire of transitions in digital cinema: "Depends on the style of the game. You can get jagged, brutal cuts, slow fades, shimmering little morphs." While such transitions disrupt the continuity produced by classical decoupage editing, the fluid navigation that is described here and occurs throughout the film seeks to produce, as Ted remarks, something more akin to the reality of lived experience.

However, this effect never materializes. Cronenberg employs the intermedial status of the digital image to interweave cinematic representation with virtual reality game simulations in a convincing but also disturbing fashion. When the final shot of the film suggests that the supposed return to a base diegetic reality might be just another game environment, the viewer's disorientation is more unsettling. In this way, the question of the potential inability to distinguish between simulation and reality applies not only to new, more sophisticated virtual reality technologies, but it extends as well to the representations of reality produced by the digitally enhanced cinematic image. In the end the viewer is left not only distrusting the simulated realities of both virtual reality games and narrative cinema, but also experiencing the disorientation as a blanket inability of both to generate an experience of reality that is grounded in an embodied past.

In Josef Rusnak's *The Thirteenth Floor* an unexpected final twist draws similar associations between digital simulation and cinematic representation. As in Amenábar's *Open Your Eyes*, the simulation is a commercial product with the potential to generate enormous profits. A multi-billion-dollar corporation, Thirteenth Floor, has created a virtual reality simulation of 1937 Los Angeles. When owner Hannon Fuller (Armin Mueller-Stahl) is murdered just as testing starts on the program, his protégé Douglas Hall (Craig Bierko) becomes the main suspect. Hall begins to question his own innocence and transports himself into the program's simulation in search of answers. The film takes us with him back into the world of 1937 Los Angeles, which appears to be more a creation of classical cinema than a realistic representation of life at the time. The locations, the settings, the characters, the action, all have the look and feel of a film about that historical period.

Given that the simulation is presented to us through the moving images of narrative film, it is not surprising that it replicates our cinematic vision of the period. However, the link between the computer simulations in the movie and the reality of mainstream film narrative becomes more substantial when Hall discovers that his own world of late 1990s Los Angeles is also an artificial reality. Until this point, the viewer, in keeping with the tacit understanding expected of the film viewer, has accepted the contemporary setting of 1990s Los Angeles as the base diegetic reality for the film. When the viewer (along with the protagonist) discovers through a dramatic visual reveal that this base reality is itself a computer simulation, the result is a pervasive uncertainty that causes us to question not only what is real in the film world, but also the very status of cinematic representation.

This uncertainty is taken a step further at the end of the film when the creator of the Thirteenth Floor corporation, David (also Craig Bierko), is killed while inhabiting Hall's body in the construct of 1997 Los Angeles. As a result, Hall's consciousness is uploaded into David's body in the year 2024. For the first time the film moves into this future world that the viewer now discovers is the base diegetic reality of the narrative. Jane Fuller (Gretchen Mol), Hannon Fuller's daughter with whom Hall has become romantically involved, reveals that he was created as a simulant and that her husband David began downloading his consciousness into his body so that he could use the simulation to kill people for pleasure. Coming to terms with the nature of his existence, Hall asks, "What do you mean? I'm not even real. You can fall in love with a dream?" Her response resonates like a line from a Hollywood love story: "You're more real to me than anything I've ever known." The dialogue and the glamorized setting of this scene, shaded in a sepia tone reminiscent of classical cinema, mark it as the happy ending of a romanticized Hollywood movie. This highly stylized ending summons up unresolved questions that have surfaced throughout the film and been lurking stubbornly as an obstacle to the expected cinematic denouement. The final shot then pulls the plug, quite literally, on this scenario. The film ends with the image collapsing as if a computer had crashed. It seems that the world of 2024 Los Angeles may be just another virtual construct like those of 1937 and 1997. As in the presentation of the Los Angeles of the past and present, this future milieu appears as a cinematically inflected film world and not the representation of a reality that could serve as the diegetic present of the film. What may seem on the surface like a restabilization of the real reveals itself to be a self-reflexive representation of cinematic reality as a virtual simulation.[2]

Like *eXistenZ, The Thirteenth Floor* clouds the distinction between virtual simulation and diegetic reality in order to highlight the overlap between cinema and digital media. Hall seems unsure of himself as he joins Jane in the future and sees her father walking along the beach with his dog. As he waves to his daughter and tells her that both he and the dog are getting hungry for lunch, the scene gives a sense that they live a benign, almost idyllic life together in this world in the future. When Hall recognizes him as Fuller, who had transferred his consciousness back to 1937 Los Angeles so that he could have sex with showgirls, he looks puzzled and unsettled. Jane tells him reassuringly, "My father. Fuller was modeled after him," and then adds in the last line of the film, "There are so many

FIGURE 7. *Jane's father Fuller, walking his dog along the beach in the final scene of* The Thirteenth Floor.

FIGURE 8. *The final, romanticized shot of Jane and Douglas Hall in the futuristic Los Angeles of 2024 in* The Thirteenth Floor.

things I need to tell you about, Doug." He smiles, apparently beginning to accept that he has escaped from the virtual constructs of the two earlier periods and is now firmly planted in reality, together with the woman he loves. The idyllic depiction of her relationship with her father and the dreamy, romantic tone of her voice tend to suggest that this might not be true. The scene plays out against the backdrop of a postmodern Los Angeles cityscape whose buildings seem not merely futuristic, but even imaginary. This is particularly true in the last shot that frames Hall and Jane from the side. The image is cast in an unnatural hazy brown hue, such that the strip of beach and buildings behind them appear almost like a painted backdrop. The viewer is probably already, at least subconsciously, beginning to wonder whether what Jane will tell Hall might be just another level of deception, when the image collapses like a computer screen going blank. The film clearly raises doubts about the ostensible return to a stable reality as it fails to offer any indication that humanity will learn to hold onto the best of the old culture that is passing and integrate it with the new digital world in a harmonious transition. Nonetheless, the two do merge de facto in the film. As this happens within a science-fiction scenario that casts doubt upon our ability to control the fast-expanding potential of virtual reality media, the transparent conclusion is that this is the new reality and that the transition to it will require finding the right path to negotiate between the old and the new.

Digital Mediations of Movement, Space, and Time

The constantly shifting, never certain status of the diegetic film world can disorient the viewer, but it also activates sensorimotor circuits in the attempt to reestablish spatial orientation. Moments of kinesthetic intensity, usually produced via digital effects, serve to transport the viewer along with the film characters from one world into another. The first transitions across time periods, whether it is between different life experiences (*Open Your Eyes*), from virtual to real environments (*eXistenZ*, *The Matrix*), or from mind-control to autonomy (*Dark City*), usually involve particularly strong, jolting action. In *The Thirteenth Floor* the transference of consciousness from one period to the other is represented by wild flashes of amorphous patterns of blue light accompanied by piercing acoustic effects. The most striking example of such transitions is the scene in *The Matrix* where Neo (Keanu Reeves) is freed from the pod and thrust into the conflict between humans and machines. When Morpheus (Laurence Fishburne) accompanies Neo into the construct to show the Matrix to him, they first strap him into a reclining chair that looks like a beat-up retro version of something one might find in a dentist's office. But here it stands in for the seat in a movie theater, where one puts the sensorimotor system into stop-action mode and becomes immersed in the stream of images moving across the movie screen. Neo is extracted from his pod in a violent series of audiovisual effects that in the diegetic reality of the film return his body to the real world.

As the protagonists in these films become more adept at negotiating the transit between different realms the scenes become less frenzied. The viewer, who like Neo is accustomed to sitting passively, is drawn along with the protagonist into more embodied

FIGURE 9. *The beat-up dentist chair in which Neo is strapped when he is extracted from the Matrix.*

involvement with the simulated screen world. These films put their audience through a form of training analogous to that which is enabling the screen characters to negotiate the simulated worlds confronting them. At the end of *Open Your Eyes* the parallel strands of physical *Bildung* converge in dramatic fashion. When César declines the chance to have his virtual life restarted in the year 2045 as an ideal existence and leaps instead off the skyscraper, the screen goes black when he hits the ground. The words of the gentle female voiceover, "Relax, relax. Open your eyes," are intended to soothe not only César but also the viewer, who, much like Neo, has been shaken out of the hypnotic trance of classical spectatorship. But neither is returned to the reality that existed before the transformative events that have transpired in the course of the film. Rather, the calming moment is the prelude to the challenges ahead where it will be necessary to recognize and adapt to new forms of mediation between the human organism and advanced technologies.

The shift to a fluid diegetic environment that promotes embodied spectatorship had begun well before the development of digital imaging. There were pronounced signs of it already at the beginning of postclassical Hollywood cinema in the late 1960s. Scenes that produced new and more powerful kinesthetic effects in the viewer played a prominent role in the success of some of the major blockbusters of that time. The use of quick-cut editing, unusual camera angles, and slow motion in scenes depicting graphic violence, as in

The Wild Bunch (Sam Peckinpah, 1969) and *Bonnie and Clyde* (Arthur Penn, 1967), produced a new kind of physical response in the spectator. The long take with a telephoto lens of Dustin Hoffman running toward the church in the climactic scene of *The Graduate* (Mike Nichols, 1967) activated other sensorimotor systems. The scene that created perhaps the strongest sensation among the film public was the classic chase scene through the hilly streets of San Francisco in *Bullitt* (Peter Yates, 1968). The camera was positioned so as to simulate the viewer's presence in the passenger seat of each car. Functioning as an invisible avatar that moves within the cognitively mapped space of the film world, the virtual embedded viewer serves as a conduit through which the physical sensation is conveyed to the body in the movie theater. The cars flying through the air as they speed up and down the hills of San Francisco produce a kinesthetic effect that is felt in the stomach of the spectator. This novel form of physical engagement with the cinematic image created a buzz among the movie-going public at the time that contributed to the film's box-office success. And according to online surveys, this sequence still remains the most popular car chase on film by a wide margin.[3]

In contemporary cinema, digital imaging generates more active participation in cinematic space and movement. In keeping with the way digital technology has altered how we orient ourselves spatially in the real world, action in movies does not take place in a coherent diegetic space. As a consequence, the invisible avatar of the viewer is not able to assume a situated, stable point of view within the scene. There is rather a constant flux of unanchored positions, a dynamic flow in which space itself moves, bends, and morphs into various forms. The action exceeds the limits of the frame in new ways, disrupting the traditional clear division of space into on-screen and offscreen. This happens in *Dark City* in the three scenes where John Murdoch (Rufus Sewell) faces the Strangers in battle. To elude and then eventually defeat them he must engage them in their own realm of experience rather than the one they have created for their human captives. In the world created by the Strangers the spatial structures that define human existence no longer hold. The diegetic space of the three scenes becomes successively more fluid as the intensity of the struggle and the kinetic energy generated by the movement in and of the frame increases. The first one plays out during the time when the humans are awake. But the confrontation takes place up on the billboard of Shell Beach alongside the outside wall of a building. It is as if Murdoch and his three attackers are suspended in mid-air, set apart from the simulated world that everyone else inhabits. When one of the Strangers falls through the planks of the walkway, we do not see him fall to the ground, but rather he seems to keep falling as if he were being catapulted out into space. The second clash occurs during the time when the other humans have been rendered unconscious. It too occurs high up above the ground among tall buildings. Because the Strangers are "tuning" the city into a different construct in these off hours, the buildings are changing shape while they fight, and Murdoch must negotiate a space that defies the natural laws of our reality as well as the principles of spatial continuity that define traditional film narrative. In the final scene Murdoch takes on the leader of the Strangers at the center of their world in a final battle for control of the Dark City. There is little directional or spatial orientation throughout the scene. It is staged as a contest between the opponents' mental abilities to overcome all physical laws and create the world around them by force of will. Digital special effects are employed to depict a physical environment that is like nothing we have experienced and that, above all else, resists any attempt to grasp it in terms of conventional spatial cognition.

The ambient image in *Dark City* produces a visual surround effect analogous to the aural effect enabled by surround sound. Together, they create an all-around audiovisual world that overturns the conventional mode of reception in which the audience watches a visual text play itself out on the flat screen in front of it. As Sean Cubitt has noted with respect to spectacle films of this period, "To control such chaos, characters gifted with a kind of spatial omnivoyance or extended proprioception populate narratives from *Desperado* (1995) to *Daredevil* (2003)" (2009, 52). The Bullet Time scene in *The Matrix* exemplifies this. When Agent Smith (Hugo Weaving) attacks Neo on the rooftop, the camera pans 360 degrees around him as he bends his body in super-slow motion to avoid the bullets. He achieves an omnivoyance that enables him to see everything around him rather than what the machines dictate he see. The viewer is neither aligned physically with Neo in this fight scene nor merely looking into the diegetic space of the film, but rather has the bodily sensation of occupying that world. The viewer becomes embedded in the scene as an avatar that has the same ability as Neo to bend space and change the time-force of moving objects. While cranes and the Steadicam enable filmmakers to enact human movement more fluidly and extend it through engineering technology, digital imaging functions to place the spectator at the center of a space open to full bodily experience rather than just audiovisual perception. Endowed with an imaginary body schema within the simulated reality of the matrix, the viewer actually experiences the sensorimotor impulses associated with Neo's action, rather than merely watching it being performed through the, in Deleuze's terminology, classical *movement-image.*

Films that employ special effects in this way also deploy digitally enhanced audio to disrupt the spectatorial orientation of the film viewer. Intensified sound works in conjunction with the digitally altered or created image to undermine the audiovisual unity of classical diegesis from within. The soundtrack bombards the audience from all sides with sounds that penetrate the body and produce a more corporeal mode of perception. Dolby digital technology accentuates the movement of sound through time and space in a way that gives it autonomy from the narrative. Exploiting sonic velocity as a "spectacle" in its own right, the contemporary action film disconnects sound from the image and employs its ability to

FIGURE 10. *Neo dodging bullets in the Bullet Time scene in* The Matrix.

penetrate the body as a cinematic effect (Sobchack 2005, 11–12; Dyson, 74–75). Employing surround-sound technology, spectacle films situate the spectator in the middle of the scene rather than as a distanced observer looking on from outside the imaginary fourth wall between the audience and the narrative space of the film world. Devoid of realistic sound perspective and visual contact with their source, these aural "images" leave the viewer groping for spatial orientation according to a new virtual body schema. Physically activated by this effect, the viewer responds to the diegetic world of the film in a more interactive embodied manner. As a result, the aesthetic sensibility that regards traditional film narratives as texts is replaced by a bodily engagement with incongruous stimuli that require multilayered sensorimotor and affective processing before they can be incorporated into a narrative context.

Even when acoustic elements are synchronized with onscreen events, they still often produce more complex forms of embodied engagement with the film image. For example, in the gun battle in the lobby of the hotel between Neo and Trinity (Carrie-Anne Moss) and a large police force there is a steady stream of loud sounds that are synchronized to the firing of the weapons, the bullets striking and tearing off chunks of the walls, and objects falling onto the hard surface of the floor. The scene plays out in a combination of regular-speed and slow-motion shots. The slowed speed of the action is necessary in part to enable the synchronization of the distinct sounds with the corresponding images. By maintaining this coordination between the audio and visual elements, the filmmakers are able to generate a richer synesthetic response to the action than would have been possible if the sounds had merely merged indiscriminately into a cacophony of overwhelming noise. As a result, perhaps the most effective moments in the scene are the two brief slow-motion shots of empty bullet cases hitting and bouncing off the floor. The momentary synchronization of the visual shot of the bullet cases with the clinking metallic sound of them hitting the floor endows the scene with an unnatural perceptual precision. The effect is to accentuate the body's attunement to the haptic force of the audiovisual image and to enhance a kinesthetic perception that folds input from the various senses into the viewing experience.

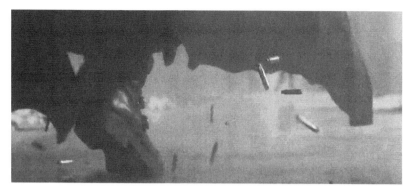

FIGURE 11. *Bullet casings bouncing off the floor in a slow-motion sequence from the lobby shootout in* The Matrix.

As a digitally enhanced cinema engages the sensorimotor systems more actively, it also promotes corresponding changes at the cognitive level. At both the microlevel of physical interaction with new technologies and the macrolevel of the conceptual grasp of these systems, cinema manifests the deep structural shifts occurring as digital technologies exert their influence throughout all areas of modern culture. This has engendered new ways of imagining virtual space and changed both how we conceive of space and how we orient ourselves in it. The result is a new hybrid conception that is constructed jointly on the basis of experience in digital media and in real, physical environments (Clark 2010, 14). Digital imaging serves as a powerful device that enables filmmakers to adapt film space to the hybrid construct formed by the convergence of physical and digital environments outside the theater. This happens both with respect to the abstract space that encapsulates the film as a whole, the space of diegesis, and the diegetic space that determines orientation and movement within a scene.

The adaptation to digitized culture at these two levels of spatial orientation are integrally linked. Theories about the relation between space and thought in such diverse fields as art criticism, linguistics, and cognitive science have contributed to a multidimensional picture of how subphenomenal processes alter spatial cognition. In his study of visual thinking in the graphic arts Rudolf Arnheim claims that the basic imagery produced by shape and motion form the primary medium in which thinking occurs. The body's rapid production of spatial perception as a result of movement is according to Arnheim an essential element of all abstract thought, which cannot be sustained purely on the basis of logical relations between semantic units (Arnheim, 118; Preston, 297–99). Lakoff and Johnson's work on metaphor (1980) supports Arnheim's thesis. They argue that the abstract relations expressed in metaphor depend on embodied experience that is structured according to movement and space. More recently, experiments in cognitive science have shown that the way the body orients itself toward objects around it in space serves as a relational model for how the mind combines cognitive contents (Spivey et al., 28; Smith and Samuelson). When applied to film viewing, these studies suggest that kinesthetic and proprioceptive elements that alter how cinema produces spatial orientation will effect changes in spatial cognition as well.

In the above examples from 1990s sci-fi films, the kinetic movement of bodies between different simulations and alternate realities happens within an alternatively constructed film world. In these movies, individual scenes fit into the space of diegesis more like entries in an archive than pieces of a narrative. This reflects the broader epistemic shift that is taking place in a computerized culture where we have fast access to a vast array of data that are detached from any larger meaningful context. In the digital age, the creation of a narrative media object, regardless of whether it is linear or interactive, involves constructing one or more interfaces to an underlying database (Manovich 2001, 228). As a result, our conceptions of space are less Euclidean. With respect to the abstract space that envelops the film as a whole, movies structured in this manner lack the kind of "coherent synthetic geography" (Gunning 1990, 91) that has been a hallmark of classical cinema. For example, in *Open Your Eyes* we have no sense of where the various sites in the film, such as the Life Extension headquarters, the clinic that performs the plastic surgery, or the prison hospital, are located in relation to each other. In *Dark City* the architecture of the city is "retuned" every night, such that there is no spatially fixed world. In keeping with this aspect of the plot, Proyas employs aesthetic means to stifle any sense of a consistent, logical relation between the various locations in the city. In *The Thirteenth Floor* the mercurial structure of the narrative space corresponds to the limitations of the computer program that generates the simulated encapsulations of 1937 or 1997 Los Angeles. Its computer power can generate isolated scenes within these simulated realities, but cannot produce a full picture of those worlds or define how all these individual scenes and moments relate to each other within such a whole. The same limitation and corresponding mode of cinematic representation apply to the simulations in *The Matrix* and the virtual reality scenarios in *eXistenZ*. What Cubitt has said about films from this period that assimilate to the digital model applies in each of these cases. They "only appear to be narrative. In fact, they are the result of one of many possible rifles through a database of narrative events whose coincidence is more structural or even architectural than temporal" (2004, 238).

There are events in these films that allude directly to the way the unity of classical cinema limits the spatial imaginary and hinders our assimilation to the hybrid space-time continuum of digitized culture. This happens in dramatic fashion in *The Thirteenth Floor*. As the computer-generated realities of other time periods stand in on one level for classical cinematic representation, they also offer a commentary on its construction of filmic space. Jerry Ashton (Vincent D'Onofrio), a simulant bartender in the virtual reality simulation of 1937 Los Angeles, discovers that he is part of an artificial existence. To confirm this, he begins driving toward Tucson. As he drives through the desert outside of Los Angeles, he is soon alone, encountering no other cars or life of any kind. He speeds past "Road Ends" signs and busts through barricades until he finally stops the car, climbs out, and stares at something that, as he says in describing the experience to Hall, "scares [him] to the depths of [his] miserable soul." The viewer is left to imagine what that is as the film cuts away from the scene after the shot of his horror-stricken face, without offering the point-of-view shot of what he sees. Only later, when Hall begins to suspect that the 1997 world he inhabits is also a virtual reality simulation, does the film give us the subjective shot of what Ashton saw. Hall drives out into the desert east of Los Angeles, in this case at night, ignoring similar road signs and crashing through barriers. When he stops and gets out, we see a comparable expression on his face, followed by a shot from behind him. In front of him, the virtual reality world of the desert gives way to phosphorescent green lines of an irregular grid stretching into the void ahead. Signaling the end of the computer simulation, where the program is no longer able to produce the images needed to sustain the virtual reality environment, this image not only marks the limits of even the most advanced media technology but also brings into question the conception of space on which cinema and the virtual reality technologies that channel the cinematic image are founded.

Dark City expresses this idea in a similar fashion. Murdoch, in his attempts to go to the coastal town of Shell Beach, also hits up against the boundaries of the simulated world created by the Strangers. In this case it is not a computer simulation but rather a more traditional science-fiction version of an alternative world: a microcosmic section of a large city created by the Strangers on a giant spacecraft or small planetoid. When Murdoch, Dr. Schreber (Kiefer Sutherland), and Inspector Bumstead (William Hurt)

FIGURE 12. *Douglas Hall staring out into the cyber grid that lies beyond the computer simulation of 1997 Los Angeles in* The Thirteenth Floor.

FIGURE 13. *John Murdoch and Inspector Bumstead staring out into space after breaking through the wall at the edge of the Dark City.*

take a boat through the canals of the Dark City in the direction of Shell Beach they end up at a door. Murdoch opens it only to find that it leads to a wall with the billboard picture of Shell Beach plastered on it. Against Schreber's warnings he and Bumstead rip off the picture and then use iron rods to break through the brick wall. It opens into the dark expanse of outer space. This scene, like its counterpart in *The Thirteenth Floor,* reflects how conventional narrative cinema establishes a self-contained space that encompasses all the locations involved in the film. By referencing it in this way, both films highlight the limitations inherent in this conception of space. Once he has defeated the Strangers, Murdoch is able to create his own alternative world that he wants to inhabit. This requires that he discover a new spatial imaginary, and that the filmmaker find a way to produce it cinematically. In terms of diegetic space, this is achieved when Murdoch, after having defeated the Strangers, opens the same door again, and this time it opens up to a flood of blinding sunlight and a pier that leads out into a vast ocean. Emma Murdoch (Jennifer Connelly), now named Anna, is standing out at the end of the pier, and Murdoch walks out to join her. His departure from the world to which he had been confined defies normal spatial logic. The ocean stretches in all directions out from the world he has left behind, seemingly endlessly. Just as the diegetic space of this scene remains undefined, the space of diegesis for the new life on which he is about to embark is also left open to the imagination. When he asks Anna whether she knows if Shell Beach is nearby, she replies, "I think that's it, just over there," and points to a nondescript strip of land jutting out into the ocean, with a lone lighthouse standing at its point.

Murdoch's ability to escape the Dark City and imagine a whole new Shell Beach is figured here as a break from both the conventional diegetic space and space of diegesis of classical cinema. Moreover, whether the creation of an advanced alien culture, as in *Dark City*, or a computer simulation, as in the other examples, the simulated reality is in essence a cinematic artifact. As such, the associated limitations allude to the notion of reality that has informed cinema's push to produce a consummate diegetic film world, questioning the idea that reality exists out in the world, separate from our embodied lived experience as a consistent, unitary entity that is accessible to everyone. They suggest that the traditional visual orientation to an outside world, the renaissance perspective figured as looking onto the world through a window, no longer configures our spatial experience in the age of digital media. The alternative construction in these films is a prosthetic extension of bodily patterns of spatial cognition that have evolved in response to a digitized cultural environment.

Just as space is no longer closed and self-contained in these films, new modes of temporality also emerge. The temporal structure becomes disjointed to the point that it is often impossible to establish a chronological timeline. Classical cinema employs various devices to break up narrative continuity (flashbacks, flashforwards, narrative frames, among others), but in most cases it offers clear markers that enable the viewer to put the events in chronological order. These temporal deviations are usually grounded in a consistent overall pattern that gathers all the various strands into a consecutively ordered narrative. This is not the case in the films I have been analyzing here. In *Open Your Eyes* César ultimately chooses his own life history over the Clause 14 existence that has freed him up from the time frames that define a human life. However, when he decides to leave the virtual reality that Life Extension enables him to create for himself, he is not returned to the same point in time where he was rendered unconscious and began his virtual life. César is empowered to create the world that he wants without being hindered by our normal construct of time. In the end, it remains unclear exactly how his experiences may fit into a logical timeline. Rather than being stymied by the jumbled temporal structure of these films, the characters are able to move fluidly between the disjointed time periods. In *The Thirteenth Floor* the viewer follows Hall as he moves back and forth between 1937 and 1997 Los Angeles, and then eventually into the year 2024. These passages occur smoothly, even though there is no temporally linked cause-and-effect relation between the events in the three time periods, and actions in one can sometimes lead to the displacement of an individual's consciousness into another time period. Instead of fitting into a chronological sequence, the various time periods are organized according to the same structural principle that establishes the space of diegesis. They too can be accessed almost arbitrarily, like individual entries pulled up from an archive, without concern for how they fit into a timeline.

As these films disrupt the structured temporal progression of narrative cinema, they enlist the viewer in the construction of an alternative reality that seeks out its own rules for ordering space and time. The most dramatic instance of this occurs in *The Matrix*. In the fight on the roof between Agent Smith and Neo the filmmakers employ time-slice special effects to show Neo speeding up his movement so as to be able to dodge the bullets fired at him by Smith. Simulating the effects of real camera movement and slow-motion filming through computer-generated imaging, they are able to have the camera move around Neo (virtually) at a normal speed, while the bullets are slowed to the point that we can watch them fly past Neo as he twists his body to avoid being hit. The effect produces a radical transformation of the time-space continuum as it is constituted by the objects onscreen. The novelty of the technique is due in part to the way it alters spatial and temporal orientation simultaneously in a coordinated manner, with one (the movement of the camera-eye through space) acting to speed up the action and the other (the slow-motion capture of the bullets) slowing it down. The scene affected the movie public in a manner much like the car chase in *Bullitt* some forty years earlier. Whereas the buzz created by the kinesthetic effect of the ride through the hilly streets of San Francisco as a virtual passenger in the speeding cars spread primarily by word of mouth, Bullet Time had its own afterlife coursing through the digital media environment. Its fame became so widespread that Warner Brothers registered the name as a trademark in connection with its Matrix video game. In both cases, the departure from classical cinematography produced a kinesthetic effect that altered film spectatorship significantly.

The Bullet Time scene in *The Matrix* represents of course a more radical break with classical spectatorship. The embodied action of Bullet Time disrupts the cinematographic boundaries of Hollywood narrative both onscreen and in the viewer, resulting in "the synaesthetic convergence of all our modalities of perception in a conjoined space-time of real, surrogate and virtual formations" (Shaw, 268). As opposed to Deleuze's concept of the time-image, where the viewer is a distanced, reflective viewer of a crystalline moment in time, here the spectator becomes caught up in the vacillating and dynamic flux of time, even when it is slowed or stilled. If the time-image replaced the focus on sequential sensorimotor action in classical cinema (the movement-image), then fully immersed embodied experience is the new register in the digital age. In this sense, Bullet Time is not merely a spectacular CGI attraction, but rather a special effect that "exposes itself as a paradigmatic form of a digital, post-cinematic media regime" (Sudmann, 304). If we take the Matrix to be a metaphor for cinema, we are watching Neo break out of the boundaries of classical cinematography both literally and figuratively. His escape from a fixed position within the Matrix to one of active production of his own reality transfers then to the spectator. As Neo and the protagonists from the other films discussed in this chapter adapt to being transported paranormally across gaps in time and space, the viewer is released from the ocularcentric spectatorship of classical cinema and adjusts to an alternative construction of the cinematic space-time continuum.

Cinema in the digital era has begun to reveal how the continuity of classical cinema is grounded in fixed, a priori conceptions of space and time. Set in a Cartesian relation to the film world, the viewing subject is detached from the spatially contained film world and partakes of it temporally through the narratively structured journey whose completion is already incorporated into it at the outset. This obscures the fact that time and space are technologies that humankind has created to help us navigate the more complex social, cultural, and material environments we inhabit. This is perhaps more obvious with respect to time. Devices such as the calendar and the clock clearly facilitate the imposing of a manmade grid onto the amorphous temporal nature of existence. An even more obvious example is the alarm clock, which helps us attune our biological rhythms to the needs and demands of a highly technocratic social system. Similarly, the concept of space is a technology used in the art of cartography and more recently in visually enhanced applications such as Google Earth to enable more effective and complex collection and transmission of spatial information.

The fracturing of temporal continuity and the setting of space in motion in digitized cinema reveal how these basic constructs for organizing experience are undergoing a radical transformation. At the conceptual level, the overarching arrangement of the spatial and temporal elements of the plot reflects how changes in the way we store and access knowledge in the world are altering both our individual and collective lives in essential ways. When these conventional constructs are upended, the equilibrium that normally forms among the senses and motor systems during film viewing is also disrupted. In response, kinesthetic, proprioceptive, and other sensorimotor systems that produce spatial awareness and cognition become activated to reestablish orientation. As a result, the new aesthetic of the digital image shuffles and restructures the bodily systems that have been extended prosthetically into culture to create our concepts of space and time. The potential for many different forms of experience is unleashed, and even if there is a natural tendency to restore the operations that were in place before the disturbance, different neural circuits are activated in the brain and new modes of spectatorship take effect.

As cinema patterns film space and time after dramatic new forms of experience in the digital age and activates sensorimotor circuits accordingly, this promotes our adaptation to the increasingly hybrid forms of structuring our bodily interaction with the world across biological and inorganic technological systems. In this respect, the Bullet Time sequence employs digital imaging differently than the more disruptive style that has been called chaos cinema.

Rather than outstripping phenomenal perception more entirely, as in the chaotic action scenes of a Michael Bay movie where the viewer can no longer discern discrete objects in the image (Denson 2016, 210–11; Shaviro 2016a, 52–56), the scene in *The Matrix* requires that the viewer adapt to different spatiotemporal structures of perception to establish continuity. It is also in this regard that one could echo Manovich's assertion that the creation of the digital moving image is a "teleological development that replays the emergence of cinema a century earlier" (1995, 186). That is, just as the film image served to adapt the sensorimotor networks of the early twentieth-century urban dweller to a faster, more highly mechanized modern culture, the digital cinematic image promotes adaptation to a new cultural environment where our lived experience is mediated extensively via digital technology.

Cinema and Singular Consciousness

These cyberspace thrillers from the end of the millennium address ambivalent feelings associated with the growing imbrication of the biological human and technology. Their visions of digital technology's potential to merge with human intelligence stir anxieties about humankind's ability to manage its own destiny, but they also give rise to feelings of transcendence. In the age of cyborgs, the traditional notion of the integrity of each human individual as an intact biological organism that cannot be penetrated by inorganic material systems had begun to lose its hold. As Hollywood cinema has turned increasingly to digital imaging, it has produced science-fiction films that fantasize about information technologies becoming self-propagating and culminating in the total digitization of the human mind/body. On the one hand, this leads to utopian ideas about a futuristic existence where the posthuman subject will be able to dispense with the body altogether. On the other hand, it gives rise to apocalyptic scenarios of alien intruders who completely supplant consciousness with an externally fabricated mental construct and relegate humans to a "body-in-the-vat" existence. This cultural ambivalence about the notion of technological determinism finds expression around the concept of singularity. Those who predict that the increasingly accelerated rate of technological development will continue to the point that machine intelligence overtakes human intelligence see it alternatively as transcendent expansion of the human or as an unpredictable end to the human era with possibly apocalyptic consequences. Before theoretical mathematical and systems models gave birth to predictions of an inevitable progression to a fusion of biological and nonbiological intelligence, McLuhan expressed a similar ambivalence about human coevolution with technology. In *Understanding Media* he speculated rather optimistically about the power of information technology to unify humankind: a "current translation of our entire lives into the spiritual form of information" might "make of the entire globe, and of the human family, a single consciousness" ([1964] 1994, 61). In his later writings, he backtracked from this enthused speculation and offered warnings about what could befall humanity if it fails to negotiate the perils of digital technology and pursues an artificial intelligence that is not grounded in the body.

Two of the films I discuss, *The Matrix* and *Dark City*, explore the question of singularity with respect to the effects digital technology is having on lived experience and postcinematic spectatorship. In *The Matrix* Morpheus explains to Neo that the machines are set off from humankind because they derive from and operate according to a "singular consciousness." The lack of interference from fragmented affective impulses and memories that punctuate individual subjectivity makes the uniform, collective knowledge— the artificial intelligence that spawned the new race of machines— more powerful than human intelligence and consciousness. They are able to turn humans' imperfect vision of the world, distorted by our inability to disengage from the past, into a prison to occupy the minds of those whose bodies are kept alive in vats to supply the machines with the small amount of electrical energy they need to function. The computer-generated world they now experience is a neural-interactive simulation modeled after the "peak of human civilization" at the end of the twentieth century. By having the Matrix replicate contemporary America, the film taps into the audience's anxiety that digital technology will soon be able to supplant our actual experiences with virtual ones. *Dark City* is also set in a dystopian future where foreign elements have used their superior intelligence to take control of the human race.

An endangered alien civilization has made earth's inhabitants the subject of a grand experiment they believe can help them stave off extinction. Analogous to the singular consciousness that defines the machine culture in *The Matrix,* the Strangers come from an advanced civilization that has only collective experience. Their technological mediation of information has advanced to the point that their civilization has eradicated all memories deriving from individual embodied experience. As Mr. Book (Ian Richardson), the leader of the Strangers, boasts to Schreber, this gives them an enormous advantage over humans: "It would take several of your lifetimes to master our gifts." And yet theirs is a dying civilization, doomed to fail in its attempt to survive by extracting from humans the secret to their existence.

Ultimately, in designing their experiment to study the human soul the Strangers were undone by humanity's own self-mythologizing. When explaining Murdoch's adaptation to Mr. Book, Schreber taunts him derisively: "Weren't you looking for the human soul? . . . Maybe you have finally found what you were looking for, and it is going to bite you on your . . ." In the final exchange with the Strangers, Murdoch makes this point in another way. Mr. Hand (Richard O'Brien), who had been imprinted with Murdoch's memories in a failed attempt to learn what it means to be human, says: "Your imprint was not compatible with my kind. But I wanted to know what it was like, how you feel." Murdoch responds: "You wanted to know what it was about us that made us human. Well, you're not going to find it in here. You went looking in the wrong place." Tellingly, Murdoch does not point to the side of his head, the customary gesture to signify the mind or intellect. Nor does he follow with the customary gesture of pointing to his chest to make the distinction between the head and the heart. Rather by pointing to his forehead he singles out the frontal cortex, the cerebral home of cognition and abstract knowledge, as opposed to the body as a whole that reacts physically to changes in the environment and adapts accordingly.

Dark City frames its depiction of an information culture where the proliferation of data flows threatens to spin out of control as a postmodern version of the Faust legend. The ambivalence expressed about the Enlightenment push toward universal collective

FIGURE 14. *John Murdoch in* Dark City: *"You're not going to find it in here. You went looking in the wrong place."*

knowledge in Goethe's *Faust* is here applied to the ability to archive and manipulate information through digital technology. As the obsessed scientist who understands "the intricacies of the human mind better than they [the Strangers] ever could," Schreber correlates to Goethe's Mephisto. As he implants the knowledge into Murdoch that will enable him to defeat the Strangers, he urges him to seize the opportunity and create the world according to his own vision. Drawing associations with Faust's romantic episode with Gretchen, he admonishes: "There is no time for romance, John. The world can be what you make it. You have the power to make anything happen. But you must act now." Schreber expects Murdoch to use the knowledge he has given him to create a simulated world of his own making, replacing what the Strangers had implanted in humans with another set of collective, shared memories that would define their existence. But rather than replace the Dark City with his own alternative reality, Murdoch opts to fashion a life for himself that is founded on the only personal memories he possesses. He accepts those created for him by the Strangers as his own and tunes a simulated version of Shell Beach where he can live a life informed by those memories. Like César in *Open Your Eyes,* Murdoch realizes that to be fulfilling, an assumed reality must be grounded in individual experience and memory, even if they are synthetic. A singular consciousness for all the inhabitants of Dark City cannot provide this essential dimension of reality, even if it is created by a benevolent fellow human rather than the oppressive Strangers. Prosthetic memories, on the other hand, do not pose a problem for Murdoch. In the context of the science-fiction story of *Dark City* they are his only option, and in the era of proliferating media they comprise an ever-growing portion of the explicit, embodied memory that constitutes the narrative self (Landsberg, 18–21, 28–32).

Murdoch's choice indicates that he has come to accept the hybrid nature of the human in a culture where our sensorium must constantly adapt to new forms of mediation between the body and the external environment. Throughout this book I have stressed the ever-expanding reciprocal agency of the biological and the technological. The previous section examined how the construction of space in digitized cinema reflects the confluence of physical and digital environments throughout contemporary culture. Chapter 1 explored how the different temporal modes of processing in computer technology (fast material processing by the hardware/slower analytical processing by software in the CPU) correspond to the dual temporalities in the body (faster sensorimotor processing/slower cognitive operations). In highlighting the failures of the Strangers, *Dark City* suggests how this hybridity exists across all areas of intersection between the biological human and the information technologies we have created. Their more advanced civilization relied completely on the accelerated flow of information that has enabled them to master knowledge more extensively and to gain powers ("gifts," as Mr. Book calls them) unavailable to humans. In doing so, however, they fell prey to the notion that the data that empowers their existence is available to them immediately, that is, it is immaterial and not linked to any physical media. The warnings that McLuhan issued in his later writings would have served the Strangers well: "As he sits in the informational control room, whether at home or at work, receiving data at enormous speeds—imagistic, sound, or tactile—from all areas of the world, the results could be dangerously inflating and schizophrenic. His body will remain in one place but his mind will float out into the electronic void, being everywhere at once in the data bank" (McLuhan and Powers, 97). The failure to remain grounded in the lived experiences that produce sensory images is what did the Strangers in, and it is the reason that their experiment with humans was doomed to fail. Having only collective knowledge, they created for the inhabitants of Dark City a singular consciousness that is not grounded in individual experience. In their attempt to learn the secrets of human existence, they put their abductees in a state that robs them of it.

In his visionary speculations about where the fusion of the human nervous system with electronic circuitry might lead, McLuhan cautions about overindulgence in the information flows offered by various modes of new media. His diverse references to numerous technologies throughout human history produced an amorphous account of the evolutionary process that could lead to the humans in the pods in *The Matrix* or those subject to the Strangers' tuning in *Dark City*—or what he called the "outering of [man's] consciousness into the computer" (McLuhan and Powers, 94). Even though they contain futuristic scenarios of such a body-in-the vat existence, the two films hold that the idea of an existence cut off from our physical being-in-the-world is a misconception, because it disregards the inevitable hybrid nature of our coevolution with technology. In the way it characterizes the successful resistance to the Strangers, *Dark City* suggests that embodied individual experience will reestablish itself when humankind begins to envision a technological singularity grounded in immaterial information flows. The Strangers' control over humans is almost total, but there are occasional exceptions, so-called strays, who are not responsive to their tuning. Murdoch's case is however special. Until he appeared, the Strangers had always found the strays and dispatched them. Frustrated by their inability to control him, Mr. Book presses Schreber for an explanation. He responds: "I don't know. Maybe he's a step up the evolutionary ladder. A freak of nature. He's adapting to survive." As this suggests, the secret that helps Murdoch fend off the Strangers is an adaptation to the world around him rather than a volitional attempt to take control. The message is not that humanity must rely on such a freak occurrence to stave off real dangers from information technology, but rather that technology is always imbricated with the biological and subject to such unexpected events that thwart the grandest plans of even the most intelligent and technologically advanced.

The choice Murdoch faces is between seeking absolute knowledge and control or affirming a life in a stream of events inflected with immediacy and emotion, even though it is clouded by the unknown. Even when he was not aware of what was happening, he paid special heed to the implicit memories that kept surfacing and disrupting the simulated consciousness that had been implanted in his brain. Following Eric Kandel's groundbreaking work on how memory is stored in neurons, cognitive neuroscience distinguishes between *implicit* (nondeclarative) versus *explicit* (declarative) memories. *Implicit memory* refers to stored memories of motor actions and other automatic bodily operations that do not attain conscious awareness. Implicit memory guides the body's actions and feeds into every aspect of our existence without being called into consciousness as mental representations. For example, implicit muscle memory determines how each individual walks and carries the body in a distinctive manner. This form of memory is passed down hereditarily, a fact that we confirm whenever we notice the child displaying the same physical mannerisms as a parent. *Explicit memory* refers to those mental representations that we produce in connection with past experiences and store in the brain as dispositional networks of neural processes that can be called (back) into consciousness. They are what we generally refer to when we talk about our memories (LeDoux, 101–19). The Strangers' civilization had become reliant on external information flows and accumulated collective knowledge to the extent that they retained only explicit memories. In the end, it is the embodiment of memory that turns out to be the key aspect of humans that the Strangers cannot understand or manipulate, as they were blinded by what Dennett has called the "Cartesian Theater" view of human nature (107).

Both *Dark City* and *The Matrix* address these issues with respect to the role visual media play in the coevolution of technology and the human. They include metacinematic references that relate the anxiety generated by their science-fiction fantasies to classical cinema's mode of representing reality as an intact world set apart from the viewer. In each case, the total simulation that has humankind under its control is linked to a conventional film culture that promotes an ocularcentric spectatorship and downplays the reach and power of the human. In *The Matrix* the minds of those whose bodies are preserved in the pods are controlled by an ersatz consciousness forged in the image of classical cinema. In this regard, *The Matrix* offers a futuristic vision of what digital technology could produce if it were used to expand classical cinema so that its film world incorporated all of our embodied responses to film. The machines' strategy for keeping the minds of humans fully occupied mirrors cinema's push to create a full diegetic reality in which every detail contributes to a complete, flawless representation of the world as we experience it. As evidenced by the public's obsession with finding breaks in continuity and consistency in films and posting them on IMDB, the adherence to representational realism has become an unquestioned convention of mainstream cinema. Similarly, the machines are intent on eliminating any such discontinuities in the Matrix. At the same time, they understand that a convincing simulation is not an ideal existence if there are no problems to overcome. It also has to mirror our existence as we experience it in terms of struggles and distress. Smith explains at one point that they had first tried to design the Matrix as a perfect world, but it was too ideal and did not work. It was a dream world from which the human mind kept trying to wake up, and "an entire crop was lost . . . as a species, human beings define their reality through suffering and misery." The prosthetic consciousness implanted in their minds had to encompass all aspects of human existence. Here too, the Matrix alludes to mainstream narrative film, which routinely involves a crisis that the protagonist must undergo, usually emerging successfully from it.

In concocting a perfected diegetic "screen" reality, *The Matrix* also comments metacinematically on its own medium. When the construct is uploaded directly into Neo's brain, he suddenly appears together with Morpheus in front of a blank white screen with two armchairs facing a 1950s television. As the camera cuts to show only the front of the television and the white screen behind it, Morpheus begins to explain to Neo that he has been living in a simulation: "This is the world that you know. The world as it was at the end of the twentieth century. It exists now only as part of a neural-interactive simulation that we call the Matrix. You've been living in a dream world, Neo." Overlaying different layers of

twentieth-century visual media in this one shot, the film marks
the Matrix as a spectatorial prosthetic consciousness informed
by the evolution of moving-image culture up to 1999. In another
allusion to cinema, as they are preparing Neo for the red pill to
kick in and extract him from the Matrix, Cypher (Joe Pantoliano)
quips, "Buckle your seatbelt, Dorothy, because Kansas is going bye-
bye." This reference to the Technicolor spectacle *The Wizard of Oz*
(Victor Fleming, 1939) equates the dream world that Neo has been
living in with the dream factory of Hollywood. Warned that he will
now see "how deep the rabbit hole goes," Neo is extracted from his
pod in a violent series of audiovisual effects that in the diegetic reality of the film return his body to the real world. Here, the process
actually reverses the transformation Dorothy experienced when
she was swept away by a tornado, or Alice when she went down
the rabbit hole in the Walt Disney film *Alice in Wonderland* (Clyde
Geronimi et al., 1951). In terms of the onscreen transformation
of the cinematic image, the digital special effects of *The Matrix*
engage the viewer in a more intensely embodied experience than
the virtual Wonderland of the Disney production or the Oz of the
MGM film. In this regard, the Kansas that has gone bye-bye is the
classically constructed film world that, in a manner analogous to
the Matrix, holds the viewer in disembodied suspension.

But *The Matrix* and *Dark City* do not imply that the classical
mode of spectatorship must be totally eliminated. Proyas's film
references itself as a cinematic love story much in the same way as
the ending to *The Thirteenth Floor*. When Emma visits Murdoch
after he has been arrested, he intimates to her that their memories
of a past life together have all been fabricated and implanted in
them. Refusing to accept this, she becomes emotional and, in a
highly melodramatic episode, pleads with the guards to give them
just one more minute before they take him back to his cell. With a
dreamy look in her eyes and a tear flowing down her cheek, Emma
says softly, "I love you, John. You can't fake something like that."
When he replies, "No, you can't," he has already made the decision, even before he is able to defeat the Strangers, to accept the
past they have scripted for him. At the end of the film, when he
creates the simulated world of Shell Beach and meets Anna out at
the end of the pier, the scene, both in its visual construction and as

FIGURE 15. *Morpheus in* The Matrix: *"You've been living in a dream world, Neo."*

a happy ending, labels itself as cinema. In both *Dark City* and *The Thirteenth Floor* what emerges triumphant is not the relationship between the protagonist and the woman he loves, but rather the cinematic theme of "love conquers all." They end on a note of nostalgia for classical cinema that signifies the loss of more than just an era of film. In the face of a changing conception of the human and reality that is not reversible, their endings express a nostalgic longing for the classical sense of the unity of existence and the corresponding cognitivist view of the human mind. This desire to turn back the clock, or to stop it in its tracks, as the Strangers did when they reconfigured human existence, is mediated through cinema's past, through its history of representing such unity in classical narratives. Figured in this way, the affirmation of love as an essential human quality is itself cast as just a product of a particular stage in a human existence that is mediated through the technologies we create. When Murdoch chooses to live with Emma in the simulated reality of Shell Beach, he does so in the knowledge that we must accept the fabricated, prosthetic nature of the lives we create for ourselves. The ending reassures that the essence of human nature, and its only possible path, has always been to evolve with new technologies regardless of where they lead.

The ending of *The Matrix* reflects similarly on the status of cinematic narrative in the digital era. Rather than resorting to a love story, it ends with a coda that addresses the goal of Neo's messianic mission. The final scene is staged as a telephone call from a phone booth within the Matrix that connects Neo to its operating system. He is delivering a message to the singular consciousness that was created at the end of the twenty-first millennium and spawned the new race of machines. When Neo finishes delivering his message, the camera moves in a single motion into and through the column of green numbers on the screen, emerges out of the telephone receiver, and slowly pulls back to reveal Neo in the phone booth. In a series of three quick, successive cuts, the camera pulls back each time, until in the final shot, the buildings and streets below appear to be little more than a pattern of geometrical lines and shapes that resemble the circuit board of a computer. The challenge he issues to the artificial intelligence ("Where we go from there is a choice I leave to you") suggests that ultimately human intelligence cannot simply jettison the biological systems that undergird all cognitive powers. This coda also marks the film's final shot as a cinematic convention that signals its own annulment. The assertion that human civilization reached its peak near the end of the twentieth century makes perhaps the most sense when taken as a self-reflexive allusion to mainstream narrative cinema. Neo flies up out of this construct toward the camera much like the figure of Superman. Not so much parodying the ending of a Hollywood superhero movie as declaring its obsolescence, the final sequence ends with the overhead shot looking down into "the peak of human civilization" from a perspective that renders it indistinguishable from the network of silicon chips that carry digital flows of information.

Even as the ending of *The Matrix* completes the film's narrative and sates a desire for closure that cinema itself has implanted in the viewer, it marks that desire as anachronistic. *Dark City* and *The Thirteenth Floor* also deny the premise of their science-fiction plots in a way that suggests their own obsolescence. At the end of both the happy ending to the romantic story is tacked onto a narrative that undermines its verity. Even when these films end on a note of nostalgia for the humanist ideals upheld by classical cinema, or *The Matrix* resorts to a contrived Hollywood superhero narrative to counter the anxieties associated with digital technologies, they reject both the embrace of the virtual as a new transcendence of the body and the reestablishment of the real as the remedy to a dangerous proliferation of new media. The persistence of conventional cinematic narrative in these films is not an indication of little change, but rather is one piece of a hybrid constitution produced by the incorporation of digital technology into cinema. Similarly, when they break with the spatial continuity of classical cinema this does not reflect a world coming apart at the seams, but rather a more dynamic world full of new potential. The loss of faith in the verifiable indexicality of the film image and the dissolution of representational realism are more than offset by cinema's enhanced ability to situate the viewer vis-à-vis the image in a way that evokes embodied being in a world mediated through digital technology.

The digital cinematic image is a hybrid in another way as well. It is composed of computer code and yet can still maintain an indexical relationship to profilmic reality. *The Matrix* reveals this dual nature of the postcinematic image and explores how the new mode of spectatorship it spawns relates to the broader challenge of adapting to a digitally mediated relationship with the world. The endless columns of streaming numerals shown at the beginning and end of the film reveal that the image is a virtual manifestation of manipulated code. The training Neo receives to negotiate the computer codes that the machines have employed to construct the Matrix applies to the construction of the cinematic image as well. Morpheus takes Neo into the downtown streets in the simulated Matrix of their training program. In the midst of the crowd of inhabitants, all dressed in drab business colors, a Marilyn Monroe-esque woman in a red dress and bright red lipstick sashays past them sexily as she stares provocatively at Neo. Her appearance captivates both Neo, who turns to look at her, and the viewer. As part of the exercise, Morpheus grabs Neo's attention, then tells him to look again. When he turns back around the woman in the red dress is gone, replaced by a simulation of Agent Smith pointing a gun at him. Here, a referential realism that is supported by ocularcentric forms of representation is undermined by new modes of comprehending the world as a system of digital code. When he completes his training and enters the Matrix, Neo is able to resist its control because of his heightened ability to see it as a system of information flows and to intervene in the writing of the code. When Morpheus takes Neo into the "construct," the loading program where the rebels arm themselves in their fight against the agents, he gives Neo the last bit of knowledge he needs to defeat them: "What is real? How do you define real? If you're talking about what you can feel, what you can smell, what you can taste and see, then real is simply electrical signals interpreted by your brain." This instruction is directed of course more pointedly at the viewer and relates to the conventional understanding of film viewing. It contradicts the notion that the spectator is situated as a self-contained observer of a classically defined reality.

My take on *The Matrix* runs counter to others who have analyzed it in the context of this set of issues. For example, Rodowick claims that even as the film employs digital imaging to capture an audience fascinated with the wondrous powers of the new technology, it codes the photographic base of cinema "as 'real,' the locus of a truthful representation and the authentic aesthetic experience of cinema" (5). Grusin overlooks how the hallucinatory world of the Matrix is linked to the classical cinema effect and thus charges that the film "fails to come to terms with the most interesting implications of digital media for contemporary cinema" (67). Similarly, Norman Bryson has described the film as "a Sleeping Beauty story, of waking out of narcotic slumber into the 'true' picture of things, the horrific hive of incubation and delusion within which posthumanity slumbers" (17). Criticizing the film for sketching a strict good/bad dichotomy between the real and the virtual, he cites its

FIGURE 16. *The Marilyn Monroe-esque blonde woman in the red dress in* The Matrix.

failure to capture how the subject exists "between technological realms," that is, between the real as captured by visual recordings and the virtual as produced internally by the body's interaction with external environments and digitally encoded images. In my reading, the film highlights the danger posed by just such a false dichotomy and suggests that to avoid it we must embrace technological innovation as an integral part of the evolving human race.

The film's lesson about spectatorship is part of its larger exploration of the new "real" as it is constructed by digital technologies. The central conflict in the film's science-fiction scenario highlights the adaptations needed to understand and evolve with increasingly complex forms of media. The key to defeating the rogue machines in *The Matrix* is not to denounce them as a force alien to humans, but rather to recognize that they are our creations and understand the reciprocal demands they place on their creators. Clinging to a humanist faith in the superiority of our intelligence, the human race at the end of the millennium had tried unsuccessfully to control them through intellectual mastery. However, as prosthetic extensions of the human organism machines necessitate that we also adapt to their operational systems, such that to a certain extent the human becomes an attendant of the machine (Hansen 2015, 73–75). This dynamic is not new in the digital age, but the exponentially greater power of recent information technology and its widespread dissemination throughout contemporary culture require more intensive intervention, even as the medium in which it occurs (computer code and nanotechnology) has become increasingly transparent. The digitized cinematic image of *The Matrix* moves the viewer in this direction by establishing a postcinematic mode of spectatorship that corresponds to lived experience in a hybrid physical-digital environment, while the film's metacinematic analysis of the effects of digital imaging drives this point home thematically.

Conclusion

A central question explored throughout this study asks, "What has been gained and what has been lost due to cinema's dominant role in visual culture since the beginning of the last century and how is that changing in the digital age?" Some media theorists have characterized the medium of cinema as a purveyor of phatic images that not only fails to promote adaptation to our increasingly mediated form of engaging and establishing control in this new cultural environment, but even impedes it in some ways. Assuming this view of cinema, Hansen looks to digital technology to break what he sees as the abiding tradition of a reductive material image. Building on the philosophy of Simondon, he sees the temporal properties of media and body technics as the major constitutive element in technogenesis. Because the digital image can engage the body's motoricity at the microtemporal level, at the stage of "primitive autocinesis" (2011, 111) it can serve as an antidote to the fixed temporality of traditional media images. Thus, he looks to technological innovation at the level of microtemporalities as the way to enhance the body's plasticity and tap into a vital source of human creativity.

For Hansen and like-minded media theorists this is necessary to substantially change the politics of the image. As correlates of phenomenological experience, traditional media images are, he asserts, more susceptible to control by social and cultural forces (2011, 109–11). By contrast, digital technologies can produce "asubjective, microtemporal images" that cohere across internal biological and external material environments and "speak directly to our brains" (2006, 14). Waging the battle for selection at the microconscious level via a wide array of mediated spaces, they have, according to Hansen, an inherent potential to disrupt and replace the fixed perceptual image with an interactive and more generative imaging process. Direct interventions of this kind can also alter how we experience the world through phenomenal consciousness. He calls for a politically charged aesthetics that will grant new media the autonomy needed not only to counter the idea that visual images insert themselves into consciousness as an already composed correlate of natural perception, but also to disrupt the media practices founded on this misconception.

While in agreement that the digital image's potential to usher in change in this way needs to be fostered, I have argued that the cinematic image should not be seen as an obstruction to this endeavor, but rather as a cocontributor in the inevitable process of mediation and remediation that drives the evolution of technology. A central thesis of this study has been that the overarching trajectory of cinema in the evolution of visual media has been to promote the transition from a disembodied spectatorial mode to a participatory mode of engaging visual images. I have taken this position even though throughout its history cinema has addressed the viewer explicitly and predominantly, although not exclusively, at the level of phenomenal consciousness. As I stated at the outset, this has likely been the main reason media theory has not focused explicitly on the convergence of film and new media and the role cinema has played in the coevolution of the human and technology. However, the remediation of digital media back into cinema alters our sensory orientation to the moving image in a way that supports adaptation to the new forms of experience in the digital age and contributes to the deterritorialization of the sensorium that results from it. Moreover, the overlapping hybridity of cinema and new media mirrors the neural architecture and genetic makeup of the human body as it has evolved over time. That is, it reflects how the human organism is a cumulative system based on the coevolution of humans with technology and the changes that technology imposes on our environment.

With respect to the current data-intensive environment where transparent feedback loops increasingly form the interface between the body's neural networks and the technology we use, conscious phenomenal and automatic subphenomenal processes are becoming more integrally conjoined hybrid operations that extend across our biological and technological systems. Adopting Shane Denson's account of what he calls "anthropotechnical . evolution" (2014, 259), a fitting way to describe this ever-changing interaction between the human biological organism and its environment is as a metabolic process. This is not merely a metaphor. If the interconnection between the biological and the technological is as integral as I have argued throughout this study, then human metabolism encompasses transformative exchanges between the individual body/mind and its technico-cultural-natural environment, as well as collectively between the entire species and the world we have created as the "medium" for our existence. Conceived in this manner, "metabolism is as much a process of media transformation as it is a process of bodily change" (Denson 2016, 208–09). As digitization has become the operational process transforming the "medium" we inhabit, its effects work their way metabolically back on the cinematic image through remediation. The postcinematic image has thus been reconstituted according to changes in the spatial, temporal, kinetic, affective infrastructure for lived experience in the digital age. This is of course just a recent, dramatic phase in an evolutionary process that has been altering the cinematic image continuously since 1900.

In reevaluating how cinema has factored historically into the cultural evolution that shapes the human, my purpose is not to boost its status or value vis-à-vis other media but rather to explore the role visual media play in the coevolution of the human with technology and, in doing so, to gain insight into the imbrication of the biological and the technological that defines our existence. To indicate how this is more than just an academic exercise, I turn again to the work of Marshall McLuhan. As signaled by the title of his seminal study *Understanding Media*, McLuhan believed that "understanding media as they extend man" is the key to gaining control over the advance of technology and mitigating "the ferocity of the winds of change" (1969). Characterizing the transition from one phase to the next as a clash of old and new media, he asserted that in his own time a shift was occurring from "the old visual culture," in which the "technologies or extensions of man were partial and fragmentary," to an electronic age where computers will dominate. Still, cinema, along with other media of the passing era, most prominently writing, would continue to exert a strong influence. In his mind, the most important thrust of his work would be to help bring the old media culture "into peaceful coexistence with the new" during this transitional period (1969).

My analysis of how cinema has factored into the process of media convergence, both as a revolutionary new medium at its outset and now as a part of the "old visual culture" that is confronting digital media, has in each case set it against the backdrop of the larger sociotechnological environment at the time. Just as the mechanized modern culture around 1900 formed a dynamic new environment that both produced the moving-image technology of film and determined how it converged with existing media, so today digital technology has dramatically altered the cultural context in which the convergence of cinema and new media is occurring. The remediation of new media back into cinema brings new forms of lived experience to bear on film viewing. Namely, digital imaging embodies new forms of interfacing with our cultural environment in the age of enhanced information technologies. As the relation between the body and the physical world is becoming more and more digitally mediated, we learn to establish control through new bodily operations and capacities that are not accessible to phenomenal consciousness. A radical consequence of this new interface with the external world is that "we are now in a position to recognize that sensibility need no longer be channeled through higher-order modes of human experience—sense perception, consciousness, attention, awareness, and so forth—in order to have experiential impact" (Hansen 2015, 160).

In the evolutionary advance of media new technologies work their way back into the existing culture, such as today's cinema, to produce hybrid forms that can become the source of both new forms of physical experience and new assumptions about the human relation to the external world. As CGI became a fixture in the standard toolkit of visual storytelling, cinema began to explore the larger social and cultural impact of our changing relation to visual images. Science fiction, the traditional genre for addressing concerns about advances in science and technology, began to turn its attention to digital technology and new media. Even before computer imaging had fully asserted its influence on film, cinema had already begun to imagine futures shaped by the ways new information and media technologies were radically altering how we see the world. *Blade Runner* and *Total Recall* explored how implanted visual memories may be able to alter individual identity and invalidate the humanist conception of personhood. In *Videodrome* (1983) David Cronenberg served up a strange, unsettling fantasy of what could happen if video technology could be implanted into the body and become one with the flesh. As the digital image continues to transform the traditional film image, the hybrid version of the human as an interface between the organic body and automatic machines yields to a new amalgamation that needs little interface. The migration of moving images onto many mobile and handheld devices contributes to this idea of a broad convergence of technologically produced material images and internal mental imagining. The big screen in the movie theater provided a much different impression of our relation to the external image. Its fixture on the oversized wall of the movie theater served "to remind audiences of the theatricality behind the movie, to assure them that they were in a place of representation, separate from the everyday world" (Rombes, 65). When it became only one among many vehicles for the digitized film image, radical new conceptions of the moving image began to surface.

Digitized data and modes of processing have also become a model for how the brain functions. The idea that we may soon no longer need our eyes has gained traction, and visual technologies have become endowed with an almost magical ability to surpass and supplant our powers of vision. Postcinematic vision refers then to a broader shift in both the way we "see" the world with our eyes and in the epistemology of vision and perception. Digital technology has introduced radical new ways of recording, projecting, and creating images in all areas of culture, with the result that the traditional privileging of vision as the sense that can best establish what is real has been brought into question. Technologies in a variety of fields offer us "optical" data that we cannot process via visual perception. From magnetic resonance imaging that enables us to detect neural activity inside complex organs such as the brain to a wide array of new microscope technologies (neutron, recurrence tracking, and field ion, among others) there are many new optical technologies that enable us to see and analyze ever smaller objects or to examine the interiors of both organic and inorganic materials without inflicting harm. Conversely, advances in telescope technologies give us the power to explore depths of space that were previously unfathomable. These instruments enable us to gather data and images of the world around us that are far more intricate and sophisticated than what the human eye can process. As they extend our vision into previously unknown realms, the idea that our eyes provide us the most dependable access to reality no longer holds. Visual perception has become a rather crude tool in comparison with scientific methods for exploring and identifying the world. There is a corresponding loss of faith in vision as a reliable access to what was considered a stable and knowable material world. As a result, our ocularcentric approach to understanding and explaining both nature and the human mind is losing ground to what are seen as immaterial forms of information. This shift has affected our view of cinema as well. In an interview promoting *Minority Report* (2002) Steven Spielberg ventured this vision of how digital imaging could change the film experience: "Someday the entire motion picture may take place inside the mind and it will be the most internal experience anyone can have: being told a story with your eyes closed, but you see and smell and feel and interact with the story" (Kennedy, 113).

As Spielberg's speculation suggests, the incorporation of digital media in cinema has brought about threshold changes in spectatorship at the neural level that alter where we direct attention, how we perceive images, how we store and retrieve memories, and how we gather all these events into a narrative about our existence. The new assumption that replaces the epistemological underpinnings of classical cinema is the idea that reality is not captured and represented on film but rather arises out of the viewer's engagement with the image. In place of a fixed relation between image and referent, cinema gains fluidity and the ability to move freely between different media (film, computer graphics, animation) and to express new modes of space and time. As the traditional mode of spectatorship is disrupted, its representationalist stance toward the image gives way to a new participatory model that increasingly evokes subphenomenal responses that demand bodily attention but not mental awareness. The remediation of digital imaging thus supports the "shift from considering cinema and the spectator as a 'disembodied eye' defined by the look and the gaze, desire and identification, to considering cinema and the spectator as an 'embodied brain,' defined by perceptions (even illusory ones), selections (even random ones), memories (even fake ones), imaginations, suggestions, and above all emotions as pure affect" (Pisters, 71). As a digitized cinema engages the viewer increasingly at the level of microsensory perception, it also promotes the development of the bodily systems needed to synthesize these sensorimotor and affective responses into conscious, integrated "human" experience.

This transition to a postcinematic mode of spectatorship promotes "understanding media as they extend man" in a key way. One bias associated with the "old visual culture" assumes that all significant contributions to our intelligence and ultimately our well-being derive from conscious, deliberate acts of thinking. The failure to understand how automatic, subphenomenal activities across a whole spectrum of extended cognitive environments unshackles our thought processes and expands our innate biological capacity to think and create leads to the apocalyptic visions of technology run amok found in *The Matrix* and *Dark City*. Indeed, these fantasies of invasive technologies that can totally supplant consciousness haunt us because we do not grasp how the reciprocal interaction of biological and technological processes at a precognitive level has always been an essential part of human intelligence and creativity. This hidden interconnection is not merely a secondary contributor to the complex system that is the human: "The most seamless of all integrations, and the ones with the greatest potential to transform our lives and projects, are often precisely those that operated deep beneath the level of conscious awareness" (Clark 2003, 34).

The alternative construction of space in these films fosters an understanding of both our evolving relation to digital technologies and our adaptation to them. These changes in the spatial properties of the diegetic film world mirror the influence that digital culture is having on the way we visualize and negotiate our environment spatially. The omnipresence of digital media has not only enhanced our ability to imagine virtual space in new ways, it has also altered how we maintain spatial orientation in our complex cultural environment. As our neural networks for automatic bodily functions dovetail with microcomputational systems, new bodily mechanisms for guiding sensorimotor responses and movement evolve. In the transition to a world defined by digital information flows, space is constructed jointly via direct contact with "natural" physical environments and on the basis of mediated experience. Digital technology has inserted itself so pervasively between the body and the external physical world that we now find ourselves increasingly interacting with mixed media and everyday material objects within a "hybrid 'digital-physical' space" (Clark 2010, 14). When cinema patterns film space accordingly, it helps both the individual viewer and the collective viewing public master spatial cognition outside the theater as well and promotes adaptation to our altered interface with the environment.

The power of digital technology also evokes apocalyptic visions of its ability to take control of the biological processes that produce consciousness and replace it with an alternative created by external agents. The idea that automatic, and perhaps inevitable, change at the level of technicity will drive human progress and evolution stokes fears that those faculties thought to be guiding civilization—free will, rational thought processes, memory, imagination, creativity—are merely products of chemical reactions and electrical flows over which we have limited influence. Those film scholars who downplay the effects of digital imaging on cinema, insisting that it has proven resilient in the face of the new technology, are motivated in part by a reluctance to cede the traditional view of human agency. Even as they emphasize the constancy of cinema, they still tend to see digital imaging as a threat. Citing how film's indexical relation to what is in front of the camera can be distorted or even completely eliminated, they declare a crisis of perception. Rather than embracing the transformative impact of moving-image technology, they cling to assumptions linked to visual media prior to 1900, such as the idea that the ontological essence of film is photographic realism (Brown, Tyron).

What is also at stake for those who mourn the loss of the indexical relation between the film image and profilmic reality is the ocularcentric regime of modernity and the spectatorial relation of the viewer to film. Stubborn adherence to this mode of spectatorship stymies the power of visual media to expand our perception and advance our understanding of how we interact with and change the world. As Hayles warned with respect to the notion of the posthuman that was emerging at the end of the twentieth century, a crucial objective must be to "keep disembodiment from being rewritten, once again, into prevailing concepts of subjectivity" (Hayles 1999, 5). The hybridity of the digitized film image destroys the illusion that we can fully represent and control who and what we are as humans at the level of phenomenal consciousness and promotes the idea that the automatic, mechanical dimension of the technological world is an essential piece of our extended cognition. The films discussed in the last chapter attest to a mutual evolution of technology and the body from which there is no return to a binary division of nature and culture, of the biological and the technological. They point to an as yet indeterminable "technologization of the body and biologization of technology" (Hotchkiss, 16) that will configure posthumanist culture. Whatever shape the new fusion of the body and technology may take, these films confirm that our mental world, like all instantiations of the virtual, emerges out of an embodiment of memory that forms the horizon for lived experience and our constructions of reality.

This posthuman conception of our body/mind becomes undeniable in the face of new forms of media that can passively record and utilize massive amounts of data without any active involvement on the part of humans. As the computer has gone from being a processor in a box on a desktop to ever smaller and more diverse units that can be installed in many different instruments and distributed across a wide range of public and domestic environments, the new generation of visual and information media has reached a stage of transparent ubiquity (Hansen 2015, 160). As the interfaces between the human and these "smart" devices have become second nature, we increasingly depend on these digital instruments as if they were an integral part of the biological organism. This kind of transparent processing is not new, but rather has always been an essential part of the human, both in internal biological systems and in the extended cognitive realm of technology. Just as our conscious thought processes inevitably depend on many unconscious operations that execute actions (thumbs typing on handheld digital "keyboards") or serve as scaffolding for higher-order abstract thinking (perception and memory recall), our mental processing finds similar support from external mechanical devices. Various forms of data mining and management systems operate transparently to supplement our mental resources, functioning in the same transparent manner as technologies that enhance our motor skills, such as autofocus cameras or antilock brakes. Without such external material assistance, our brain would not be able to solve a multitude of problems we face in our complex sociotechnological environment. In this regard, when today's smart phone carries out so many complex functions without any conscious input on our part it is working no differently than "the pen with which we write, the hand that holds it while writing, or the various neural subsystems that form the grip and guide the fingers" (Clark 2003, 28–29).

These enhancements to our cognitive capabilities also produce new sensibilities and new ways of orienting ourselves to the world around us. Not only do they enhance our capacity to make sense of things, they also change how we assign meaning and establish identity. This is the essence of Morpheus's commentary on the real. The taste of the juicy artificial steak that explains Cypher's betrayal of the rebels and Neo's response to the blonde in the red dress are only electrical signals, and in this case ones stimulated by virtual images (visual and tactile), but they determine what we taste, feel, and desire. As these devices assume an ever-expanding role in both the affective and deliberative sides of our decision-making, they will alter how we feel about what we are doing, where we are going, and how we may be able to accomplish our goals, and ultimately also our idea of who and what we are. In this respect, the threshold transition from the figure of the cyborg to the posthuman vision of the human-machine merger entails the full acceptance of the idea that external, technological resources are as integral a part of the biotechnical system that determines our intelligence, capacities, and desires as what exists inside "the good old biological skin-bag" (Clark 2003, 33). The extensions of the biological are no longer seen as simply additional resources that enable the real cognitive being to devote its attention and intelligence to more important matters. We are nearing the stage in the human-machine merger where humans will, as Clark forecast in 2003, realize their latent status as natural-born cyborgs. And, when we accept this view of who we are, these extensions will begin "dovetailing back in earnest," such that "more and more parts of the world will come to share the moral and psychological status of parts of our brains" (Clark 2003, 34). The same evolutionary process of scaffolding that has enhanced our mental powers by extending cognition into the external physical world has also led to other forms of technological innovation that promote and constrain social and cultural evolution. These include complex sociopolitical institutions such as legal systems as well as prevailing conceptions of the human. They are part of "the specific sociotechnological matrix in which the biological organism exists" (Clark 2003, 33) at each point in human history, and which forms the framework for further human evolution. As digital media engage and intermesh more pervasively with our neural networks, this sociotechnological matrix gains extended control over human subjectivity. The resulting expansion and deterritorialization of the human sensorium leads to a posthuman culture where increasingly "the *propensity of the situation* as a whole holds sway over any delimited agency" (Hansen 2015, 252).

In our current media-saturated environment where technology is fast assuming an ever-greater role in our decision-making and identity formation, an understanding and acceptance of our posthuman existence will be required to stave off "the ferocity of the winds of change" (McLuhan 1969). Fear of losing our dominion over all other forms of existence on earth produces the worst-case scenarios where foreign agents (the machines in *The Matrix* or the Strangers in *Dark City*) can bypass the individual's production of consciousness to impose their own agenda onto humans. Our minds, steeped in the self-image of the traditional humanist subject, fail to grant cognitive agency to the nonbiological material world or to accept that it is an essential part of "human nature." Only when we deny our coexistential relation to machines and alienate ourselves from them do we envision the invisible transactions conducted by increasingly sophisticated computers as an imminent threat to our autonomy. A digitally altered cinema supports the transition to a liberated posthuman subject working in conjunction with intelligent machines by promoting an enhanced *response-ability* that is not diminished by a prejudgment of what constitutes reality (Abel, xii–xvi and 10–19). This expansion and deterritorialization of the human sensorium strengthens our ability to fend off nefarious attempts at delimitation and control, not only from imagined alien threats, but also from the marketing strategies of the business world or manipulative political instruments. Following this reasoning, I have portrayed cinema and digital media as joint agents in the evolutionary rebound from cognitive biases that are themselves a product of our evolutionary heritage. Both belong to a set of modern media that strikes a more balanced engagement of embodied and cognitive responses, one that better reflects how we establish and manage our existence in the external world we have created for ourselves.

Notes

Introduction

1. For others who have speculated about the end of cinema due to the rise of new media see Dixon, Gaudreault and Marion, and Usai. One can also find of course an abundance of claims or declarations of the death of cinema in the popular press and online, including by such famous directors as Martin Scorsese and Ridley Scott (https://qz.com/878002/the-movies-are-dead-according-to-martin-scorsese-and-ridley-scott/) and Quentin Tarantino (http://www.bbc.com/culture/story/20140612-the-death-of-cinema).

1. Film and the Embodied Mind

1. For a similar view see *Man the Tool-Maker* by the British physical anthropologist Kenneth P. Oakley. He writes in the introduction, "Employment of tools appears to be [man's] chief biological characteristic, for considered functionally they are detachable extensions of the forelimb." Cited in Hayles 1999, 34.

2. Mark Hansen's view of technogenesis coincides for the most part with Stiegler's account of *epiphylogenesis* (i.e., biological evolution occurring outside of the realm of biological life), but not on this point. The difference is evident in their interpretations of how the first tool use functioned as the originary moment in the coevolution of the human and technology. Stiegler stresses the central role of mental representations in the external object, claiming that the tool serves as a medium that archives the mental process needed to reproduce it (as *tertiary memories*, in his terminology). Hansen contends, however, that it occurs through nonconscious activity at the level of the pre-individual "in the more indirect technical mediation of an environmental sensibility shared by living beings prior to and independently of their subsequent psychic individualizations as perceivers, subjects, or consciousnesses" (Hansen 2012, 48).

3. Hansen emphasizes this aspect of *human* evolution when he takes issue with Stiegler's account of *epiphylogenesis*: "As the actualization of

pre-individual potential in the form of mediation, *technical objects furnish the support for transindividuation* and in so doing actualize the epiphylogenetic dimension of human evolution" (Hansen 2012, 48; emphasis added).

4. For a good account of Gottlieb's theory see Oyama.

5. While Clark's work has meshed well with that of researchers focused on the embodied component of the 4EA model, his view of the extended mind has met with resistance and remains debated within the larger philosophical movement emphasizing embodied experience. In particular, some entrenched supporters of enactivism and related thinkers who draw heavily on phenomenology have resisted this adjustment to their view of how cognition derives from the activity of a *situated living body*.

6. Gerald Edelman, whose work on binding and the production of consciousness coincides with Damasio's in broad strokes, while also differing in some significant ways, claims that it did not evolve via specific selection. He contends that consciousness emerged according to a process of natural selection of neural systems, but not due to "selection for consciousness itself" (2003, 5520).

7. The key thinkers who have pushed the idea that some of the most important operations in the brain, and in particular those associated with cognitive functions, entail modules that evolved discretely to support distinct functions include Jerry Fodor (1983), Zenon Pylyshyn (1984), and Leda Cosmides and John Tooby (1992).

8. Other important models that explain consciousness on the basis of synchronicity include Edelman's theory of reentry, Damasio's concept of convergence zones, and Dennett's "multiple drafts" explanation. For a good overview of these and similar views see Taylor, 110–17. For a good concise account of his theory of *neuronal group selection* and *reentry* that explains the "spatiotemporal coordination" required to bind synchronous events into primary consciousness see Edelman 2003. See also Metzinger, 25–40.

9. My account of Llinás's work follows the description on the McGill University website The Brain from Top to Bottom: http://thebrain.mcgill.ca/flash/a/a_12/a_12_cl/a_12_cl_con/a_12_cl_con.html.

10. In my analysis of Werner Herzog's *Cave of Forgotten Dreams* (Cook 2013) I see cave painting having a more expansive influence on the interconnection between the sensory systems of the body and their external mediation into audiovisual images. For a similar reading of the film that also emphasizes the dynamic audiovisual effect of cave painting see Koepnick.

11. For an alternative view see Cook 2013.

12. The explanation was formally disproved by experiments in 1912 (Wertheimer). Nonetheless, film scholars have continued at times to use it to explain the perception of motion (Anderson and Anderson).

13. Some prominent instances are Furman et al.; Hasson, Furman et al.; Hasson, Landesman et al.; Levin and Wang; Magliano and Zacks; and Zacks et al. For a study designed by a humanities scholar that uses electroencephalographic (EEE) measurements to compare brain activity during reading versus screen viewing see MacDougall. This last study also offers a good overview of some of the difficulties and limitations associated with using EEE and similar investigative tools (such as, CAT, PET, and fMRI) in media research (102–04).

14. David Bordwell makes a similar claim with respect to our ability "to organize images and sounds into a unique whole" (2009, 357).

15. On this point compare Manovich 2001, 86.

16. Brian Carr also argues that SQUID technology cannot make good on its promise to convey the complete subjective experience of the wearer because the lived experience of the user intervenes and interferes with the vicarious experience (199–200).

17. Recent studies suggest that autism may well stem from distortions in these connections and dysfunctions in the mirror neuron system that are related to them (Ramachandran 151–52).

18. Without linking it to mirror neurons and automatic bodily responses, Dennis Perri makes a similar observation. He argues that, because all the characters in his world are his own creations, César is deprived of an essential piece of the input provided by fellow humans: "The other possesses a 'surplus of seeing' unavailable to the self even by means of the mirror" (95).

19. See Shaviro (2014), Hansen (2015), and Ivakhiv (2013). Ivakhiv's formulation that describes Whitehead's philosophy of the universe as relations in process—"subjects-in-the-making and objects-given-to-that-making" (Ivakhiv 2016, 744)—reveals its close affinity to the concept *codependent arising*.

20. For a discussion of *codependent arising* see Varela et al., 219–26, 233–35.

2. 1900: Film Transforms the Media Landscape

1. Daniel Morgan gives a good overview of how Bazin's theory has been interpreted in different ways in recent years. Stressing the need for a fresh look at Bazin's work, Morgan argues that the standard reading has overemphasized the role of indexicality in his notion of cinematic realism. For an account of Bazin's notion of "total representation" that

stresses both its ambiguity and its tendencies toward representationalism see Shaviro 2007, 37–40.

2. See also Manovich 2001, 104–9.

3. See also in this regard Armstrong, 218–19.

4. In discussing his two books *Cinema 1* and *Cinema 2*, Deleuze states that he did not set out to offer either a history or a theory of cinema, but rather to isolate what he calls cinematographic concepts (1986b, ix). He characterizes his study as an exploration of the system of signs and structures that constitute the cinematic image and calls the "special discipline" that he pursues a taxonomy (1990, 67).

5. A New York newspaper article (*New York Mail and Express*, October 17, 1896) on the 1896 reality film *Empire State Express*, which shows a train approaching quickly and then zooming past the camera, reported: "Two ladies in the boxes on the left-hand side of the horseshoe, which is just where the flyer vanishes from view, screamed and nearly fainted as it came apparently rushing upon them. They recovered in time to laugh at their needless excitement" (quoted from Musser 1990, 153–55).

6. For Rodowick, the "impression of reality" that cinema invokes is a misguided attempt at representation, one that goes back to what for him is the essential error in the conception of the realism effect of film: that is, the mistaken notion that the essential ability of the photograph to capture moments of reality depends on spatial correspondences between the profilmic objects and the photographic image (102). In practice this idea of how film produces an "impression of reality" prolonged "Hollywood cinema's long-standing stylistic goal of producing spatial transparency or immediacy" (103). Although he does not state this view explicitly, Rodowick's critique of the pursuit of an impression of reality in mainstream filmmaking attributes a legitimate realism effect to the photographic image of film. It is the temporal indexical relationship between the image and a real event in the past. For Gunning, it is precisely this notion of indexicality that leads to false conceptions of film's ability to generate realism and, in practice, to cinema's pursuit of the *illusion of reality*.

7. For a good discussion of this aspect of Leroi-Gourhan's argument see Frabetti (10–11).

8. For an insightful discussion of this aspect of McLuhan's work see Mitchell, 399–400.

9. See among others the two recent books *Kafka und der Film* by Peter-André Alt and the anthology *Mediamorphosis: Kafka and the Moving Image* (Biderman and Lewit).

10. With this one exception, the date I give for Kafka's works is, for those that were not published in his lifetime, the last year that he is known to have worked on them, and for the others, the year of publication.

11. For an extensive list of critical literature to "Before the Law" see Engel and Auerochs, 206–7.

12. In discussing the move away from a cinematic form of narration in *The Castle* Alt focuses on the overall narrative structure. He argues that Kafka's plan for his two late novels requires more narrative flashbacks, diegetic narration, and extensive dialogue and thus has less visual description of episodic scenes than was typical of his earlier works (186–87).

13. Tracing what we know of Kafka's travels in the region around Friedrichstal where he spent three weeks at a health resort in August 1921, Alt documents the likelihood that his model for the castle was Oravsky hrad, the castle F. W. Murnau used as the setting for *Nosferatu*. However, Kafka would not have had the opportunity to see the film before he wrote all the pieces that comprise his unfinished novel.

3. 2000: Cinema and the Digital Image

1. For a good entry point into this area of scholarship see the collection of articles edited by Tino Balio.

2. On this point, Lia Hotchkiss offers a diametrically opposed view of *The Thirteenth Floor* and *The Matrix*. Juxtaposing them with *eXistenZ*, she argues that they offer essentialist resolutions to the threat posed by simulated realities. She maintains that their narratives perform "the restabilization of an absolute real" that is external to our bodies. This leads, she claims, back to a dualist view of nature versus culture rather than to the messy imbrication of our bodies and technology that we find in *eXistenZ*.

3. http://money.cnn.com/2005/07/12/Autos/funonwheels/car_chases/index.htm.

Bibliography

Abel, Marco. 2007. *Violent Affect: Literature, Cinema, and Critique after Representation*. Lincoln: University of Nebraska Press.

Abraham, Ulf. 2008. "Kafka und Recht/Jutiz." In *Kafka-Handbuch: Leben—Werk—Wirkung*, edited by Bettina von Jagow and Oliver Jahraus, 421–37. Göttingen, Germany: Vandenhoeck & Ruprecht.

Alt, Peter-André. 2009. *Kafka und der Film: Über kinematographisches Erzählen*. Munich: C. H. Beck.

Altman, Rick. 2007. *Silent Film Sound*. New York: Columbia University Press.

Anderson, Joseph D. 1996. *The Reality of Illusion: An Ecological Approach to Cognitive Film Theory*. Carbondale: Southern Illinois University Press.

Anderson, Joseph D., and Barbara Anderson. 1993. "The Myth of the Persistence of Vision Revisited." *Journal of Film and Video* (Spring): 3–12.

Antunes, Luis Roches. 2015. "Neural Correlates of the Multisensory Film Experience." In *Neuroscience and Media: New Understandings and Representations*, edited by Michael Grabowski, 46–61. New York: Routledge.

Armstrong, Tim. 1998. *Modernism, Technology, and the Body: A Cultural Study*. Cambridge: Cambridge University Press.

Arnheim, Rudolf. 1969. *Visual Thinking*. Berkeley: University of California Press.

Baddeley, Alan. 2007. *Working Memory, Thought, and Action*. Oxford: Oxford University Press.

Balázs, Béla. 2010. *Visible Man or the Culture of Film*. Translated by Rodney Livingstone. In *Béla Balázs: Early Film Theory*, edited by Erica Carter, 1–90. London: Berghahn.

Balio, Tino, ed. 2014. *Hollywood in the Age of Television*. New York: Routledge.

Bartels, Andreas, and Semir Zeki. 1999. "Toward a Theory of Visual Consciousness." *Consciousness and Cognition* 8: 225–59.

Bazin, André. 1967. *What Is Cinema?* Volume 1. Translated by Hugh Gray. Berkeley: University of California Press.

Beicken, Peter. 2000. "Kafka's Mise-en-Scène: Literary and Cinematic Imaginary." *Journal of the Kafka Society of America* 24, no. 1–2 (June/December): 4–11.

Beicken, Peter. 2011. "Kafka's Visual Method: The Gaze, the Cinematic, and the Intermedial." In *Kafka for the Twenty-First Century*, edited by Stanley Corngold and Ruth V. Gross, 165–78. Rochester, N.Y.: Camden House.

Benjamin, Walter. 1969a. "On Some Motifs in Baudelaire." In *Illuminations: Essays and Reflections*, edited by Hannah Arendt, translated by Harry Zohn, 155–200. New York: Schocken.

Benjamin, Walter. 1969b. "The Work of Art in the Age of Mechanical Reproduction." In *Illuminations: Essays and Reflections*, edited by Hannah Arendt, translated by Harry Zohn, 217–51. New York: Schocken.

Bergson, Henri. (1907) 2011. *Creative Evolution*, translated by Arthur Mitchell. New York: Henry Holt.

Biderman, Shai, and Ido Lewit. 2016. *Mediamorphosis: Kafka and the Moving Image*. New York: Wallflower.

Bolter, Jay David, and Richard Grusin. 1999. *Remediation: Understanding New Media*. Cambridge, Mass.: MIT Press.

Bordwell, David. 1985. "Space in the Classical Film." In *The Classical Hollywood Cinema: Film Style and Mode of Production to 1960*, edited by David Bordwell, Janet Staiger, and Kristin Thompson, 50–59. New York: Columbia University Press.

Bordwell, David. 1989. "A Case for Cognitivism." *Iris* 9 (Spring): 11–40.

Bordwell, David. 2006. *The Way Hollywood Tells It: Story and Style in Modern Movies*. Berkeley: University of California Press.

Bordwell, David. 2009. "Cognitive Theory." In *The Routledge Companion to Philosophy and Film*, edited by Paisley Livingston and Carl Plantinga, 356–67. New York: Routledge.

Brown, William. 2009. "Man Without a Movie Camera—Movies Without Men: Towards a Posthumanist Cinema?" In *Film Theory and Contemporary Hollywood Movies*, edited by Warren Buckland, 66–85. New York: Routledge.

Bryson, Norman. 2003. "Introduction: The Neutral Interface." In *Blow-Up: Photography, Cinema and the Brain*, edited by Warren Neidich, 11–19. New York: Distributed Art Publishers.

Burch, Noël. 1982. "Narrative/Diegesis—Thresholds, Limits." *Screen* 23, no. 2: 16–33.

Carr, Brian. 2002. "*Strange Days* and the Subject of Mobility." *Camera Obscura* 17, no. 2 (September 1): 191–217.

Chion, Michel. 1994. *Audio-Vision: Sound on Screen*. Translated and edited by Claudia Gorbman. New York: Columbia University Press.

Clark, Andy. 2003. *Natural-Born Cyborgs: Minds, Technologies, and the Future of Human Intelligence.* New York: Oxford University Press.

Clark, Andy. 2010. "Minds in Space." In *The Spatial Foundations of Language and Cognition,* edited by Kelly S. Mix, Linda B. Smith, and Michael Gasser, 7–15. Oxford: Oxford University Press.

Clark, Andy, and David Chalmers. 1998. "The Extended Mind." *Analysis* 58, no. 1: 7–19.

Clarke, Arthur C. 1973. *Profiles of the Future: An Inquiry into the Limits of the Possible,* rev. ed. New York: Harper and Row.

Cohn, Dorrit. 1978. *Transparent Minds: Narrative Modes for Presenting Consciousness in Fiction.* Princeton, N.J.: Princeton University Press.

Cook, Roger F. 2011a. "Correspondences in Visual Imaging and Spatial Orientation in Dreaming and Film Viewing." *Dreaming: Journal of the Association of the Study of Dreams* 21, no. 2: 89–104.

Cook, Roger F. 2011b. "Hollywood Narrative and the Play of Fantasy: David Lynch's *Mulholland Drive.*" *Quarterly Review of Film and Video* 28, no. 5: 369–81.

Cook, Roger F. 2013. "Cinema Returns to the Source: Werner Herzog's *Cave of Forgotten Dreams.*" *Film International* 56, no. 2: 24–41.

Cook, Roger F. 2015. "Embodied Simulation, Empathy, and Social Cognition: Berlin School Lessons for Film Theory." *Screen* 11, no. 1: 153–71.

Corngold, Stanley, and Benno Wagner. 2011. *Franz Kafka: The Ghosts in the Machine.* Evanston, Ill.: Northwestern University Press.

Cosmides, Leda, and John Tooby. 1992. "The Psychological Foundations of Culture." In *The Adapted Mind: Evolutionary Psychology and the Generation of Culture,* edited by Jerome H. Barkow, Leda Cosmides, and John Tooby, 19–136. Oxford: Oxford University Press.

Crary, Jonathan. 1990. *Techniques of the Observer: On Vision and Modernity in the Nineteenth Century.* Cambridge, Mass.: MIT Press.

Crary, Jonathan. 1999. *Suspensions of Perception: Attention, Spectacle, and Modern Culture.* Cambridge, Mass.: MIT Press.

Cubitt, Sean. 2004. *The Cinema Effect.* Cambridge, Mass.: MIT Press.

Cubitt, Sean. 2009. "The Supernatural in Neo-Baroque Hollywood." In *Film Theory and Contemporary Hollywood Movies,* edited by Warren Buckland, 47–65. New York: Routledge.

Curtis, Robin. 2008. "Deixis, Imagination und Perzeption: Bestandteile einer performativen Theorie des Films." In *Deixis und Evidenz,* edited by Horst Wenzel and Ludwig Jäger, 241–60. Freiburg: Rombach.

Damasio, Antonio. 1999. *The Feeling of What Happens: Body and Emotion in the Making of Consciousness.* San Diego: Harcourt.

Damasio, Antonio R., and Hannah Damasio. 1996. "Making Images and Creating Subjectivity." In *Mind-Brain Continuum: Sensory Processes,* edited by Rodolfo R. Llinás and Paula Smith Churchland, 19–27. Cambridge, Mass.: MIT Press.

Deacon, Terence W. 1997. *The Symbolic Species: The Co-evolution of Language and the Brain*. New York: W. W. Norton.

Deacon, Terence W. 2012. *Incomplete Nature: How Mind Emerged from Matter*. New York: W. W. Norton.

Deleuze, Gilles. 1986a. "Le cerveau, c'est l'ècran, entretien avec Gilles Deleuze." *Cahiers du Cinéma* 380 (February): 24–32.

Deleuze, Gilles. 1986b. *Cinema 1: The Movement-Image*, translated by Hugh Tomlinson and Barbara Habberjam. Minneapolis: University of Minnesota Press.

Deleuze, Gilles. 1989. *Cinema 2: The Time-Image*, translated by Hugh Tomlinson and Roberta Galeta. Minneapolis: University of Minnesota Press.

Deleuze, Gilles. 1990. *Negotiations: 1972–1990*, translated by Martin Joughin. New York: Columbia University Press.

Dennett, Daniel C. 1991. *Consciousness Explained*. New York: Little, Brown and Company.

Denson, Shane. 2014. *Postnaturalism: Frankenstein, Film, and the Anthropotechnical Interface*. Bielefeld: Transcript-Verlag/Columbia University Press.

Denson, Shane. 2016. "Crazy Cameras, Discorrelated Images, and the Post-Perceptual Mediation of Post-Cinematic Affect." In *Post-Cinema: Theorizing 21st Century Film*, edited by Shane Denson and Julia Leyda, 193–233.

Denson, Shane, and Julia Leyda, eds. 2016. *Post-Cinema: Theorizing 21st Century Film*. Sussex, U.K.: Reframe Books. http://reframe.sussex.ac.uk/post-cinema/.

Derrida, Jacques. (1967) 1997. *Of Grammatology*, translated by Gayatri Chakravorty Spivak. Baltimore: Johns Hopkins University Press.

Diederichs, Helmut H. 1996. *Frühgeschichte deutscher Filmtheorie: Ihre Entstehung und Entwicklung bis zum Ersten Weltkrieg*. Frankfurt am Main: Habilitationsschrift im Fach Soziologie am Fachbereich Gesellschaftswissenschaften der J. W. Goethe-Universität. http://www.gestaltung.hs-mannheim.de/designwiki/files/4672/diederichs_frueh geschichte_filmtheorie.pdf.

Dixon, Wheeler Winston. 2001. "Twenty-Five Reasons Why It's All Over." In *The End of Cinema as We Know It: American Film in the Nineties*, edited by Jon Lewis, 356–66. New York: New York University Press.

Doidge, Norman. 2007. *The Brain That Changes Itself: Stories of Personal Triumph from the Frontiers of Brain Science*. New York: Viking.

Donald, Merlin. 1991. *Origins of the Modern Mind: Three Stages in the Evolution of Culture and Cognition.* Cambridge, Mass.: Harvard University Press.

Dubuc, Bruno. 2015. "Neuronal Assemblies and Synchronization of Brain Activity." The Brain from Top to Bottom (website). http: //thebrain mcgill.ca.

Dudai, Yadin. 2008. "Enslaving Central Executives: Toward a Brain Theory of Cinema." *Projections: The Journal for Movies and Mind* 2, no. 2: 21–42.

Dyson, Frances. 1996. "When Is the Ear Pierced? Clashes of Sound, Technology and Cyberculture." In *Immersed in Technology: Art and Virtual Environments*, edited by Mary Ann Moser and Douglas MacLeod, 73–102. Cambridge, Mass.: MIT Press.

Edelman, Gerald M. 1990. *The Remembered Present: A Biological Theory of Consciousness.* New York: Basic Books.

Edelman, Gerald M. 2003. "Naturalizing Consciousness: A Theoretical Framework." *PNAS* 100, no. 9 (April 29): 5520–24.

Edelman, Gerald M. 2006. *Second Nature: Brain Science and Human Knowledge.* New Haven, Conn.: Yale University Press.

Edelman, Gerald M., Joseph A. Gally, and Bernard J. Baars. 2011. "Biology of Consciousness." *Frontiers in Psychology* 2, no. 4: 1–7.

Engel, Manfred, and Bernd Auerochs, eds. 2010. *Kafka-Handbuch: Leben—Werk—Wirkung.* Stuttgart and Weimar: J. B. Metzler.

Fodor, Jerry A. 1983. *Modularity of Mind: An Essay on Faculty Psychology.* Cambridge, Mass.: MIT Press.

Frabetti, Federica. 2011. "Rethinking the Digital Humanities in the Context of Originary Technicity." *Culture Machine* 12: 1–22.

Friedberg, Anne. 1994. *Window Shopping: Cinema and the Postmodern.* Berkeley: University of California Press.

Friedberg, Anne. 2006. *The Virtual Window: From Alberti to Microsoft.* Cambridge, Mass.: MIT Press.

Furman, O., N. Dorfman, U. Hasson, L. Davachi, and Y. Dudai. 2007. "They Saw a Movie: Long-Term Memory for an Extended Audiovisual Narrative." *Learning and Memory* 14: 457–67.

Gallese, Vittorio. 2005. "Embodied Simulation: From Neurons to Phenomenal Experience." *Phenomenology and the Cognitive Sciences* 4: 23–38.

Gallese, Vittorio. 2009. "Mirror Neurons and the Neural Exploitation Hypothesis: From Embodied Simulation to Social Cognition." In *Mirror Neuron Systems: The Role of Mirroring Processes in Social Cognition*, edited by Jaime A. Pineda, 163–90. New York: Humana Press.

Gaudreault, André. 2009. *From Plato to Lumière: Narration and Monstration in Literature and Cinema*, translated by Timothy Barnard. Toronto: University of Toronto Press.

Gaudreault, André, and Philippe Marion. 2015. *The End of Cinema? A Medium in Crisis in the Digital Age*. New York: Columbia University Press.

Gibson, James J. 1986. *The Ecological Approach to Visual Perception*. Hillsdale, N.J.: Lawrence Erlbaum.

Goebel, Rolf J. 2000. "Kafka's Cinematic Gaze: Flânerie and Urban Discourse in *Beschreibung eines Kampfes*." *Journal of the Kafka Society of America* 24, no. 1–2 (June/December): 13–16.

Goebel, Rolf J. 2011. "Kafka in Virilio's Teleoptical City." In *Kafka for the Twenty-First Century*, edited by Stanley Corngold and Ruth V. Gross, 151–64. Rochester, N.Y.: Camden House.

Grau, Oliver. 2007. "Remember the Phantasmagoria! Illusion Politics of the Eighteenth Century and Its Multimedia Afterlife." In *MediaArtHistories*, edited by Oliver Grau, 137–61. Cambridge, Mass.: MIT Press.

Gray, Jeffrey. 1995. "The Contents of Consciousness: A Neurophysiological Conjecture." *Behavioral and Brain Sciences* 18, no. 4: 659–76.

Grieveson, Lee, and Peter Krämer. 2004. "Introduction: Cinema and Reform." In *The Silent Cinema Reader*, edited by Lee Grieveson and Peter Krämer, 135–44. London: Routledge.

Grush, Rick. 2004. "The Emulation Theory of Representation: Motor Control, Imagery, and Perception." *Behavioral and Brain Sciences* 27: 377–422.

Grusin, Richard. 2016. "DVDs, Video Games, and the Cinema of Interactions." In *Post-Cinema: Theorizing 21st Century Film*, edited by Shane Denson and Julia Leyda, 65–87.

Gunning, Tom. 1989. "An Aesthetics of Astonishment: Early Film and the (In)Credulous Spectator." *Art & Text* 34 (Spring): 31–45.

Gunning, Tom. 1990. "Non-Continuity, Continuity, Discontinuity: A Theory of Genres in Early Films." In *Early Cinema: Space-Frame-Narrative*, edited by Thomas Elsaesser, 86–103. London: British Film Institute.

Gunning, Tom. 1991. *D. W. Griffith and the Origins of American Narrative Film: The Early Years at Biograph*. Urbana: University of Illinois Press.

Gunning, Tom. 2004. "From the Opium Den to the Theatre of Morality: Moral Discourse and the Film Process in Early American Cinema." In *The Silent Cinema Reader*, edited by Lee Grieveson and Peter Krämer, 145–54. London: Routledge.

Gunning, Tom. 2007. "Moving Away from the Index: Cinema and the Impression of Reality." *differences: A Journal of Feminist Cultural Studies* 18, no. 1: 29–52.

Hansen, Mark B. N. 2004. *New Philosophy for New Media*. Cambridge, Mass.: MIT Press.

Hansen, Mark B. N. 2006. *Bodies in Code: Interfaces with Digital Media*. New York: Routledge.

Hansen, Mark B. N. 2011. "From Fixed to Fluid: Material-Mental Images between Neural Synchronization and Computational Mediation." In *Releasing the Image: From Literature to New Media*, edited by Jacques Khalip and Robert Mitchell, 83–111. Stanford, Calif.: Stanford University Press.

Hansen, Mark B. N. 2012. "Engineering Pre-Individual Potentiality: Technics, Transindividuation, and 21st-Century Media." *SubStance* 41, no. 3: 32–59.

Hansen, Mark B. N. 2015. *Feed Forward: On the Future of Twenty-First-Century Media*. Chicago: University of Chicago Press.

Hasson, Uri, Orit Furman, Dav Clark, Yadin Dudai, and Lila Davachi. 2008. "Enhanced Intersubject Correlations during Movie Viewing Correlate with Successful Episodic Encoding." *Neuron* 57 (February 7): 452–62.

Hasson, Uri, Ohad Landesman, Barbara Knappmeyer, Ignacio Vallines, Nava Rubin, and David J. Heeger. 2008. "Neurocinematics: The Neuroscience of Film." *Projections: The Journal for Movies and Mind* 2, no. 1: 1–26.

Hayles, N. Katherine. 1999. *How We Became Posthuman: Virtual Bodies in Cybernetics, Literature and Informatics*. Chicago: University of Chicago Press.

Hayles, N. Katherine. 2006. "Unfinished Work: From Cyborg to Cognisphere." *Theory, Culture, and Society* 23, no. 7–8: 159–66.

Hayles, N. Katherine. 2012. *How We Think: Digital Media and Contemporary Technogenesis*. Chicago: University of Chicago Press.

Hayles, N. Katherine. 2014. "Cognition Everywhere: The Rise of the Cognitive Nonconscious and the Costs of Consciousness." *New Literary History* 45, no. 2: 199–220.

Hayles, N. Katherine. 2017. *Unthought: The Power of the Cognitive Nonconscious*. Chicago: University of Chicago Press.

Heath, Stephen. 1976. "Narrative Space." *Screen* 17, no. 3 (Autumn): 68–112.

Hoffmeyer, Jesper. 2008. *Biosemiotics: An Examination into the Signs of Life and the Life of Signs*, translated by Jesper Hoffmeyer and Donald Favareau, edited by Donald Favareau. Scranton, Penn.: University of Scranton Press.

Hofmannsthal, Hugo von. 2004. "The Substitute for Dreams," translated by Lance W. Garner. In *German Essays on Film*, edited by Richard McCormick and Alison Guenther-Pal. New York: Continuum, 53–56.

Holl, Ute. 2012. "Cinema on the Web and Newer Psychology," translated by Allison Plath-Moseley. In *Screen Dynamics: Mapping the Borders of Cinema*, edited by Gertrud Koch, Volker Pantenburg, and Simon Rothöler. Vienna: SYNEMA.

Hotchkiss, Lia M. 2003 "'Still in the Game': Cybertransformations of the 'New Flesh' in David Cronenberg's *eXistenZ*." *The Velvet Light Trap* 52 (Fall): 15–32.

Hurley, Susan L. 1998. *Consciousness in Action*. Cambridge, Mass.: Harvard University Press.

Ivakhiv, Adrian J. 2013. *Ecologies of the Moving Image: Cinema, Affect, Nature*. Waterloo, Conn.: Wilfrid Laurier University Press.

Ivakhiv, Adrian J. 2016. "The Art of Morphogenesis: Cinema in and beyond the Capitalocene." In *Post-Cinema: Theorizing 21st Century Film*, edited by Shane Denson and Julia Leyda. 724–49.

Jahraus, Oliver. 2008. "Kafka und der Film." In *Kafka-Handbuch: Leben—Werk—Wirkung*, edited by Bettina von Jagow and Oliver Jahraus, 224–36. Göttingen, Germany: Vandenhoeck & Ruprecht.

James, William. 1961. *The Varieties of Religious Experience*. New York: MacMillan.

Janouch, Gustav. 1951. *Gespräche mit Kafka*. Frankfurt am Main: Fischer.

Jay, Martin. 1988. "Scopic Regimes of Modernity." In *Vision and Visuality*, edited by Hal Foster, 3–23. Seattle: Bay View Press.

Kaes, Anton. 1978. *Kino-Debatte: Texte zum Verhältnis von Literatur und Film 1909–1929*. Munich: Deutscher Taschenbuchverlag.

Kafka, Franz. 1965a. *The Diaries of Franz Kafka, 1910–1913*, edited by Max Brod, translated by Joseph Kresh. New York: Schocken.

Kafka, Franz. 1965b. *The Diaries of Franz Kafka, 1914–1923*, edited by Max Brod, translated by Martin Greenberg. New York: Schocken.

Kafka, Franz. 1973. *Letters to Felice*, edited by Erich Heller and Jürgen Born, translated by James Stern and Elisabeth Duckworth. New York: Schocken.

Kafka, Franz. 1994. "Der Fahrgast." In *Drücke zu Lebezeiten*, edited by Wolf Kittler, Hans-Gerd Koch, and Gerhard Neumann, 27–28. Frankfurt am Main: S. Fischer.

Kafka, Franz. 1998a. *The Castle*, translated by Mark Harman. New York: Schocken.

Kafka, Franz. 1998b. *The Trial*, translated by Breon Mitchell. New York: Schocken.

Kafka, Franz. 2007. *Kafka's Selected Stories: New Translations, Back-*

grounds and Contexts, Criticism, translated and edited by Stanley Corngold. New York: W. W. Norton.

Kafka, Franz. 2016. *The Metamorphosis: A New Translation, Texts and Contexts, Criticism*, translated by Susan Bernofsky, edited by Mark M. Anderson. New York: W. W. Norton.

Kennedy, Lisa. 2002. "Spielberg in the Twilight Zone." *Wired* 10, no. 6 (June): 113–20.

Kittler, Friedrich A. 1999. *Gramophone, Film, Typewriter*, translated by Geoffrey Winthrop-Young and Michael Wutz. Stanford, Calif.: Stanford University Press.

Kleitman, Nathaniel. 1982. "Basic Rest–Activity Cycle—22 Years Later." *Journal of Sleep Research and Sleep Medicine* 5, no. 4 (December): 311–17.

Kluszczynski, Ryszard W. 2007. "From Film to Interactive Art: Transformations in Media Arts." In *MediaArtHistories*, edited by Oliver Grau, 207–28. Cambridge, Mass.: MIT Press.

Koepnick, Lutz. "Herzog's Cave: On Cinema's Unclaimed Pasts and Forgotten Futures." *The Germanic Review: Literature, Culture, Theory* 88, no. 3: 271–85.

Kracauer, Siegfried. (1926) 1987. "Cult of Distraction: On Berlin's Picture Palaces." *New German Critique* 40 (Winter): 91–96.

Kracauer, Siegfried. 1997. *Theory of Film: The Redemption of Physical Reality*. Princeton, N.J.: Princeton University Press.

Lakoff, George, and Mark Johnson. 1980. *Metaphors We Live By*. Chicago: University of Chicago Press.

Landsberg, Alison. 2004. *Prosthetic Memory: The Transformation of American Remembrance in the Age of Mass Culture*. New York: Columbia University Press.

Langdale, Allan. "S(t)imulation of Mind: The Film Theory of Hugo Münsterberg." In *Hugo Münsterberg on Film: The Photoplay: A Psychological Study and Other Writings*, edited by Allan Langdale, 1–41. New York: Routledge.

LeDoux, Joseph. 2002. *Synaptic Self: How Our Brains Become Who We Are*. New York: Penguin.

Leroi-Gourhan, André. 1993. *Gesture and Speech*, translated by Anna Bostock Berger. Cambridge, Mass.: MIT Press. Originally published in 1964 as *La Geste et la parole*. Paris: Albin Michel.

Levin, Daniel T., and Caryn Wang. 2009. "Spatial Representation in Cognitive Science and Film." *Projections: The Journal for Movies and Mind* 3, no. 1: 24–52.

Lowenstein, Adam. 2015. *Dreaming of Cinema: Spectatorship, Surrealism, and the Age of Digital Media*. New York: Columbia University Press.

MacDougall, Robert C. 2015. "Seeing In, and Out, to the Extended Mind through an Analysis of Page and Screen Reading." In *Neuroscience and Media: New Understandings and Representations*, edited by Michael Grabowski, 89–107. New York: Routledge.

Mach, Ernst. 1914. *Analysis of Sensations and the Relation of the Physical to the Psychical*, translated by C. M. Williams. Chicago: Open Court.

Magliano, Joseph P., and Jeffrey M. Zacks. 2011. "The Impact of Continuity Editing in Narrative Film on Event Segmentation." *Cognitive Science* 35: 1–29.

Manovich, Lev. 1995. "What Is Digital Cinema?" In *The Digital Dialectic: New Essays on New Media*, edited by Peter Lunenfeld, 172–92. Cambridge, Mass.: MIT Press.

Manovich, Lev. 2001. *The Language of New Media*. Cambridge, Mass.: MIT Press.

Manovich, Lev. 2006. "Visual Technologies as Cognitive Prosthesis." In *The Prosthetic Impulse: From a Posthuman Present to a Biocultural Future*, edited by Marquard Smith and Joanne Morra, 203–19. Cambridge, Mass.: MIT Press.

Maturana, Humberto R., and Francisco J. Varela. 1987. *The Tree of Knowledge: The Biological Roots of Human Understanding*. Boston: Shambala.

McLuhan, Marshall. 1969. "Playboy Interview: Marshall McLuhan: A Candid Conversation with the High Priest of Popcult and Metaphysician of Media." *Playboy Magazine* 16, no. 3 (March, 1969).

McLuhan, Marshall. (1964) 1994. *Understanding Media: The Extensions of Man*. Cambridge, Mass.: MIT Press.

McLuhan, Marshall. 1995. "Is It Natural that One Medium Should Appropriate and Exploit Another?" In *Essential McLuhan*, edited by Eric McLuhan and Frank Zingrone, 180–90. New York: Basic Books.

McLuhan, Marshall, and Bruce R. Powers. 1989. *The Global Village: Transformations in World Life and Media in the 21st Century*. New York: Oxford University Press.

McMahan, Alison. 2006. "*Chez le Photographe c'est chez moi*: Relationship of Actor and Filmed Subject to Camera in Early Film and Virtual Reality Spaces." In *The Cinema of Attractions Reloaded*, edited by Wanda Strauven, 291–308. Amsterdam: Amsterdam University Press.

Media Literacy Project. "About Media Literacy." https: //medialiteracy project.org/learn/media-literacy.

Merleau-Ponty, Maurice. 2002. *The Phenomenology of Perception*, translated by Colin Smith. New York: Routledge.

Merleau-Ponty, Maurice. 2004. *The World of Perception*, translated by Oliver Davis. London: Routledge. Originally published as *Causeries*, 1948.

Metz, Christian. 1990. *Film Language: The Semiotics of Cinema.* Chicago: University of Chicago Press.

Metz, Christian, and Alfred Guzzetti. 1976. "The Fiction Film and Its Spectator: A Metapsychological Study." *New Literary History* 8, no. 1: 75–105.

Metzinger, Thomas. 2009. *The Ego Tunnel: The Science of the Mind and the Myth of the Self.* New York: Basic Books.

Milner, A. David, and Melvyn A. Goodale. 2006. *The Visual Brain in Action,* 2nd ed. Oxford: Oxford University Press.

Mitchell, W. J. T. 2007. "There Are No Visual Media." In *MediaArt Histories,* edited by Oliver Grau, 395–406. Cambridge, Mass.: MIT Press.

Mitry, Jean. 2000. *The Aesthetics and Psychology of the Cinema,* translated by Christopher King. Bloomington: Indiana University Press.

Moholy-Nagy, László. 1922. "Produktion-Reproduktion." *De Stijl* 5, no. 7 (July): 97–100.

Moholy-Nagy, László. 1934. "An Open Letter to the Film Industry and to All Who Are Interested in the Evolution of the Good Film." *Sight and Sound* 3, no. 10: 56–57.

Moholy-Nagy, László. 1947. *Vision in Motion.* Chicago: Theobald.

Morgan, Daniel. 2006. "Rethinking Bazin: Ontology and Realist Aesthetics." *Critical Inquiry* 32: 443–81.

Münsterberg, Hugo (1916) 2002. *The Photoplay: A Psychological Study.* In *Hugo Münsterberg on Film:* The Photoplay: A Psychological Study *and Other Writings,* edited by Allan Langdale, 45–162. New York: Routledge.

Musil, Robert. (1906) 1978. *Die Verwirrungen des Zöglings Törless.* Hamburg: Rowohlt Taschenbuch.

Musser, Charles. 1990. *The Emergence of Cinema: The American Screen to 1907.* New York: Charles Scribner's Sons.

Musser, Charles. 2004. "Moving Towards Fictional Narratives: Story Films Become the Dominant Product, 1903–1904." In *The Silent Cinema Reader,* edited by Lee Grieveson and Peter Krämer, 87–102. London: Routledge.

Ndalianis, Angela. 2004. *Neo-Baroque Aesthetics and Contemporary Entertainment.* Cambridge, Mass.: MIT Press.

Neidich, Warren. 2003. *Blow-Up: Photography, Cinema and the Brain.* New York: Distributed Art Publishers.

Noë, Alva, and J. Kevin O'Regan. 2001. "A Sensorimotor Account of Cision and Visual Consciousness." *Behavioral and Brain Sciences* 24: 939–1031.

Novalis. 1981. *Schriften: Die Werke Friedrich von Hardenbergs* vol. 2, edited by Richard Samuel, 3rd ed. Stuttgart, Germany: W. Kohlhammer.

Oakley, Kenneth P. 1949. *Man the Tool-Maker*. London: Trustees of the British Museum.

Oyama, Susan. 2000. *The Ontogeny of Information: Developmental Systems and Evolution*, 2nd ed. Durham, N.C.: Duke University Press.

Panksepp, Jaak. 1998. *Affective Neuroscience: The Foundations of Human and Animal Emotions*. Oxford: Oxford University Press.

Perri, Dennis. 2009. "Amenábar's *Abre los ojos* (Open your eyes): The Posthuman Subject." *Hispanofila* 154 (September): 89–98.

Pisters, Patricia. 2012. *The Neuro-Image: A Deleuzian Film-Philosophy of Digital Screen Culture*. Stanford, Calif.: Stanford University Press.

Plunkett, John. 2013. "'Feeling Seeing': Touch, Vision and the Stereoscope." *History of Photography* 37, no. 4: 389–96.

Poissant, Louise. 2007. "The Passage from Material to Interface," translated by Ernestine Daubner and Jason Martin. In *MediaArtHistories*, edited by Oliver Grau, 229–50. Cambridge, Mass.: MIT Press.

Preston, Joan M. 2006. "From Mediated Environments to the Development of Consciousness II." In *Psychology and the Internet: Intrapersonal, Interpersonal, and Transpersonal Implications*, 2nd ed., edited by Jayne Gackenbach, 277–307. San Diego: Academic Press.

Protevi, John. 2012. "One More 'Next Step': Deleuze and Brain, Body and Affect in Contemporary Cognitive Science." In *Revisiting Normativity with Deleuze*, edited by Rosi Braidetti and Patricia Pisters, 25–36. London: Bloomsbury.

Pylyshyn, Zenon. 1984. *Computation and Cognition: Toward a Foundation for Cognitive Science*. Cambridge, Mass.: MIT Press.

Quartz, Steven, and Terence Sejnowski. 1997. "The Neural Basis of Cognitive Development: A Constructivist Manifesto." *Behavioral and Brain Sciences* 20: 537–56.

Ramachandran, V. S. 2011. *The Tell-Tale Brain: A Neuroscientist's Quest for What Makes Us Human*. New York: Norton.

Revonsuo, Antti. 2003. "The Reinterpretation of Dreams: An Evolutionary Hypothesis of the Function of Dreaming." In *Sleep and Dreaming: Scientific Advances and Reconsiderations*, edited by Edward F. Pace-Schott, Mark Solms, Mark Blagrove, and Stevan Harnad, 85–109. Cambridge: Cambridge University Press.

Revonsuo, Antti. 2006. *Inner Presence: Consciousness as a Biological Phenomenon*. Cambridge, Mass.: MIT Press.

Rizzolatti, Giacomo, Lucio Riggio, and Boris M. Sheliga. 1994. "Space and Selective Attention." In *Attention and Performance XV: Conscious and Nonconscious Information Processing*, edited by Carlo Umiltà and Morris Moscovitch, 231–66. Cambridge, Mass.: MIT Press.

Rodowick, D. N. 2007. *The Virtual Life of Film*. Cambridge, Mass.: Harvard University Press.

Rombes, Nicolas. 2009. *Cinema in the Digital Age*. London: Wallflower.

Sahli, Jan. 2006 *Filmische Sinneserweiterung: Làzlò Moholy-Nagys Filmwerk und Theorie*. Marburg, Germany: Schüren.

Schefer, Jean-Louis. 1995. *The Enigmatic Body: Essays on the Arts*, translated by Paul Smith. Cambridge: Cambridge University Press.

Schivelbusch, Wolfgang. 1986. *The Railway Journey: The Industrialization of Time and Space in the Nineteenth Century*. Berkeley: University of California Press.

Shaviro, Steven. 1993. *The Cinematic Body*. Minneapolis: University of Minnesota Press.

Shaviro, Steven. 2007. "Emotion Capture: Affect in Digital Film." *Projections: The Journal for Movies and Mind* 1, no. 2: 37–56.

Shaviro, Steven. 2010. *Post-Cinematic Affect*. Winchester, U.K.: Zero Books.

Shaviro, Steven. 2014. *The Universe of Things: On Speculative Realism*. Minneapolis: University of Minnesota Press.

Shaviro, Steven. 2016a. "Post-Continuity: An Introduction." In *Post-Cinema: Theorizing 21st Century Film*, edited by Shane Denson and Julia Leyda, 51–64.

Shaviro, Steven. 2016b. "Splitting the Atom: Post-Cinematic Articulations of Sound and Vision." In *Post-Cinema: Theorizing 21st Century Film*, edited by Shane Denson and Julia Leyda, 362–97.

Shaw, Jeffrey. 2002. "Movies after Film: The Digitally Expanded Cinema." In *New Screen Media: Cinema/Art/Narrative*, edited by Martin Rieser and Andrea Zapp, 268–75. London: British Film Institute.

Simmel, Georg. 1997. "The Metropolis and Mental Life," translated by Kurt H. Wolff. In *Simmel on Culture: Selected Writings*, edited by Mike Frisby and David Featherstone, 174–85. London: Sage.

Simondon, Gilbert. 2017. *On the Mode of Existence of Technical Objects*. Translated by Cécile Malaspina and John Rogove. Minneapolis: Univocal.

Singer, Ben. 2004. "Manhattan Nickelodeons: New Data on Audiences and Exhibitors." In *The Silent Cinema Reader*, edited by Lee Grieveson and Peter Krämer, 119–34. London: Routledge.

Singer, Wolf. 2010. "Neocortical Rhythms: An Overview." In *Dynamic Coordination in the Brain: From Neurons to Mind*, edited by Christoph von Marlsburg, William A. Phillips, and Wolf Singer, 159–68. Cambridge, Mass.: MIT Press.

Smith, Linda B., and Larissa K. Samuelson. 2010. "Objects in Space and Mind: From Reaching to Words." In *The Spatial Foundations of*

Language and Cognition, edited by Kelly S. Mix, Linda B. Smith, and Michael Gasser, 188–207. Oxford: Oxford University Press.

Sobchack, Vivian. 1992. *Address of the Eye: A Phenomenology of Film Experience*. Princeton, N.J.: Princeton University Press.

Sobchack, Vivian. 2004a. "The Scene of the Screen: Envisioning Photographic, Cinematic, and Electronic 'Presence.'" In *Carnal Thoughts: Embodiment and Moving Image Culture*, 135–62. Berkeley: University of California Press.

Sobchack, Vivian. 2004b. "What My Fingers Knew: The Cinesthetic Subject, or Vision in the Flesh." In *Carnal Thoughts: Embodiment and Moving Image Culture*, 53–84. Berkeley: University of California Press.

Sobchack, Vivian. 2005. "When the Ear Dreams: Dolby Digital and the Imagination of Sound." *Film Quarterly* 58, no. 4: 2–15.

Spaulding, Shannon. 2014. "Embodied Cognition and Theory of Mind." In *The Routledge Handbook of Embodied Cognition*, edited by Lawrence Shapiro, 197–206. London: Routledge.

Spivey, Michael J., Daniel C. Richardson, and Carlos A. Zednik. 2010. "Language Is Spatial, Not Special: On the Demise of the Symbolic Approximation Hypothesis." In *The Spatial Foundations of Language and Cognition*, edited by Kelly S. Mix, Linda B. Smith, and Michael Gasser, 16–40. Oxford: Oxford University Press.

Stanzel, Franz Karl. 1984. *A Theory of Narrative*, translated by Charlotte Goedsche. Cambridge: Cambridge University Press.

Stiegler, Bernard. 1998. *Technics and Time 1: The Fault of Epimetheus*, translated by Richard Beardsworth and George Collins. Stanford, Calif.: Stanford University Press.

Sudmann, Andreas. 2016. "Bullet Time and the Mediation of Post-Cinematic Temporality." In *Post-Cinema: Theorizing 21st Century Film*, edited by Shane Denson and Julia Leyda, 297–326.

Taylor, John G. 1991. *The Race for Consciousness*. Cambridge, Mass.: MIT Press.

Theweleit, Klaus. 1992. "Circles, Lines, and Bits." In *Incorporations*, edited by Jonathan Crary and Sanford Kwinter, 256–64. New York: Zone Books.

Thompson, Kristin. 1985. "Classical Narrative Space and the Spectator's Attention." In *The Classical Hollywood Cinema: Film Style and Mode of Production to 1960*. David Bordwell, Janet Staiger, and Kristin Thompson, 214–30. New York: Columbia University Press.

Tollefsbol, Trygve. 2014. "Transgenerational Epigenetics." In *Transgenerational Epigenetics: Evidence and Debate*, edited by Trygve Tollefsbol, 1–9. London: Elsevier.

Tomasello, Michael. 1999. *The Cultural Origins of Human Cognition.* Cambridge, Mass.: Harvard University Press.

Tyron, Chuck. 2009. *Reinventing Cinema: Movies in the Age of Media Convergence.* New Brunswick, N.J.: Rutgers University Press.

Uleman, James S. 2005. "Introduction: Becoming Aware of the New Unconscious." In *The New Unconscious,* edited by Ran R. Hassin, James S. Uleman, and John A. Bargh, 3–15. Oxford: Oxford University Press.

Usai, Paolo Cherchi. 2001. *The Death of Cinema: History, Cultural Memory, and the Digital Dark Age.* London: British Film Institute.

Valiant, Leslie. 2013. *Probably Approximately Correct: Nature's Algorithms for Learning and Prospering in a Complex World.* New York: Basic Books.

Varela, Francisco J., Evan Thompson, and Eleanor Rosch. 1991. *The Embodied Mind: Cognitive Science and Human Experience.* Cambridge, Mass.: MIT Press.

Virilio, Paul. 1994. *The Vision Machine.* Bloomington: University of Indiana Press.

Walsh, Denis M. 2017. "'Chance Caught on the Wing': Metaphysical Commitment or Methodological Artifact?" In *Challenging the Modern Synthesis: Adaptation, Development, and Inheritance,* edited by Philippe Huneman and Denis M. Walsh, 239–60. New York: Oxford University Press.

Wertheimer, Max. 1912. "Experimentelle Studien über das Sehen von Bewegung." *Zeitschrift für Psychologie* 61: 161–265.

Wexler, Bruce. 2010. "Shaping the Environments that Shape Our Brains: A Long Term Perspective." In *Cognitive Architecture: From Biopolitics to Noopolitics: Architecture & Mind in the Age of Communication and Information,* edited by Deborah Hauptmann and Warren Neidich, 142–67. Rotterdam: 010 Publishers.

Wiener, Norbert. (1948) 1961. *Cybernetics: Or Control and Communication in the Animal and the Machine.* 2nd revised edition. Cambridge, Mass.: MIT Press.

Wiener, Norbert. 1954. *The Human Use of Human Beings: Cybernetics and Society,* 2nd ed. Garden City, N.Y.: Doubleday.

Wilson, Robert A., and Lucia Foglia. 2015. "Embodied Cognition." In *The Stanford Encyclopedia of Philosophy,* http://plato.stanford.edu/entries/embodied-cognition/.

Woolf, Virginia. 1925. "The Cinema." In *Collected Essays,* vol. 2, 268–72. New York: Harcourt, Brace & World.

Young, Paul. 2006. *The Cinema Dreams Its Rivals: Media Fantasy Films from Radio to the Internet.* Minneapolis: University of Minnesota Press.

Zacks, Jeffrey M., Nicole K. Speer, Khena M. Swallow, and Corey J. Maley. 2010. "The Brain's Cutting-Room Floor: Segmentation of Narrative Cinema." *Frontiers in Human Neuroscience* 4 (October 1, 2010). https://doi.org/10.3389/fnhum.2010.00168.

Zischler, Hanns. 2003. *Kafka Goes to the Movies*, translated by Susan H. Gillespie. Chicago: University of Chicago Press. Originally published 1996 as *Kafka geht ins Kino*.

Index

(continued from page ii)

Roger F. Cook is professor of German studies and director of the Film Studies Program at the University of Missouri.